HON◯R &
Commitment
STANDARD *life* OPERATING GUIDELINES
FOR **FIREFIGHTERS** & THEIR **FAMILIES**

Lori Mercer

©2016 by Lori Mercer
ISBN: 978-0-692-68697-3

Cover image by Jason Jones, www.jonesphoto.weebly.com

*Dedicated to the one man who has stayed committed to me,
to himself, to our family and the fire service.*
Thank you for being brave, vulnerable and
sharing your heart with me.

To My Fire Wife Sisterhood

To those who touched my life for a season, for a reason,
and especially for those who are here for a lifetime, much fire
wife love. I am grateful for both the encouragement and challenges
you bring me. You girls make me a better wife, mom and friend.

CONTENTS

SECTION 3: A NEW LEVEL OF COMMITMENT

INTRODUCTION

Honor and Commitment. Those two words undeniably describe what's required of a firefighter. It's an honor to be chosen as one who can handle this challenging service. And it takes a commitment like none other to say you'll submit yourself to dangerous settings in order save life and property. Firefighters are undoubtedly admired for what they do.

But most firefighters do not like the word "hero." And shrug off the limelight. Because to them, they signed up for this and knew what they were getting into. And many other professions also require dangerous work so to single out firefighters seems a bit selfish. They are men and women who said yes and were in the right place at the right time to give aid.

Firefighters are also real people. Who have spouses and children and moms and dads and side jobs and volunteer as scout leaders and coaches. They live real lives and most will say they never really stop being firefighters even when they are away from the station. See how that works? They are always firefighters who are honored and committed. So follow me here—honor and commitment are also words that describe marriage, yet the state of marriage in our world so often paints a very different picture. To honor our marriage and be committed to our spouses and families makes us the subject of ridicule in some circles. I see an opportunity. And a way to help others. This is how we work, us firefighters and their family members. We help others.

How can we take those admirable firefighting traits—honor and commitment—and demonstrate them in all aspects of our lives? **Can firefighters be admired in their community also for how they honor** and are committed to their families? Sure, why not? This world certainly can use a few more role models, on and off "the court." And that's the mission of this book: **To equip firefighters and their families to live a life of honor and commitment at home and on the job.** And it starts with equipping our own fire families with training and knowledge and fortitude and love and patience and commitment.

Through our personal story and those of many others who have joined the 24-7 COMMITMENT community, we want to see the same honor and commitment that is admired in firefighters carry over through our own families. At the end of the day, it's a less obvious yet also life changing way to "save" our communities. And it requires your entire family to participate. So let's take the best of the firefighting world and the best of strong marriages and families and meld them together as we unpack the **Standard *Life* Operating Guidelines for Firefighters and their Families.**

Who am I? I'm just another girl who fell in love with a firefighter. And then I wrote a little story about the good, the bad, the beautiful, and the ugly, and a community of women married to firefighters said "Finally. Someone who understands my life." That was July of 2012 on our 10th wedding anniversary. Today with more than 100,000 fans, followers, subscribers, donors, volunteers—whatever title you put on the people who have said "yes" in some way, 24-7 COMMITMENT is alive and ready to make that path a little easier on a lot of firefighters and their families.

I'll be fully honest here (because that's the only way I know how to be) and share that there was a season of our life together that **I really disliked the fire service.** I could never imagine giving so much of myself, as I do now leading 24-7 COMMITMENT, to an entity that I truly felt was jeopardizing my marriage. But the fire service was just one of the causes of the challenges in our marriage and family life and an easy target, especially because I didn't have any resources to help me learn about it and there was no community stepping up at the time to help me or my husband understand. In fact, the opposite happened. **Guys who were admired senior mentors to my husband told him to leave me.** They said I wasn't cut out for this gig. Ouch. (Luckily he didn't tell me that until recent years or I may have had a fight to pick!) And huge credit to my rookie firefighter for side stepping that piece of advice, listening to some other wise counsel and making the commitment to our marriage.

Now that we are well past that challenging season, I can reflect back and see that **the fire service wasn't entirely to blame**. All marriages have their own set of baggage to work through as well but the fire service can certainly ignite some ugly fires that might have otherwise smoldered out (all cheesy fire puns intended in this book.)

And looking back, I am so grateful for the small handful who came alongside us and said "you can work it out," and encouraged us to do so. I did cry on the shoulder of a fire wife whom I didn't even know that well, but who gladly took that phone call from me. And her husband came alongside mine to remind him that marriage is hard work but so worth it. Most people aren't so excited to dump their personal struggles on someone else's ear and ask for that help, at least not until it's maybe too far gone.

So for you who are here reading this, I hope it lays a foundation to prepare a strong, enduring fire marriage and shortcut that challenging cycle my husband and I experienced.

Now, I must credit the fire service for some amazing positives as well. I have a husband who has a job that he LOVES. Not many women can say that. And while it does take them away from home a lot, it also allows for some fantastic long breaks and time away. One day off = 5 days off on some schedules. And those "Kelly Days" (if you're new to this life we'll cover these fire terms throughout this book.) And to be married to someone who is making a very personal difference in the lives of many, well, it's truly one of the reasons I first fell in love with him. Firefighting takes a big heart. Even the grumpiest, saltiest, potty-mouthed firefighters who I know have big hearts for serving. I don't think there's any other way to do this job. It's about honor and commitment.

So why are you here with this book? For whatever reason you've flipped it open, I believe there is a purpose. Nothing is wasted in my opinion. It's all part of the journey.

We believe that to be the best firefighter, you must have your whole life in focus. Sure you can put out a fire and run a cardiac arrest but then if you go home and constantly bicker with your wife and are emotionally absent for your children, is that living your best life? No way. Your role as a husband/wife/father/mother will long outlast the title of firefighter in your life. And no firefighter is at their best when their home life is challenging and a distraction on their mind in the middle of a rescue. We're here to build the best all around firefighter—mentally, physically, and relationally. And you have the best edge at firefighting when your home team—your family—is supportive and encouraging through it all.

The same is true for the spouse of a firefighter. We must get ourselves "right" to be the best spouse/parent/(insert your career role here) as well. And yes your spouse the firefighter isn't on some pedestal superior to your role in life. This is your first crew, your family together. It is possible to find that balance in the midst of the fire life, which, by the way, is envied and admired by many. You are one lucky family to have this opportunity to be living out the traits of honor and commitment.

We call that the 24-7 COMMITMENT. At all times and in all roles we want to be performing our best. That's the philosophy with which we approach this book. **We want to give you the information and tools to create the fire life that works for your family.**

Who is this book for?

Firefighters and their spouses.
Each chapter includes sections written to the firefighter and then one separately written to the spouse. We encourage you both to read both sections.

Newlywed couples and Academy Grads.
We hope you get off on a strong foundation with resources that have previously never existed. Real life "fire life" as it's called, with stories by real firefighters and family members.

What if I'm not a newlywed or a new firefighter?
We hear so often "I wish this program was around when I was a newly-wed," or that "I wish I had this 5 years ago before my divorce." Yes, even old dogs can see things in a new light. So don't hesitate to pick it up. Perhaps you've never read anything like this in your entire firefighting career. And can I just warn you? One of the side effects of wives of

firefighters becoming a part of our community is that their love life really fires up. Just FYI. We think that's why all the men encouraged this group to keep doing what we're doing.

What will this book cover?

This book is the "A to Z" (not in alphabetic order by the way) of topics in the fire service that influence a family and situations in a family life that influence firefighting. It's broken into sections such as:

- Balancing firefighting and family
- Worry & Fear
- Managing Schedules
- Kids of Firefighters
- Transitioning to/from home
- Family visits to the firehouse
- Connecting to your extended fire family
- Healthy Communication in Your Marriage
- Trust in Your Marriage
- Staying Intimately Connected
- Jealousy and Female Firefighters
- Dealing with difficult calls
- Line of Duty Death Preparedness and Support
- Holidays Away
- Academy, Medic School, Training and Promotional Processes
- Physical Health and Wellness

I want more than a book.

I so hear you. I've got piles of great books I've read, act on for a week or two, and then those thoughts get shoved out of my brain with another topic. What I really need is accountability and continual change and growth. Because you don't just read it and suddenly you change. It takes effort over time. So firstly, this book can be used as an ongoing reference and we've included some note and journaling spaces along the way. Secondly, there are lists of resources, specific to each topic, at the end of each section, including more articles, videos and specific support communities. Thirdly, our vision is that all fire families become living and breathing examples of a positive fire life that changes the culture and morale in your local fire department and demonstrates honor and commitment to marriage and family in your own communities. So you can be that positive influence amongst the other firefighters and families as well. Yes, we expect this book to build a positive movement. We dream big but we've seen it already on a small scale and know that it's a good thing. All good things must prevail.

A few thank yous...

So much credit for the creation of this book goes to the community at 24-7 COMMITMENT. The crazy thing is that we started with community and then backed up into resources like our Marriage On Fire video series and this book. Three years of writing articles on our websites (247commitment.org and FirefighterWife.com) have culminated in this book, hopefully the first of many print resources in production.

Our online community grew up grass roots from a couple raw blog posts and a social media following. And the conversations, friendships, understanding ears and encouragement there inspired much of the content that was written over the years. Best of all are the friendships we've all formed through this connection. Those friendships which have withstood the trials with which a new non-profit struggles and have outlasted differences of opinion, tiny budgets, long hours, ridiculous silliness and heartfelt moments these words can't even begin to describe.

But you may be new here and all that talk bores you. So I'll stop with the thank yous and let you get on to the experience. We hope you walk away inspired, encouraged and eager to connect with and grow your own 24-7 COMMITMENT community so our firefighters and families can continue to be beacons of hope, honor, courage and inspiration in our communities, not just protecting their community but as positive role models for commitment to marriage and family.

Sincerely yours,
Lori Mercer

A Personal Note to Wives (or soon to be wives) of Firefighters

It's important for you to know these things about me before reading this book.

Other firefighter wives used to make me uncomfortable. I didn't get a warm welcome from them. They seemed have been lifelong friends and I was the new girl they gave the once over. No one was reaching out to me. When I tried to chime in, they were harsh and bitey with their replies, as if what I added was so very juvenile.

In hindsight, these particular wives were somewhat hardened and bitter towards what the fire life had done to their men and the marriages. My fresh, energetic, young love they probably envied a bit. I just couldn't partake in their sarcastic, somewhat husband bashing, banter. It wasn't honorable and I was committed to my marriage....two words I didn't associate with it at the time.

There were other wives who seemed much nicer but they were just busy. So busy taking care of their own families I really didn't want to interrupt. They had a flow and a routine and no need for me. I admired their take charge attitude and ability to get things done and seemingly strong spirit. Maybe they just hid their frustrations well or didn't want to spill them on the new girl.

There were wives I never met. Perhaps their husband shielded them from the fire service or they self-selected out. Either way they never visited the station nor social events, and I couldn't pick them out on the street if I saw them.

Anyhow, none of them lived very close to us and my husband was so tired of the firehouse by the time he got home, he didn't want to hang out with the other firefighters off duty. (See that? Don't compare yourself to the 'brotherhood' that does everything for each other. It may be more of an internet perpetuated rarity than the norm.) So I settled into my career and our family and my husband his job, and we worked through those early years of marriage with very little social engagement with the firehouse and certainly not much positive support.

See, there are many paths to walking this fire life. And until our 10-year wedding anniversary when I wrote that blog post, "The Raw, Ugly and Revealing True Story of a Fire Marriage," I would have been just as happy continuing to live semi-detached from the fire service and annoyed at the stress and frustrations it gave my husband. That blog post brought to me a community of women who did think like me and struggle with the same things. And for the first time in my adult life, I had found girlfriends who got me. Before then, I didn't realize just how much my husband being a firefighter impacted our schedules, our priorities and even our conversations and thoughts. What a huge blessing that has been.

It may look like I'm all wrapped up in being a fire wife. Truth is I'm not. I'm wrapped up in being a Godly woman, his wife, a mom and serving my purpose here on this planet. I don't worship him for being a firefighter. I never call him hero nor let him walk all over me just because he's a firefighter. Heck there are days I have wished this wasn't his profession (and has he.) The only reason I wear fire wife t-shirts is because of my friendships here in the Fire Wife Sisterhood (before all of this I felt very weird wearing his department t-shirt or even identifying myself with where he works.)

So please, this is your invitation to read this and be you. Be what works for your family (notice I didn't say "fire family"). I hope you find some real life tidbits you can relate to because these are stories from real life fire families. Not the results of some research paper or psychological study or skewed data points that allowed someone to get a government grant (no grants here. Nada. They're not down with our real life living.)

Just in case you're reading this thinking you're going to "fix him", let me give you the most important piece of marriage advice EVER. Not exaggerating there at all. You may be frustrated at him, his habits, his behaviors, his fire schedule, the way he talks to you or sleeps all day when we gets off shift. It doesn't matter.

The most important person you can change is yourself.

Changing yourself changes your marriage. It changes your family and your home. I'm not saying to change who your authentic self is. I'm saying to just smooth the rough places, fill in the gaps and slightly mold into a more refined and beautiful you.

And when you change, your husband will notice. And he's likely to want to make some improvements in himself as well. Change for the better, is a very sexy, seductive and attractive feature in your spouse. You have nothing to lose if you try it.

So if your husband has ever felt frustrated with your viewpoint on the fire service and how it affects him and your family, consider this list. **This is my summary of what it may look like to rock this life married to a man who happens to be a firefighter.**

It isn't about being all gaga over those brave, heroic, sexy hunks of firefighters we are married to. Attracted? Sure. Proud? Absolutely. But it's DEFINITELY not about letting them run roughshod over our lives. Firefighting isn't any kind of excuse to not wholly participate in a healthy marriage. However, it is a big part of the man you married and you must embrace that to love him wholly.

You've actually already been tested by fire and are stronger because of it. Fires in your marriage. With parenting. Health issues. Job loss. Death of a loved one. All the tough stuff. You've survived and you've done a lot of it on your own while he is off serving the community.

You understand the challenges of the fire service but you accept it and embrace it. Missed holidays. Unexpected overtime. Sleepless nights resulting in irritable firefighters at home. Discussions of scenes no human should ever have to witness.

Death is very real to you. You have frequent discussions about how quickly our lives can be taken away. You've imagined life as a widow. So all your piddly first world problems....yeah, you don't sit around whining and complaining about those.

You can bend and not break. With grace. Unplanned overtime. Dinner time pages. Weekend training. The need to drop everything and discuss a terrible call the moment he walks in the door.

You are flexible and compassionate. You hug him. You smile. You say you understand. And although it's frustrating, in your heart you know it's the right way. You still have some weak areas but you're working like mad to make yourself stronger every day.

Physically strong. Fit and able to take on life and the house chores as a single mom when he's gone.

Emotionally strong. Girls cry. Sob even. It's ok. But we know WHY we cry and it only makes us stronger. Don't cry without hope.

Mentally strong. No weapon formed against you shall stand. Fear. Worry. Guilt. Shame. Take captive every thought. Don't whirlwind into hopelessness.

Spiritually strong. Anyone who spends this much time in the face of life or death (or discussing it intensely with someone who does, like your firefighter) has thought about life after death and knows their beliefs. When life is crazy all about you, a spiritual foundation is what you cling to for strength.

It means not everyone can relate to your life. But it's ok. Because you are strong and blessed with this special gift. (and if needed you have a community of strong women to turn to at FirefighterWife.com)

This life is yours. Authentically yours. You are a strong, capable woman who holds down the fort (and likely a career!) for more than just an 8-hour office day, while your husband runs off to save the world.

This isn't for someone who wants to whine and complain.

Firefighting is noble, honorable, courageous, committed—traits that many admire—if you're lucky, there's a wise old salty firefighter reminding you of this. If you're super lucky, there's a salty firefighter married for 35 years with a sweet wife ready to be your listening ear and advice giver.

This book is meant to show that you aren't the only one.

Firefighters typically don't ask for help nor do they show fear and worry… on the outside. But they will show it to you, their safe place, if you make it that for them. But from the rest of the world home problems are hidden and compounded if not addressed. As the wife, you know first and you know the real deal when your husband is upset. That, along with all the other already important life roles you have, is what sets you apart for the additional bonus title "firefighter's wife." There was no one else made to be his wife aside from you in this moment right now. It's an honor and a commitment.

So don't compare yourself to any other "fire wife" who's emblazoned her Facebook page with everything fire. That's just one way to walk the fire life and what works for her. Do it your way. That's the best way. The way that you and your husband together find brings the most joy and satisfaction to your life (but I'm certain there are a few tips and tricks in this guidebook to help you along the way.)

Signed,

Just another girl who fell in love with an amazing man.....
who happened to be a firefighter

Now a Word from the Firefighter Husband

So exactly what does my husband have to say about all of this? A lot of really good things when he has a few moments away from his demanding fire service career and our family (we strive to keep our fire family balance lest we be called hypocrites in the face of what we are doing here). The times he is able to step away and write or speak for 24-7 COMMITMENT bring immensely powerful messages to the community. Without a husband who is so caring, loving and approving of the raw transparency with which I have shared our life, none of this would exist. It's truly not many men who are courageous enough to let their emotional junk hang out all over the internet. Those who do, that is a moment I won't hold back from using the word brave. It doesn't take a far stretch to imagine exactly how these stories wind up in firehouse pranks, jabs and verbal right hooks. So although his writing is of less volume than what myself and other wives have contributed, we hang on every word. It's not often enough we get to see into the minds of men, let alone firefighter's whose gifting is more laden with brute strength and testosterone than language arts finesse. With no further ado, my husband's words to all of you on commitment.

◆◆◆ "Commitment: Is It Worth It?" By Dan Mercer ◆◆◆

I'm sitting in the cold February Ohio crispness doing what you do when you have a sick kid home from school with a fever and vomiting. I contemplate. OK, contemplate, do some laundry, maybe work out in the garage, but a lot of contemplating. I'm wondering, does he just have the flu? Did I drag it home and give it to him or did he get it at school or with the hockey team traveling together all weekend? What's tomorrow look like if he doesn't get any better? Where's the break over point where we stop feeding him Motrin and Tylenol and perhaps call the pediatrician? What if he gives this crap to his Mom or I? Worse yet passes it on to one or all of his three siblings? Contemplating...

The circumstances have me revisiting the old standard that I've come to know over the past 14 years or so, "Parenting is difficult." There's no instruction manual, no SOG's to follow and no two of the little boogers responds the same to the same methods. It's a thankless task filled with preschooler tantrums, elementary school fears and tears, pre-teen drama, and high school age eye rolling in my direction. None of them will say Lori and I were right about nearly anything until they're like 25 and even then, only if we stay the course, fight the fights and come out on the other side having raised a productive member of society, we may not get a thank you for it. It can leave you thinking, if you let it, is it worth it? My answer is of course it is. It's worth every moment of effort and every second of concern. The sense of love and pride I have in our four children is nothing I ever could have imagined. There are moments of disappointment to be sure. (We aren't raising saints). But the joy derived from seeing them work their way through the ups and downs of life, sharing in their wins and comforting them in their losses is priceless. Its an experience I had no idea I was going to enjoy so much and that i wouldn't change now for any reward.

As I sat this morning contemplating these circumstances of life, the thought occurred to me of just how paralleling the circumstances can be with regard to our choice to serve in the fire and emergency services profession. Doing this job can be difficult. I don't need to go on and on revisiting the topics we discuss at length that make the job unique in its stress and effort required. We can name them off the top of our head at this point. Sleep deprivation, exposure to circumstances that aren't ideal to witness, potential to miss meals, being unable to be present for a special occasion with your family, are all things we encounter that we know have an effect on us both in the moment and over time. Dealing with how you and your family make the best of each of these and the numerous other difficult scenarios that arise from our job are a personal decision. I so enjoy seeing the examples from the community we've built of people who have found healthy ways to navigate the winding road of career and family balance. But It can be hard. And it can leave one asking oneself at times the same question we find ourselves asking about parenting. Is it worth it? I believe, just as I do about parenting, that it is.

Now let me empathize with you a little if you're more of the cynical type and think that it takes a bit more than a rainbow colored glasses article or blog post to create truth. I hear you. I soooo hear you. We're working in an era of culture change in the fire service right now. Living in what I think you'll see go down in the manuals of the future fire academies as an awakening and professionalization period. The fire service has been an ever evolving profession as time has passed but there had always been a great pride in the fact that we had not allowed popular culture to change us. We are proud of the way we've gotten the job done for this long and we're proud that we've been able to do it all the while hanging onto our traditions of commitment and courage. This is an admirable quality that I still believe the fire service, and we as firefighters, should cling to. We however shouldn't stifle professional progress in that same effort. So without making this about the ever changing fire service, lets agree that what was difficult to be part of in the first place is even more difficult to be part of when it's going through some changes. What's the saying? Change is hard? So it's hard. The question was, and still is, is it worth it?

I find it worth it in the pride I feel in knowing that I may have been the only person an elderly person had a conversation with that day. (Are your grandparents still alive? If so, stop reading this and call them.) I find worth in knowing that when a poor family's world has been rocked upside down by a room in content fire in the back of their home that has ruined nearly every personal belonging they have to their name I can be there to help them recover what's left of their stuff and hopefully reestablish some sense of normal to their world again. I find worth in it shoving Narcan up a young girl's nose, watching her begin to take breathes again, and understanding that no matter how messed up she might be at this very moment, somewhere there's a dad just like me who didn't get the worst phone call of his life tonight. I find worth in it in the laughter around the dinner table last night at the station as we ate…together…like a family. I find worth in it in the effort I see my fellow crew members putting into their workouts and the skills drills we do, trying hard to never be the one that would feel as though they let each other down. It's worth it when I hear the pride in my 8 year old daughters voice when she tells someone what I do for a living. When I hear what SHE believes we're about, what SHE believes we're capable of, what SHE believes we're devoted to. It's worth it.

Things can be hard. Family, kids, work, your relationship with your spouse. All of them will present us with challenges along this crazy road called life. Things will come along that feel like a huge kick in the teeth at times. Tremendous joys will be derived from the same source. It's our responsibility as husbands, wives, fathers, mothers AND as professionals to understand and stay focused on the commitment that we've made. I've lost focus before. I'll get sidetracked again. There's no doubt. But staying connected to a group of people who share my same belief in dedication to a promise I made is one of the best tools I have in not running this train that is my life off the rails. Both in the online community and in personal relationships we should all seek out people who will hold us accountable to the understanding that regardless how difficult the "job" at hand becomes, its all worth it.

Daniel Mercer,
Husband, Father, Firefighter, Co-Founder 24-7 COMMITMENT

Memo to Fire Departments: Why Your Firefighter's Healthy Marriage Is Important to Your Success

We know the pressures firefighters are under on the job. PTSD and suicide are very real issues. Do you know what trigger often pushes them "over the edge"? It's not the one bad call. It's home life.

If the home life is stable, they have a safe place to rest and recover from the stress of the fire service. When it's in turmoil, suddenly everything is too much.

While there are no official statistics regarding divorce in the fire service, the evidence is around you. Count the members of your crew who are separated, divorced or on a second or third marriage. Even the marriages that survive have many scars along the way.

Home life can in fact be the healer and difference maker in a successful fire service career simply because of the support and stability they receive allowing them to endure the difficult runs, long hours and often politically charged environment.

Supporting this are research findings that share how marriage makes you healthier, happier and believe it or not, wealthier:

- Married women are about 30 percent more likely to rate their health excellent or very good than the same-aged single women were. Married men showed similar advantages over unmarried men. Married men and women are also less likely than singles to suffer from long-term chronic illness or disabilities.[1]

- Married men and women report less depression, less anxiety and lower levels of other types of psychological distress than do those who are single, divorced or widowed.[2]

1 Mike Murphy, Karen Glaser, and Emily Grundy, "Marital Status and Long-term Illness in Great Britain" *Journal of Marriage and the Family* 59 (1997) 156-164.
2 John Mirowsky and Catherine E. Ross, *Social Causes of Psychological Distress* (New York: Aldine De Gruyter 1989), 90-92

- Researchers have found that the act of getting married actually makes people happier and healthier; conversely, getting a divorce reverses these gains - even when we take into account prior measures of mental and emotional health.[3]

- The cost of divorce is high. Even if the income is divided fairly between the former spouses, the standard of living of the family drops by about 25 percent. No amount of child support can change the basic math: It costs more to live separately than together, and the money must come from somewhere

While it may not feel professional to involve your personal life with your job, it is practical for employers to provide resources as preventive measures to support their best asset—their employees.. When the home life balance tilts into an unhealthy space, your firefighter is no longer as focused on the job and at risk for injury, accident or worse.

It's an easy fix to make resources available to your fire department and that is the mission of 24-7 COMMITMENT:[4] *To Honor, Strengthen and Encourage First Responder Marriages and Families with resources, events and community support for both the firefighter and their spouse.*

Please share the attached resources with your department and consider providing more support tools to your firefighters. This is not a topic you need to add to your busy training agenda. It simply needs awareness and visibility and your encouragement as a leader who cares for their people, in all aspects of their life.

Sincerely, Dan & Lori Mercer, Founders of 24-7 COMMITMENT
Committed Firefighter, Husband and Father / Wife and Mother
refusing to be another statistic

---

3 Nadine F. Marks and James D. Lambert, "Marital Status Continuity and Change among Young and Midlife Adults: Longitudinal Effects on Psychological Well-being", *Journal of Family Issues* 19 (1998) 652-686

4 About 24-7 COMMITMENT: We are a federally approved 501(c)3 non-profit organization funded primarily by individual donors and supporters.

SECTION 1

Fire Life Basics

I commit to honor, with my thoughts,
words and actions, all of the good,
the little bit of bad, and most of all,
the beautiful memories of our life as
a family (that happens to include a
firefighter).

Family First Firefighting
Committed to the Right Priorities

To many, firefighting is more than a profession; it's a calling. It is part of who they are. To others, it's simply a job description (an awesome one that they are grateful they are paid for), but the job ends when they leave the station. For family members it's the same way. Some strongly identify with being a "fire family" or "fire wife," and for others it's just one piece of who they are. Here's the good news, no matter how your family looks at it, you can make it work for you. While marriages around you in the fire service may be dropping like flies, the mere fact that you have picked up this book is a strong indicator that you won't be one of them. Our marriage was almost a statistic, but our stubborn selves had already been divorced once and refused to walk that path again. So when the balance in our fire family life was off, some changes had to be made.

Balance is actually an ugly little word. Kind of flat and boring and, well, actually unachievable. There are moments you want and need to sail full force into something for your family or your career. A more appropriate way to think about this is to have a rhythm, or a cadence, and to learn to recognize the signals that knock you out of rhythm long before there's a crash.

■ ■ ■ ■ ■ ■ ■ ■ ■ ■ ■ ■ ■ ■

"Have a rhythm, or a cadence, and learn to recognize the signals that knock you out of rhythm long before there's a crash."

■ ■ ■ ■ ■ ■ ■ ■ ■ ■ ■ ■ ■ ■

First, I'll tell you a little more about our personal story so that you can relate better as I write this. I never dreamed about nor planned on marrying a firefighter. In fact, the person who introduced me to my husband was a dear college friend. And when he abandoned his degree path and said he was going to be a firefighter, our tight circle of friends were like "What? That's crazy!" Of course it turns out that he's a great firefighter and I'm forever grateful. As I was wrangling the madness of single mom life, this was one set of friends who stood beside me, and led me to meeting my husband, Dan. But I was stepping into the fire life with little experience or exposure. My cousins were volunteer firefighters so I got a bit of that lifestyle, but dating a man in a uniform was never something on my "must have" list of potential candidates. Nevertheless, I fell hard for that giant, giving heart that I believe is at the core of every firefighter. To do this job, there must be a desire to sacrifice and serve the community. Fast forward 14 years and here we are. I'm writing a book about it. Life is a wild ride.

■ ■ ■ ■ ■ ■ ■ ■ ■ ■ ■ ■ ■

"While I always admired what my husband did and enjoy that little giddy feeling I get when telling people 'my husband is a firefighter,' that's where it ended. I didn't define myself as a 'fire wife.'"

■ ■ ■ ■ ■ ■ ■ ■ ■ ■ ■ ■ ■

So I wasn't stepping into this world with a lot of education or expectations. While I always admired what my husband did and enjoy that little giddy feeling I get when telling people "my husband is a firefighter," that's where it ended. I didn't define myself as a "fire wife" and it wasn't until that little blog post I wrote in 2012 blew up that I owned my own fire department t-shirt. In fact, we didn't really interact much with the fire department at all. Our lives were pretty full with raising kids, other work interests and hobbies, extended family, neighborhood and church activities and so on. The fire department was 30 minutes across town and while we didn't take it for granted, our lives didn't revolve around it. Well, except for the number of hours and energy it sucked from our lives before we had a good "balance" for our family. I keep saying "balance" like that in quotes because it's such an overused and possibly unrealistic word that some of you are probably air quoting and rolling your eyes as you read it. I'm right there with you but roll with it and see if we can't overcome that perception.

■ ■ ■ ■ ■ ■ ■ ■ ■ ■ ■ ■ ■

"We must seek balance that doesn't let one part of our lives skew our perspective on others or completely dominate time, attention, conversation or finances."

■ ■ ■ ■ ■ ■ ■ ■ ■ ■ ■ ■

Like everything in life balance is necessary for some stability, mostly elusive and ever-evolving. It's ok to have some out-of-balance seasons. I don't think we should seek balance that leaves us in that mediocre, boring, complacent place. But we must seek balance that doesn't let one part of our lives skew our perspective on others or completely dominate time, attention, conversation or finances.

From 5 Straight Shifts to Family of 5: How We Found Our Rhythm

Our friends, retired Chief Rick Lasky and retired Chief John Salka, who are both authors and speakers, were the first men in the fire service I ever heard say to give your "first family" the importance it deserves. When my husband first heard them speak back in 2003, my heart found hope for our marriage, our family, and the fire service. Here were two well experienced and admired firefighters who were telling others the importance of keeping this balance, and my husband was respectfully listening!

Back then, my husband was a young(er), new(er) firefighter motivated to leave a mark in this tight brotherhood that does so much good for our communities, and totally one of the reasons I fell so madly in love with him. However, in a span of 2 years he went from spending 5 nights in a row hopping from firehouse to firehouse to network and make connections, to being a husband, stepdad and father to his first newborn daughter, and the announcement 10 months later that baby #3 was on the way. He also had to do that all with me, a woman who was quite new to the fire life and a bit (ok, maybe a lot) resistant. Can I just continue to be transparent here and say that we were arguing so much we couldn't possibly imagine how we were pregnant again? It was that bad.

My take was this: You are spending way too much time away from your family. We never see you. Is the fire department more important than us? I resent the fire service for what it does to our family.

His take was this: I was born to be a firefighter. This is what I do. It's how I provide for our family and this is what it takes to be the best firefighter ever.

And there was a bit of truth in both of those statements.

{Enter scene left—wise, respected and admired fire service all stars} The words "first family first" began to bridge the gap between my husband's viewpoints of his home and the firehouse.

He got the reassurance he needed to not have to sacrifice his life away for the fire service. The tension he was building in himself about how to best love on his new wife, stepson and baby girl, began to resolve itself. By the way, that internal tension was never spoken to me, the wife. That's, of course, pretty common of men right? It was only after years of reflection and objectively viewing the situation without emotion that I could see he didn't really like it either. Those words freed him to be a husband and dad first and foremost, and still be a darn good firefighter.

■ ■ ■ ■ ■ ■ ■ ■ ■ ■ ■ ■

"Those words freed him to be a husband and dad first and foremost, and still be a darn good firefighter."

■ ■ ■ ■ ■ ■ ■ ■ ■ ■ ■ ■

I finally saw with an open heart and mind, good men in the fire service speaking about whole life viewpoints and respecting and honoring their families. I saw my husband soak in those words and begin to make changes. **It helped to melt my resentment towards the fire service. The Fire Service was never really the problem. It was the**

way my husband was engaging with it, and he realized that as well. When my words and heart softened, it became easier for him to see the forest from the trees. I remembered one of the reasons I fell in love with this man—he was born to do something so giving, requiring such hard work and dedication, that not every man is made for. My husband was born to be a firefighter. The fact that he would back off of that a bit for the sake of our family, well, be still my thumping out of my chest heart.

■ ■ ■ ■ ■ ■ ■ ■ ■ ■ ■ ■ ■

"When my husband talked within the fire service about my complaining about his time away, highly regarded senior mentors told him to divorce me. 'She's not cut out for this.'"

■ ■ ■ ■ ■ ■ ■ ■ ■ ■ ■ ■ ■

Like all common marriage tension, we both gave a little, met in the middle and the love (and a bit of stubbornness) held us together. So what is the "right" healthy boundary for firefighting and family life? No one can tell you what those boundaries should be. It's up to you and your spouse to discuss and define what works for you. The problem for us in our young marriage was that there were few places to turn to know how to do that. We saw a lot of other unhappy marriages and unhealthy examples. Those outside the fire service were able to give us great marriage and life advice but when we talked about his schedule, all they had was "Wow, that's a lot." And when my husband talked within the fire service about my complaining about his time away, highly regarded senior mentors told him to divorce me. "She's not cut out for this." So here we are with some suggestions and discussion topics from real fire families to help you find that balance.

~ for the firefighter ~
Family First Firefighting
Committed to the Right Priorities

Here's a hint for the guys: You probably know the look on your wife's face when she has heard enough tales from the firehouse for one day, just like she knows the look on yours when you've heard enough about her passion project. While we want to be there for each other in all aspects of our lives, we need to agree upon some healthy boundaries. It's also ok to go all in on one area for a season when you both agree on it—going back to school, taking a short term lower paying job for opportunities in the future, or even those unexpected imbalances with health changes or family crises. Agree on this and be all in as a team.

■ ■ ■ ■ ■ ■ ■ ■ ■ ■ ■ ■ ■

"Stepping outside the fire service is going to give you perspective, fresh insights and refuel you for the grueling profession that it is."

■ ■ ■ ■ ■ ■ ■ ■ ■ ■ ■ ■ ■

(Warning for some strong words here…. but written by a woman so it might not slap you upside the head like a direct blow from a salty captain on your crew.). **There is way more to life than just firefighting. Actually stepping outside the fire service is going to give you perspective, fresh insights and refuel you for the grueling profession that it is.** No one ever dies saying they wish they'd worked more right? Well, except we have all met those firefighters who just can't and won't stop. We will boldly go on record here and say that you are first a husband/wife, father/mother, even son/daughter, and friend, before firefighter. Firefighting is a profession that could be taken away from you with one quick swing of the halligan resulting in a career-ending injury.

Yes, you may be made for it, but you were also made to do many other amazing things. No man is defined solely by their career, and if they are, then they've missed out on a lifetime of blessings. I know that might sting for some of you, and I pray those words don't make you put this book down. Can you promise to keep on reading and see just how fulfilling your fire family life can be?

■ ■ ■ ■ ■ ■ ■ ■ ■ ■ ■ ■ ■

"Firefighting is a profession that could be taken away from you with one quick swing of the halligan resulting in a career-ending injury."

■ ■ ■ ■ ■ ■ ■ ■ ■ ■ ■ ■ ■

Firefighters, you've got the job of a lifetime. The job so many little boys and grown men dream of. It may feel like you won the lottery but you know all the hard work that went into it working at multiple part-time departments, volunteering time everywhere, and spending off-duty time getting to know the fire service community. Even through your first rookie year there are so many expectations of your time and activities. **But no one expected you to abandon your marriage and family for this job.**

■ ■ ■ ■ ■ ■ ■ ■ ■ ■ ■ ■ ■

"Even through your first rookie year there are so many expectations of your time and activities. But no one expected you to abandon your marriage and family for this job."

■ ■ ■ ■ ■ ■ ■ ■ ■ ■ ■ ■ ■

Understanding Your Spouse's Perspective

- Comparison can be the thief of joy but it can also bring eye opening perspective. Your spouse is likely to be surrounded by others whose life revolves around a Monday through Friday, nine to five schedule. This may be a realization of how many waking / sleeping hours are spent apart in a fire family compared to others, while you are surrounded by firefighters who are used to that schedule.

- She knows that you must go into the firehouse for work. She's not being unrealistic and wanting you to quit or stay home, but recognizing those feelings she is having is important. She just wants you to hear that it's hard on her too and that she is lonely sometimes.

- If she does not understand how the overtime, vacation time, or training schedules work, she may feel you are choosing to be away from your family and be at the firehouse instead.

■ ■ ■ ■ ■ ■ ■ ■ ■ ■ ■ ■ ■

"She may feel you are choosing to be away from your family and be at the firehouse instead."

■ ■ ■ ■ ■ ■ ■ ■ ■ ■ ■ ■ ■

Your spouse and family should never be made to feel that the fire department is more important than your family.

~ for the spouse ~
Family First Firefighting
Committed to the Right Priorites

Spouses,

He (or she but we will tend towards the "he" language here in this book for simplicity of language and writing sake) got the job. Celebrate! You're married to someone who is a hard worker and just landed their dream career. Perhaps you've already spent a lot of time apart while he was training and working multiple jobs trying to get on a full-time fire service career. Your most important job is to never make him feel bad for doing a job he loves, and to learn to love him for the man he is, which includes being a firefighter.

■ ■ ■ ■ ■ ■ ■ ■ ■ ■ ■ ■ ■

"He was made to be a firefighter. So many people never know what they were born to do in life. You've got a spouse who does and loves it and is providing for your family."

■ ■ ■ ■ ■ ■ ■ ■ ■ ■ ■ ■ ■

But, you also have a right to have some expectations for your marriage and family. And some responsibilities to discuss and communicate that as well. Here are our best suggestions for you as you learn to find that right priority setting for your family:

- Make the commitment to embrace his love for the profession. It really isn't all bad. There are some amazing things about being a fire family. Clinging onto the resentment is simply going to keep negativity stirred up in you and your home. He was made to be a firefighter. So many people never know what they were born to do in life. You've got a spouse who does and loves it and is providing for your family. That's already a huge win.

- Understand where your frustrations are coming from so when you have a discussion about family priorities, you can do so with rational thinking and calmness. Inserting extra emotion is going to slow down that process

- I dislike the saying "He's a firefighter. You knew what you were getting into. Deal with it." Firefighting doesn't trump everything else in life. So if you feel the urge to suck it up and deal, it's only going to delay a blow up of frustrations. If you feel something out of whack, have the courage to have that conversation and address it.

- Learn about the fire service and what the demands are on your spouse. This will help you to have clear expectations and understand where you must be patient and where there is room to negotiate some balance. For your firefighter to be the best at what he does, which includes staying safe and focused on the job, he needs to know you are on his team and committed to his success. You don't have to be all enamored with it like he is. I get tired of watching videos of fires too. But, like your spouse gives you time for your hobbies and important conversations, you should learn about their passions as well.

- Assume positive intent. When something comes up that changes the schedule, assume that your spouse has done the best they can to avoid it, instead of assuming they didn't try to make it work for your family. Assuming positive intent defuses rough situations. No one expects it and even if they didn't have positive intent, they will remember your expectations of that and make different choices down the road. It feels good to know that someone thought the best of you.

Throughout this book we have the honor of people from many walks of life in the fire service contributing their thoughts and knowledge. Our first contributor is an author and speaker, Frank Viscuso. When we first heard Frank speak, it was another refreshing breath of air. It had been over a decade since Chief Lasky and Chief Salka spoke words into our family that reminded us the fire service has people who get this whole family and life thing. Now that we are mid-career, that starts to look different and Frank brings a motivating new spin on this topic of honor and commitment for firefighters and their families. As a husband and father, but more importantly as a leader, his motivating talks bring the best of leadership in general and apply it to the fire service specifically. My husband and I left his workshop massively pumped up and re-energized to continue our efforts with 24-7 COMMITMENT and Frank continues to be a cheerleader for this cause. That's our personal introduction now here are the formal props for this great firefighter.

Frank Viscuso is a career deputy chief, nationally recognized speaker, and author of six books, including the best-seller *Step Up and Lead* (PennWell, 2011) and the newly released follow-up book *Step Up Your Teamwork*. Frank is also co-creator of FireOpsOnline.com, a website that provides valuable free training, drills, and tips for firefighters who are serious about advancing their career.

As a speaker, Frank has the ability to move people to action. Over the past decade he has spoken to audiences in and outside the fire service on many topics that include leadership, team building, officer development, and customer service. His seminars are designed to introduce people to the top traits associated with leadership and to equip them with the skills needed to lead, inspire, and motivate their teams.

Frank works as a Tour Commander in Kearny, NJ. He and his wife reside in Toms River with their three boys.

"Balance" By Frank Viscuso

What exactly is balance anyway? Perhaps you are like me. I have always been in awe of people who seem to have found a perfect life balance. You know the type of person—beautiful family, thriving career, strong faith, great attitude, perfect teeth. Okay, moment of truth. Perhaps I have not always been in awe of these people. Maybe at one point in my life I held a bit of resentment towards them. After all, I was going through a failed relationship, my career was stuck, and I had more spiritually related questions than answers. Most of my energy was spent fighting a shallow depression that stemmed from a misdirected focus on all of my flaws; and trust me, I had many.

Fast forward twenty years. My life is almost unrecognizable from the one I just described. Today I have a beautiful family, thriving career and strong faith. I still have flaws and imperfect teeth but they work, and I still have my hair, for now.

■ ■ ■ ■ ■ ■ ■ ■ ■ ■ ■ ■ ■

"I don't know much about balance. In fact, I sometimes become obsessed with certain projects for a short period of time, but I do know that wherever I am at any given moment, I commit to being in that moment."

■ ■ ■ ■ ■ ■ ■ ■ ■ ■ ■ ■ ■

Recently I was being interviewed on a radio program when the host began to inquire about how I have been able to write six books and raise three boys while still working full time. He mentioned that he had seen my posts on social media and I appeared to have a very happy and balanced life. Balance—there is that word again. He asked what my secret was. I replied by saying that I don't know much about balance. In fact, I sometimes become obsessed with certain projects for a short period of time, but I do know that wherever I am at any given moment, I commit to being in that moment. It doesn't matter where: with my wife and kids, writing a chapter for a book, working at a 3 alarm fire, speaking to an audience, wherever it is, I commit to being in that moment. Life is a wonderful journey, but so many people are physically in one place while their mind is in another, which can contribute to anxiety, stress, insecurity and fear. Have you ever battled those four demons?

Balance is something worth striving for, but balance doesn't mean you are thriving in all areas in life. It simply means that you value the important things in life and that you are committed to making progress. We are talking about family, faith, health, recreation and career. I can't tell you what order to put those things in because every person is different, but you would be much better off if you set goals and focused on the activities that would enable you to improve in the areas that are important. If your relationship is struggling, find time alone with your partner so that you can focus on each other. If your health is failing, make working out and eating better a daily priority. If you're stressed out because of work, get away with the people you love to be around and do something that makes you happy.

Everyone agrees that goal setting is important, yet the average American can't answer the simple question, "what are you goals for the next 12 months?" Without attainable goals in various areas of your life, it's easy for people to become distracted by things like unhealthy habits and workplace drama. People on a path of purpose don't have time for those types of distractions. They are too busy being in the moment and focusing on making progress. Progress, now that's a great word. I like it better than the word balance, because making progress in the areas that are important to people is what makes people happy.

Since we have come full circle, I want to propose these four simple steps to help you enhance your life:

1. Decide what is important to you.

2. Set goals in those areas.

3. Be in the moment.

4. Commit to making progress in all areas.

Welcome to a balanced life.

Deputy Chief Frank Viscuso

■ ■ ■ ■ ■ ■ ■ ■ ■ ■ ■ ■ ■

We've already sung the praises of Retired Chief John Salka and are grateful for his contribution to this book so that all of you can also be inspired by this honorable and committed man. Chief Salka is the kind of fire chief who connects well with people like my husband because he's really been in the action and lived it. John served with the FDNY for over 33 years, the past 15 years a battalion chief in the 18th Battalion in the Bronx. Prior to being promoted to battalion chief, Chief Salka was assigned as the Captain of 48 Engine also in the Bronx.

He is a New York State certified instructor and also lectures nationally. John served as the co-lead instructor for the H.O.T. Firefighter Safety and Survival program at FDIC for over ten years, serves on the FDIC advisory board, and is the co-host for the radio show "The Command Post" heard on Fire Engineering Talk Radio. Chief Salka has also found the time to work for the NIOSH Firefighter Fatality Investigation and Prevention Program.

John is the author of the best-selling books "First In Last Out Leadership Lessons from the New York Fire Department" and "The Engine Company." He received the 2001 FDIC Training Achievement Award for his Get Out Alive firefighter survival training program and travels extensively training firefighters throughout the 50 states and Canada in tactics, strategy, leadership and safety & survival. Chief Salka has also served as a volunteer firefighter for over 30 years. He has been married to his wife Dawn for 32 years and together they have 5 children.

◆◆◆◆◆◆ "Separate But Equal" By John Salka ◆◆◆◆◆◆

I've been in the fire service for 40 years this year and the trip has been unbelievable. I started out as a volunteer firefighter in the Mineola, NY fire department on Long Island, made a short stop as a career firefighter in Titusville Florida, came back North to join the FDNY, and finally joined the local volunteer fire department in South Blooming Grove, where I now live. I have been in two career and two volunteer departments and I can tell you that each place has its own character. So what does this have to do with my personal life, my family and my wife? Everything!

Everyone handles their job, their family and their better half differently. Some of us just get it right and some don't. Sometimes you think you have this complex set of relationships down pat and sometimes everything is falling apart. Let me tell you a little about how I have gotten along being a firefighter, a father, a husband and a man.

I have had great success living the various segments of my life independently from each other. Not completely, but to a large degree I traveled from segment to segment as the months and years went by. There were times when I would have a busy and complicated 24 hour shift in the Bronx firehouse and after being relieved and heading home I would put that shift, all of the issues and all of the people there in my duffel bag with the other items I was bringing home. I could be home for three or four days and never really talk about the job or worry about anything that I would have to deal with when I returned to work a few days later. Many times I would be driving up the driveway after a shift and just as I got out of my vehicle, one of the kids or my wife would say, "go pick up Brian at the football game!" I would be back in the car and heading down the driveway for my first "family" task and I hadn't even gotten in the house yet. This "family" segment of my life would continue for a number of days and involve my interactions with the kids and my wife, and all of the other elements of a typical home life. In the summer yard work, swimming and vacations and in the winter shoveling snow and chopping wood for the fireplace. During this time is when I spent my almost undivided time on my family relationships. I consciously tried not to interrupt these days with fire department activities. I do realize that sometimes an event or an emergency comes up, or even a scheduled training day, but I tried to keep my time at home for the people at home. I do remember having to be reminded about this a few times by my wife who let me know that I had been spending more time at work and work related events, and less with her and the kids.

Then I would go to work for 24 hours, and as I drove away from the house my thoughts would turn to work. I drive about an hour to the firehouse and most of the things I would think about on the way would be job related. I would think about the last shift and if I had to finish anything that wasn't completed, or I might have a few new ideas for the upcoming shift. Once I arrive at the firehouse I'm off and running. Talking with the chief I'm relieving and getting physically ready for work. I can tell you right now that I might even work the entire overnight portion of my shift without either calling home or getting a call from my wife. We would eventually talk via phone but it was always short and sweet and I almost always immediately returned to my work.

■ ■ ■ ■ ■ ■ ■ ■ ■ ■ ■ ■ ■

"Chief, what advice can you give us about how we can be more successful and satisfied in our future careers?' I thought for a moment and told them to 'spend more time at home.'"

■ ■ ■ ■ ■ ■ ■ ■ ■ ■ ■ ■ ■

This "separation of church and state" worked well for me and for us. Like many other aspects of our lives it might not be how you live yours, but it worked well for me. I know firefighters who have successfully blended their fire service life and their personal life effectively. I know other firefighters who are divorced because they could not put the job on the back burner. I also know firefighters who come to work and do what required and don't stay a minute later so that they can get home to their wife and children. Whatever it is that works for you it is a balancing act that you must stay on top of.

The last item I want to mention is the answer that I gave during a presentation to a large group of firefighters at a conference I was presenting at several years ago. The question from the firefighter was, "Chief, what advice can you give us about how we can be more successful and satisfied in our future careers?" **I thought for a moment and told them to "spend more time at home."** I think they were expecting a discussion about studying for promotion, attending training or having passion, but it was not. I told them to spend more time at home with their wife and keep that relationship healthy and growing. **When the career is over, when the fires are all out, we will still be with our wives and families.**

Ret. Chief John Salka, FDNY

– for discussion –

In each chapter we will provide a list of discussion questions. These are meant to be thought provoking for you individually, to be discussed as a couple or to be used in a small group book study together. I believe that reading does wonders to expand the mind but taking action on the results is what really sets apart those who change and grow in life. Journaling is a powerful tool as you work through your thoughts as well. Consider keeping an "Honor and Commitment" journal as you read through this book.

- Do you know personally firefighters who focus too much on firefighting at the expense of their family? What does that look like from the outside perspective?

- What triggers in the fire life set off those frustrating emotions? Unplanned overtime? Another training outside of shift hours? The informal social and support events for the "brotherhood"? Think about why these are triggers and practice not reacting with emotion then have those courageous conversations together about how to adjust, if needed.

- Talk together about your first commitment to each other, your first family. If firefighting went completely away in your life for some unfortunate reason, you would be there for each other because of that first commitment to your marriage. Just reflecting on that scenario will bring some new perspectives to you.

- What's on your bucket lists for life outside of the fire service? Are there timelines and goal dates to complete those by? Looking outside the fire service and realizing how many short years we really have on this earth, will bring perspective to your priority setting discussions.

- Who do you admire in the fire service who is a top notch, honorable and committed firefighter who is also equally or more so honoring and committed to their family? What is it about them you admire? What choices do they make to do and not do in the fire life?

RESOURCES

Each chapter in this book includes a full set of resources available on our website from articles to videos to other books, speakers, partners and our online community discussions.

All resources mentioned in this chapter can be found at HonorAndCommitment.com/Chapter1

Some resources include:

- Back Off! That's Our Time—Protecting Your Fire Family Schedule: An article on balancing family time in the fire life

- A True Love Story: The original articles that launched Fire fighterWife.com—the raw and revealing story of the first years of our marriage which detail a lot of the balance struggles we worked through.

- Frank Viscuso, CommonValor.com

- Chief Rick Lasky and Chief John Salka's book *Five Alarm Leadership*

Shift Days Apart
The Good, The Bad, The Honorable Commitment

When we were first dating and newlyweds, shift days made me cry. Oh boy did I miss him like crazy! Not only did I miss him but I was a tinge bit (maybe a lot bit) jealous. This man loved his job, loved the people he worked with, and got to spend his days (when at the slow department) fitting in a work out, eating healthy and delicious meals he didn't have to make and clean up by himself, enjoying fresh baked cookies delivered by the local mom's groups, perhaps catching a game of basketball and inevitably, watching that movie we had planned to watch together. The icing on the cake would be when they planned a meal for dinner that I already had thawing in the fridge for our meal together the next night! Oh yes. It took me some time to learn to share him with his firehouse crew and not be jealous of those moments they had together.

For me, there was a stark contrast in our lives then because, when he was on shift, my days consisted of getting 1, 2, or 3 infants and toddlers dressed, out the door, situated for childcare, and get myself off to a job that provided well for our family but wasn't really my passion at that moment. Then back home, tired myself, to the same kitchen that didn't magically clean itself after breakfast and face 1, 2, or 3 young children who were just as tired, hungry, and grumpy as me. So when we'd finally connect by phone and he was so cheerful and beaming about his great workout and meal, I wasn't really in the mood to hear about it. (In fact, read the chapter on communication and it may explain some of the reasons he stopped telling me what they had for dinner!)

I wonder sometimes why God made us go straight from the honeymoon season of couplehood where you could do almost anything you wanted together, into that infant / toddler season which requires so much selflessness and sacrifice. What a giant leap. Truly once the children were all in school, life was much better adjusted. It could be simply that we are all more mature by then, or that life is easier when toddlers stop dumping bowls of spaghetti-o's on their head and the dog 5 minutes before you need to leave the house (on a shift night of course).

Learning to Love the Time Apart

Once you get beyond the "I can't stand for your eyes to be out of my sight" stage of a relationship, you do get used to the time apart. In fact, every single wife of a firefighter I've ever met has stated that those days apart have saved their marriage, and re-adjusting to having him home every night as a 40-hour officer, or once he retired, was an even bigger adjustment. Let's not go there yet. I'm not ready, and the thought of a 40-hour job some days makes me hyperventilate.

Time apart is healthy in marriage. Yes, we joke about watching what we want on the TV and eating what we want for dinner, but the best part is being a person who can stand solidly on their own two feet and take care of themselves. Confidence is one of the most sexy and attractive features in a partner. Spouses of firefighters who spend a lot of time apart, holding down the home front, exude confidence. (Perhaps we exude so much confidence we scare others off, hence my initial fear of other fire wives. Something to think about.)

And absence surely does make the heart grow fonder. Think of it like this. You just spent 24 or more hours apart. One of you was on call for the city should disaster or emergency strike. A noble calling. The other of you was single handedly managing your job, the household and family so your firefighter didn't have to worry while he was gone. Then you take all that confidence and testosterone back into the same room for what's only another 24- or 48-hour time period and you'll want to make the most of it. That's the heartbeat of a firefighter marriage right there. You don't know what's coming next, but you know you've got it and you've got each other.

What's the Good part of a shift day?

- Time apart to be you.
- Absence makes the heart grow fonder.
- Doing what you love.
- And with kids, special bonding time just for you and them.

What's the Bad part of a shift day?

Murphy's Law. It's bound to happen. Well, actually, it's not statistically proven it's just that it's way more noticeable and inconvenient to have something else pile on while one-half of you is completely unavailable to help. It is true that many firefighters can get time off for emergencies at home, but with limited vacation and personal time most of us try to avoid burning that for an emergency that can we can wrangle alone.

A sampling of Murphy's Law from our 14 years so far:

- 14 stitches to the forehead and a ride to Children's Hospital by Medic (neighbors covering childcare for the rest of the children)
- Our au pair arrested for drunk driving at 1 am (it was her last day of employment with us)
- Kitchen and basement flooded when a second floor laundry installation went bad
- Countless bouts of bodily fluids hurled about at all hours, from multiple people at once
- Locking ourselves out of house and cars
- Snow storms that only happen on shift days (I swear one winter my husband didn't have to shovel a single time because it only snowed on his shift day!)

■ ■ ■ ■ ■ ■ ■ ■ ■ ■ ■ ■ ■

Are there days I just want to be the damsel in distress and have him sweep in and take care of everything? Absolutely.

■ ■ ■ ■ ■ ■ ■ ■ ■ ■ ■ ■ ■

When Nature Strikes, It's a Tag Team Event

Then there are these things that aren't exactly Murphy's Law because everyone is dealing with them, such as natural disasters in your local area. For instance, windstorms that knock out power for 5 days and ice storms that do the same while preventing you from driving anywhere. Normally these are excuses for families to hunker down together and make the most of the frontier like fun times, but not fire families. If your firefighter is on crew when it strikes, chances are he'll need to hold over. If he's not on crew, chances are he gets called in. And when he does make it home, he's hot / cold, tired, exhausted, and needing some rest and TLC. This leaves you to pull out the generator, get 'er started up and clear away whatever challenge nature threw your way—wind, water, ice, snow, or heaven forbid, forest fires. It's an adventure. It's always an adventure. Are there days I just want to be the damsel in distress and have him sweep in and take care of everything? Absolutely. (And he may not say it but he wants that occasionally as well, right guys?)

These moments are when you realize how strong and capable you truly are as an individual. You get to be a problem solver. Your children see you tackle and accomplish big stuff. Your words can convey a confident attitude that you may not know exactly how you will fix this but you will get through it. These are the moments you need a support network around you and to not be afraid to ask for help. You get super creative and most of all, you make memories. The ice storm Christmas of 2004 we had no power, a 4 year old, 2 year old and 6 month old. I warmed formula on the gas log fireplace, fed the toddlers dry cereal and wrapped up in blankets in front of the fireplace reading books. When they were settled for a moment, I arranged for Santa to visit us in a hotel a few miles away that still had power. When my husband got home, we drove to that hotel, grabbed dinner and worked our Santa magic to come back to a hotel room full of gifts. Three hours later around 11 PM, we got word that our power was back on and we bundled everyone up and headed home to the comfort of our own warm beds. The kids were too little to remember but my husband and I will never forget how we tagged team those parenting moments without a hitch or a panic attack. We had it all the way. Life is meant to be an adventure.

What's the Beautiful Part of a Shift Day?

Natural disasters and Murphy's Law are all exceptional situations for sure. A question we get even more often is how to simply pass the time while apart (for the spouse, not the firefighter who is clearly busy being of service to the community.)

■ ■ ■ ■ ■ ■ ■ ■ ■ ■ ■ ■ ■

"If you find yourself restless and lonely on a shift day, spend time soul searching about your own purpose in life."

■ ■ ■ ■ ■ ■ ■ ■ ■ ■ ■ ■ ■

Being someone who loves to stay busy, this was never a challenge for me personally. I always have a queue of projects way bigger than my lifetime could ever accomplish, and a pre-kids shift day meant I was going to dive into one of those. Reading, scrapbooking, crafts, home decorating and DIY projects topped my list. Shift days are also great times to catch up with your girlfriends or even visit a grandparent. Volunteer work is another great option, especially if you live in a community with volunteer fire departments and want to get to know a little more about what's involved with the fire service.

Let me reach out for a moment to some girls who struggle with this topic on a more personal level. If you find yourself restless and lonely on a shift day, spend time soul searching about your own purpose in life. Yes, I do believe each of us was ordained specifically to be our husband's wife. And that role is possibly more important than anything else you may ever do in life. But being a good wife doesn't mean 24-7 care and attention. In fact, a doting wife can sometimes be an annoying wife. Goodness, it's a tough balance we all try to strike as husband and wife in marriage. Husband's need to read our minds to know if we are exuding confidence or having one of our damsel in distress moments. And wives need to be nurturing caregivers, but at the same time, not so needy and hands on that we don't give them enough space.

That's the beautiful thing with the shift schedule. You can settle into your own heartbeat rhythm in your marriage of time together/time apart so you are both equally filled up while away and eager to reunite when back together. It's a healthy balance that gives both space and the desire of those missed moments together. Can you see that and love it for what it is?

There are a few more logistical issues to face on these shift days we'd be remiss to leave out.

Attending Events Without Your Firefighter

Even if you have a great relationship with your in laws, that moment arrives when you first attend a family function without your spouse because they are on shift. Awkward. A wee bit or possibly even a lot. There's only one way to make this more comfortable over the years and that is to be sure first and foremost that the two of you as husband and wife have the same opinion and approach to handling this. Some couples decide to only attend if both of you can be there. In other cases, you can agree it's good to attend even without the firefighter who is on shift, but that may require a few conversations with the in-laws to be sure everyone is ready to make a new spouse feel welcome and part of the family. In the worst case, there are families who do not understand nor appreciate the shift schedule and will cast blame, or worse, towards the firefighter and their spouse. I'm so sorry if you are having to deal with that. You can't pick blood family right? Remember the title of this book? Honor and Commitment. This is one of those moments to maintain being honorable, remember your commitment first to your marriage, and let the spouse whose family is involved take the lead. Family drama is another one of those high ranking marriage struggles you must commit to not let interfere in your relationship. Meddling mother-in-laws come in all shapes and sizes and maturity levels. But you, you are a couple committed to honor in all walks of your life. Honor thy mother and father. Yes, it stings, but realize there are ways to be honorable and respectful without getting walked on and without harming your relationship. Here's hoping you have just a minimally awkward getting to know each other stage and it's all love from there. These are the people who birthed and raised a firefighter and will be grandparents to your littles.

Feeling Safe on Shift Nights

Dogs, guns, security systems and lots of training to feel comfortable with them all. I could end this section here but it wouldn't feel complete. This is a topic that might jump up and surprise you. Perhaps you live in a very safe community when suddenly there are a series of break-ins and home invasions. Or possibly just neighborhood teenagers playing "Ding Dong Ditch" at 1:30 am. Talk about a heart attack! I realize guns are not legalized in all states, but I happen to live in one where they are. It's taken me a few years to get comfortable and realize the importance of being able to protect my home if my husband is not there. This is such a personal decision we don't need to dwell on the details. I just didn't want to skip over it as an important discussion point—are you feeling safe when you are home alone? What should you put in place to do so?

Passing the Time with Kids on a Long Shift Day

You know what makes a 24 seem short? A 48! It's one of our favorite memes of all time we share on our social media pages because it's the truth. Wives miss their husbands. Husbands miss their wives. Kids miss Mom/Dad. Mom/Dad miss kids. If we dwell there it's pretty dismal. So we look at the positives and things we decide to do to make it special, like making a blanket fort and camping on the living room floor, ice cream sundaes for dessert, or saying yes to that new playground on the other side of town.

■ ■ ■ ■ ■ ■ ■ ■ ■ ■ ■ ■

Shift days. It's all about your perspective. It can feel like watching paint dry or you can make it an adventure.

■ ■ ■ ■ ■ ■ ■ ■ ■ ■ ■ ■

Our favorite family tradition for a shift night is the reward of who gets to sleep with mom. I hear you. Octopus-legged toddlers need not apply. This is another topic that can send groups of women into separate corners over parenting choices. No matter what you decide, this is certainly a fun tradition for many fire families. We've grown so accustomed to it in our house that I worry if I'll be lonely (and cold!) once they are all too big to want to share my bed. (So far the 8-year-old girl and 11-year-old boy are still in on it.....shhhhhhh!) Like everything else in this book, I just wanted to give you permission to not feel guilty or judged for taking this path as a fire family if it works for you.

Shift Day Meal Specials

If you don't yet have kids, let us also give you permission to eat a bag of popcorn for dinner. Or a plate of nachos. Or a crazy combination of yesterday's leftovers. No one is judging. If you have kids to feed, it gets a little more complicated. With toddlers, I would make them a healthy finger food combination with a PB&J and eat the leftovers for my meal. It served a dual purpose. No wasted food and less clean up. Remember those are the rough seasons. I don't recommend that as a standard. Help is on the way from about 300 fire families though. Read on.

Despite the fact that my cooking skills are so very challenged, our organization launched a cookbook called "Eat Like A Firefighter". Food is a love language. It connects you over conversation and all the senses of sight, smell, taste and touch. It commemorates special occasions and even people. This cookbook includes slow cooker meals, freezer meals, simple and healthy meals, and lots of other great options for that spouse who loves to cook. Without a doubt, the cookbook was a great hit. However, as the director of this organization I felt I must contribute something of value in the way of a recipe, not just the concept and design and writing. Then it hit me, "Snacky Dinner." Next to a bowl of cereal or oatmeal, this is our fire family's favorite shift night meal. Just for you, we'll share it here as well.

SNACKY DINNER (247commitment.org)

Dan & Lori Mercer
Founders of FirefighterWife.com and 24-7 COMMITMENT
Columbus, Ohio

Raisins
Celery and Peanut Butter
Cut Up Apple Slices
Carrot Sticks
Cheese Sticks
Shredded Cheese in a Dish
Cheese Slices
Cheese in any format really
Almonds, Cashews or any Nuts
Hard Salami
Deli meats in general
Ranch Dip or French Onion
　　Chip Dip
Nacho or Regular Chips
Crackers
Nutella
Small portions of leftovers from
　　the fridge
Grapes
Strawberries
Easily heatable freezer
　　appetizers such as Tacquitos
　　or Pizza Bagel Bites
Yogurt
Cottage Cheese
Apple Sauce

This meal is dedicated to every mom who's husband is pulling long shifts at the firehouse and by the end of the day, you can't imagine dirtying up your kitchen for a hot meal that will take your children 1 minute and 30 seconds to eat and you 1 hour and 30 minutes start to finish to prepare and clean up. Pick any of the above items in combination. Put them on a serving tray. Provide paper towels or paper plates and let your family select buffet style. The rule is this. There must be at least one protein and one fruit and one vegetable in each person's selection. It's fun. It's healthy. It's easy. And it totally counts as dinner.

Note: Lori Mercer is a fire wife and mother of 4 who has also managed a full time career. She rarely cooks. But her kids have not starved and are incredibly healthy and her husband tolerates it all. She prays to find quick, easy and healthy choices for people whose talents are not in the kitchen. Hence was born Eat-LikeAFirefighter.com and we're grateful you are here!

Shift days. It's all about your perspective. It can feel like watching paint dry or you can make it an adventure. Then, you can look forward to the 48 hours your fire family can spend together. Let's summarize some tips for both the firefighter and the spouse.

~ for the spouse ~
Shift Days Apart
The Good, The Bad,
The Honorable Commitment

For Firefighters

Our best "Honor and Commitment" tips for supporting your spouse at home on a shift day:

- Praise and recognize your spouse's efforts to keep it all under control. It's honorable.

- Notice when they need a little boost of energy and encouragement and send an extra sweet text or give them permission to just let it all ride until you are home. (Did you know the most productive hour of cleaning is 1 hour before shift ends? If a clean house isn't as important to you, some shift days that can be a wonderful gift to give your spouse. That's commitment through thick and thin.)

- When it truly is an emergency, you know you have a brother firefighter who can help by either working for you or checking in on your family.

- Suggest ideas for hobbies or entertainment for your spouse to participate in even without you. Are you playing on a co-ed softball team? Encourage her to still play even if you have a shift night.

- Get on the same page regarding attending your family functions without you. Some families are close and others not. This could either be a very comfortable setting or quite awkward. She needs you to be clear and clearly on her team as these decisions are made together. It's honorable.

- Have your home stocked and prepared for various natural disasters and teach your spouse where to find and how to use these items. Weather radios, flares, flashlights, generators, bottled water, and yes even weapons and security systems.

- Send flowers. Just because. It really helps sometimes.

~ for the firefighter ~
Shift Days Apart
The Good, The Bad,
The Honorable Commitment

For the Spouse

Our best tips for managing a shift day:

- This might sound harsh or obvious and if so, it probably doesn't apply to you. Someone needs to hear it though because it's the honorable way to support your spouse. Don't blame your firefighter for not being able to be there and help. They are off supporting your family financially with their work. I'm going to use the direct male delivery my husband always shares on this topic "You married someone who is gainfully employed in a respected job and providing for his family. You're already winning." (If he's working too much, refer to the Chapter 1 on priorities!)

- If something isn't a huge deal, don't stress your firefighter with it on a shift day. Take into consideration they may worry about you or feel bad that they can't be there to help. I know sometimes us girls just want to vent, but sometimes our men just want to fix, and it can be frustrating for them to not be able to fix anything while they are at work.

- Find YOU! Be comfortable and happy with who you are and find your own hobbies and passions to carry on in the time you have alone. A strong you makes an even better marriage. Note, however that working at the station does not count as downtime for your firefighter. He also needs downtime and hobbies that will mean your grace and encouragement to do so during his possibly rare off duty times.

- Find friends who appreciate the shift schedule and will spend time together on shift nights yet understand why the nights he is home are so special.

- Don't worry needlessly but be prepared and ready in the case of disasters. Be sure you are aware of and trained on all the safety and security items in your home.

- If you have kids, make it a fun special time and a normal part of their routine.

– for discussion –

1. Spouse: What are your favorite ways to spend a shift day?

   Firefighter: Do you like to hear about these adventures while on shift or after you get home?

2. Family Events apart: Where is the comfort level with the spouse attending alone? Any conversations that the firefighter can have with their family to make this more comfortable?

3. Safety: Is your home equipped to handle an emergency and everyone trained on being prepared?

4. Spouse: What do you need to work on in yourself to feel more confident in handling a shift day solo?

   Firefighter: Where are you finding time to care for your soul with hobbies and down time off shift?

RESOURCES

All resources mentioned in this chapter can be found at HonorAndCommitment.com/Chapter2

Commitment
Over Worry and Fear

This is a very common issue for new fire wives but one that may drive their firefighters crazy. Sometimes it can sneak up on us out of the blue in various life seasons. The goal here is to help you know that fear and worry are normal (within reason), give you some basic tools to deal with it, and recognize when you need further help.

Firefighters, if you don't mind, we're going to speak mostly directly to the wives in this section. But please still read it, and check out the summary points specifically for you. As a firefighter, you've already tackled many worrisome and fearful scenarios and probably have this issue knocked down (if not, you won't be the first nor last firefighter to struggle with some anxieties so be sure to reach out for support from your crew members.) Your commitment to your spouse includes through these kinds of hurdles and getting over them together will only make you stronger.

To the spouses: This may not be a struggle for you but if it is, it's one of the most real and vicious mental enemies you can face. But it's totally possible to overcome this. We're going to show you how.

Congratulations! You married a hero. A total hunk. The man of every girl's dreams. Every day he does brave and noble and honorable deeds to serve his community. Bringing back someone from cardiac arrest. Sweetly calming an anxious, elderly widow. Rescuing a toddler from a second floor window of a burning building. Tearing a door off a mangled car to smile at an unscathed infant locked safely in her seat.

Even serving up a plastic fire helmet to kids who are stopping by the fire house. He's off saving the world! And you are SO PROUD!

Until....

Until you hear the door shut behind him in the morning before the sunrise. You get up and get busy enjoying your day but the worry and fear thoughts still come at you. Is he ok? Should I turn on the scanner? He hasn't returned my call. Should I text him again? You turn on the news and see stories of fires, murders, and train derailments, all with firefighters working on the scene. In turnout gear, almost any of them could be your man.

Fears. Irrational, ridiculous fears hit you. Thoughts that you are certain most other women aren't thinking about their husbands. If he dies on the job, will the chief or the assistant chief call me? Will his body be recognizable if he dies in a blaze? Does his partner really know how to keep him safe and protected?

Then comes nightfall. The thoughts quicken. Your heart races. The strange noises pick up around the house. Before too long it's time to climb into that big, empty bed alone. You're searching for peaceful slumber not knowing what the love of your life is doing at any given moment. In the worst cases you toss and turn and barely blink your eyes shut as you suffer through another restless, sleep-deprived night.

Yes, you are proud. But this fear, worry, and sleeplessness is the side of the glamorous fire wife life that you never anticipated. You ask yourself, "Did I really sign up for this?"

Statistic: You are not alone. "Anxiety disorders affect about 40 million American adults age 18 years and older (about 18%) in a given year, causing them to be filled with fearfulness and uncertainty," and "Women are 60% more likely than men to experience an anxiety disorder over their lifetime." (Statistic from the National Institute of Mental Health, http://www.nimh.nih.gov/health/topics/anxiety-disorders/index.shtml)

Ok, so some of you may be thinking my description of fire wife anxiety is a bit exaggerated. Or at least you are not in this mode every day. But certainly in a fire wife's life, she has experienced at least one or two days of this worry and fear running around in her mind.

Statistic: "Anxiety is a normal reaction to stressful and uncertain situations. It's your body telling you to stay alert and protect yourself..."

(Anxiety and Depression Association of America. http://www.adaa.
org/understanding-anxiety/generalized-anxiety-disorder-gad/gad-vs-
general-anxiety-about-economy)

Not every day is this hard. Some days fly by with friends, fun, and
confidence. As the years wear on, you find ways to enjoy your "you
time" when he's away. Your movies. Your dinner favorites. Your choice
of how to spend the time.

But some days are this difficult. And for some people, it can go on
and on and on. It doesn't matter if this is an ongoing problem, a once
in a while occurrence, or even if you've long grown out of this season
of your fire wife life. Worry, fear, and interrupted sleep patterns are all
thieves of your joy and peace. These are not the places any of us need to
be spending our mental energy. 86,400 seconds in a day is truly a very
short amount of time, and your fireman does not want you to be sitting
around fretting the day away. In fact, what probably turns your fireman
on the most is the worry-free, confident woman you were designed to be.

■ ■ ■ ■ ■ ■ ■ ■ ■ ■ ■ ■ ■

*"Living a stressful life has been found to atrophy the cortex
of the brain. Did you read that? Your worrying is
literally killing your brain cells!"*

■ ■ ■ ■ ■ ■ ■ ■ ■ ■ ■ ■

Dr. Nussbaum, a Clinical Neuropsychologist, Adjunct Professor of
Neurological Surgery at the University of Pittsburgh School of Medi-
cine, and President of Brain Health Center, Inc., says, "Living a stressful
life has been found to atrophy the cortex of the brain, the critical part
that processes information consciously. Stress also can cause damage in
areas of the brain the regulate emotion." (http://www.fitbrains.com/
blog/2012/12/06/stress-damaging-to-the-brain/)

Did you read that? Your worrying is literally killing your brain cells!
So if this constant stress and worry is actually going to shrink and damage
your brain and wear on you emotionally, then there's only one logical thing
to do...End the Bad Thought Patterns Now! Clear the nasty thoughts
from your memory bank and replace them with ideas of confidence and
peace. This doesn't mean you are in denial of the possibilities, but rather

that you have faced them head-on. You are prepared if the worst happens, but you won't allow those thoughts to steal away a single moment of life in between the now and the what-ifs.

When I was a kid, I'd always get that nervous stomach feeling whenever I was trying something new, under pressure to perform, or even just the night before a fun vacation. It got bad in 5th grade when I had a mean math teacher in the first period and felt sick to my stomach waiting on Fthe bus each morning. By high school, I was that track athlete who physically threw up 5-10 minutes before every race (that might be 4 times in one day before each event) yet feeling high as a kite two steps after the gun went off. I was disguising it better by college, but I became a giant irritable stressed out bridezilla who didn't eat anything but crackers for 48 hours during my first wedding. I somehow managed to jet set my pre-children years around the country for my corporate job in my mid-twenties. I would clench my jaw tight and try to meditate my way to calmness for the entire flight. By then, I had developed TMJ so bad I had constant massive headaches and soon found myself sitting in the office of a psychologist, convinced I had a brain tumor and was going to die. (And a husband, who is now ex, who had zero words to say to me to help me through it except, "I don't get it." But that's a story for another training).

What I experienced, my friends, is a classical diagnosis of anxiety. (And if you are exhibiting any crazy symptoms like those, we highly encourage you to seek professional help to get that anxiety under control!)

I am here to tell you that I am successfully, 110% "cured" from that kind of debilitating anxiety, and if you are anywhere on the anxiety spectrum it is totally possible for you as well. You can overcome the anxiety that would make you find excuses from participating in certain life events like roller coaster rides. I'm not going to go into the hows of that cure except to say that I did it without medication, which was very important for me. I truly wanted to get to the root of my broken thinking and fix it. And that's essentially what I did through a combination of:

- Professional Counseling
- A small, professionally-led support group for those struggling with anxiety
- Massage therapy and aromatherapy

- An amazing women's Bible study that first introduced me to Beth Moore (can I get a "Glory"?)

- Reading almost every self-help, positive thinking book under the sun

- Keeping my fitness routine consistent and including activities I loved

- Learning many mental and physical coping techniques through journaling, prayer and meditation

I still get nervous sometimes. Everyone does. It is very natural. But now it doesn't run off in a whirlwind cycle of doomsday thinking leaving me paralyzed and stealing my joy.

■ ■ ■ ■ ■ ■ ■ ■ ■ ■ ■ ■ ■

"I've been paralyzed with worry and anxiety and too focused on the negative what-ifs. I don't want anyone else to sit trapped in that pit any longer than necessary."

■ ■ ■ ■ ■ ■ ■ ■ ■ ■ ■ ■

Why do I share this? Because some of you may be looking at me speaking up on stage, shooting videos for all our fans here at FirefighterWife.com and spouting out all this hope and inspiration and think, "She's really got it together." I definitely have it more together than I did in my twenties (a statistically high season of life for mental health topics to raise their ugly heads by the way). But I want you to know that I've been there. I've been paralyzed with worry and anxiety and too focused on the negative what-ifs. I don't want anyone else to sit trapped in that pit any longer than necessary. It's time to share this story and get you all back up on that mountain of positive thinking and confidence while leading a vibrant life. Are you ready to make that commitment?

What Does a Case of the Worries Look Like for a Fire Wife?

So now you see a bit about how the brain works and what we are up against in this worry and anxiety battle. Let's apply it specifically to the life of a Fire Wife. We've done all the worrying for you. Here is a list of things you could worry about your husband's role as a firefighter and ways to turn those thoughts in a positive direction:

My worry: He might get hurt and can't work for a while.

The irrational level of worry: Feeling that every time he goes to work, he's going to get injured, lose his job, have no benefits, and land your family into a pit of debt and despair.

My Commitment to Turn That Thought Around: Injury is possible, but this is why the firefighters train regularly, take continuing ed classes, and have protective gear and equipment. If something were to happen, this is the reason you have insurance. You are also part of a large fire family who will help if you need it.

My worry: He could get sick from being exposed to something contagious on a call.

The irrational level of worry: He will catch some new superbug from strange and vicious germs on a call and bring it home to you and your children and your fate will be unknown.

My Commitment to Turn That Thought Around: There is a chance of exposure, but there are also many precautions to prevent this: masks, gloves, sharps containers, specific protocol while handling sharps, training, etc.

My worry: He could develop cancer from his exposure to carcinogens during fire calls.

The irrational level of worry: He's going to die of cancer at a young age and suffer a lengthy, gruesome death, leaving you as a single parent, widowed, and raising young children.

My Commitment to Turn That Thought Around: Carcinogens are everywhere, but a healthy immune system is key to avoiding cancer. Some firefighters receive yearly physicals. Learn to avoid cancer risks at home and work. Study healthy, clean living for your whole family. Knowledge is empowering, emotionally freeing, and benefits the entire family for a lifetime.

My worry: He might get hit by a car while working on a roadside accident scene.

The irrational level of worry: He is struck and thrown into the lane of oncoming traffic while working an accident. His body is so badly damaged that you aren't even allowed to see him before you bury him.

My Commitment to Turn That Thought Around: As fearless as he may seem to you, your firefighter is a smart man with enough fear in him to also be a cautious one. Every accident scene has a specific way of staging apparatus so that firefighters, EMS, and law enforcement are protected inside the staging area. If you want to know more, ask him how they do it. He'll be happy for the opportunity to brag on some fire department info.

My worry: He has had to battle fires near gas tanks before and you worry about a gas explosion.

The irrational level of worry: You see on the news that FFs are battling a fire with a gas leak. You feel in your heart that the gas tank is going to blow, leaving no trace of any person who was working to fight it. You just know you'll never see your firefighter again.

My Commitment to Turn That Thought Around: Ask yourself, "What does my fireman know about fires near gas? What training do they have? What are their SOPs on these?" You say a prayer and put his fate in the knowledge and training of his FD and in God.

My worry: He might get caught in a flashover.

The irrational level of worry: The next big fire will certainly be his last, because after watching that movie last night, you know that every fire has a flashover, despite what he's told you. He must be trying to calm your fears, but you know better than to believe him about it! He's going to die in a Hollywood-style inferno and be unrecognizable as his Brothers carry his body from the rubble.

My Commitment to Turn That Thought Around: Think of all the times you've watched firefighting on TV and your FF sat there, shouting that, "These are the warning signs! That's not how it looks! They wouldn't have survived. They would be headed out already because of the unstable conditions." Have faith that if he recognizes a flashover is imminent on TV, he will recognize an out-of-control fire in real life and get to safety first.

My worry: He could fall through a floor during a fire.

The irrational level of worry: He will fall through a floor into a burning basement and suffer a slow and painful death as he desperately calls for help, then panics and rips his mask off.

My Commitment to Turn That Thought Around: You know your fireman well enough that he has a healthy fear of burning to death and will always take precautions to prevent that, including not going interior in an unstable building with floors that will collapse.

My worry: He might fall off a ladder.

The irrational level of worry: You've seen him stumble and fall off the step stool at home. He probably learned nothing and is so clumsy he will fall to his death on the very next fire or training scenario involving the ladder.

My Commitment to Turn That Thought Around: You run through a list in your mind of all the training classes you remember where he's been away from home extra time, but has come home excited about all the fun ropes and ladder training they did like high angle rescue when he was dangling off the side of a water tower.

■ ■ ■ ■ ■ ■ ■ ■ ■ ■ ■ ■

"He trains for this. All the time. It doesn't mean it would prevent it from happening, but what do the firefighters do way more than fight fires? Train for them."

■ ■ ■ ■ ■ ■ ■ ■ ■ ■ ■

My worry: His fire truck could get in an accident.

The irrational level of worry: His fire truck is going to be involved in a horrible accident someday and you just know that if anyone survives, your FF will not. He will be the one everyone else will try desperately to extract, before they have to back away from the fire taking over the fire engine and your fireman.

My Commitment to Turn That Thought Around: Fire trucks are massive vehicles. They are highly visible on purpose. They rarely wreck. The chances of you and your family being in an accident in your personal vehicle are much more likely than your husband wrecking in the fire truck.

In summary, here is why there is absolutely no reason to worry about him:

- He trains for this. All the time. It doesn't mean it would prevent it from happening, but what do the firefighters do way more than fight fires? Train for them.

- He was made for this; born for it, most likely. Not every man out there wants to run into a burning building. I believe God gave that gift only to men and women who want to do it and know what they're doing.

- Statistically speaking, it's not going to happen. While it may seem like you are always hearing about a LODD, the reality is they are way lower in the fire service than in other professions such as police. Go with the statistics. They don't lie.

- Even if something does happen, there is almost always a way out. Being trapped in a building like the guy in Ladder 49? That's Hollywood's version, made for the movies. You know that, right? Go back to those statistics. That one is a crazy low probability.

Now we aren't saying to live in denial. Because heaven forbid something does happen. You will most likely be really messed up by those thoughts. Here is what we are saying.

1. Come to terms with the fact that he could die on his job. (And you could die tomorrow in a car accident or a freak fall in the shower. That's the reality of life.)

2. Remind yourself that he is trained and prepared and protected by all kinds of angels who do a lot of extra protecting of men who work such dangerous jobs.

3. Focus on something other than the worry. That's the only healthy way to approach this. If you turn into a freaky, whimpering, vulnerable mess of a girl over this topic all the time, it's going to be a challenge in your marriage.

Here's a story from our fire family life to illustrate called "What I Didn't Know Didn't Hurt Me."

This is one of those situations where I probably could have worried more during the event had I actually known it was happening. But instead, I learned later just how close my fireman had come to losing his life falling through a burning floor. That just added fuel to the mental fire of worry. I hadn't imagined that one yet and now I had something new to imagine. You see, I come from a long line of worrying women.

My great-grandma and her 7 daughters made a career out of worrying and could carry on hours of conversation just fretting about the what-ifs. It's so bad that we pretty much never tell any of them when we are traveling by plane. Despite my awareness of this, the worry gene has not escaped me. When I make a particularly irrational worry statement, my husband jokingly says, "Ok Grandma Ann," which is my cue to relax a bit on the mental worry tornado swirling through my head!

My husband didn't immediately tell me what happened in that house fire. A couple days later, I sat there with my jaw dropped to the floor as he recounted how the kitchen floor gave way underneath him into a fiery basement and how, luckily, he got hung up on his pack. Then his partner at the time (who thank the good Lord was a ginormously strong muscle builder) added superhuman strength and grabbed him up out of there by his pack without even thinking twice. They are both darn lucky the whole floor didn't cave in on them.

So he's fine. All is well. Another heroic rescue and many angles of the story to retell around the coffee pot in the firehouse kitchen. All is well, except for my brain that is. It now has a new scene to play over and over. Because THAT was a scenario I had not pictured before. I had not yet worried about a flaming basement swallowing my husband. In some ways, I realize that's how I did survive our early years of marriage. I didn't really understand all the intricacies of firefighting back then, so scenario after scenario was archived in my brain as "things to worry about." He went to ropes training and was learning about knots. I ask why. What do they use them for? Out comes a dozen examples of needing the rope for various escape and rescue methods when you are stuck somewhere. 2nd floor windows being a prime example.

Key lesson here is that **if you are going to learn about all the terrifying what if scenarios, you must also pack your brain with all info about their training and safety.** And if you know there are people on his crew who are, well, not as safe or as fit as others, it's probably best not to ask who will have his back that day. If you ask, be able to let go of those what if thoughts before they take over your brain.

HONOR GUARD

~ for the firefighter ~
Commitment
Over Worry and Fear

Ok firefighters, have you been taking notes? There are some really basic things you can do to support your spouse through these fears and worries.

- Feelings are real, even if they aren't quite accurate. Acknowledge the feelings first. It shows empathy and allows you to be more effective in helping your spouse to work through these emotions.

- Just be prepared. Fear of the unknown is usually worse than the fear itself so having open dialogue about risks and dangers and an action plan in place should something happen will calm some worries.

- Don't feed into the fears and worries. Give your spouse the gift of your confidence in your training and your crew. When they see a confident firefighter, their worries may subside. (If you aren't confident in your abilities or your crew, please, please, please be taking steps to make the necessary changes in your life to get there.)

- Be aware of your spouse's triggers and warning signs of heading into an anxietous episode. World events, local events or something that hits close to home can really flare up those anxieties.

~ for the spouse ~
Commitment
Over Worry and Fear

Spouses this entire chapter was very directed at you. Instead of rehashing those points, we want to leave you with one final powerful example of just how strong you can be as a fire family.

This story comes to us from Heather Baker in California, a fire wife who experienced a justifiable near death experience with her firefighter. Heather shares with us the emotions and advice for other fire families who we pray do not experience this, but know you will be prepared to face those fears.

February 6th, 2012:
The Incident of My "Fire Wife Career"
by Heather Baker

A question that is often asked of me by the non-fire wife or a new firefighter wife is "How do you not worry about your husband getting hurt?" My usual answer is "I believe that God is ultimately in control; my husband could get hurt crossing the street, driving his car, or going into a burning building. Therefore, I learned long ago to lay that fear at my Savior's feet." However, little did I know that on February 6th, 2012, my words and faith would be tested more than ever before in my life.

The day began with my normal routine as I was stuck in traffic coming home from work while worrying that I wouldn't have dinner on the table in time for my husband. I always like to have dinner on the table for him after a long day at work. Thankfully, I got home in time to prepare our meal. I was about ready to start dinner, when I received a text from my husband, stating he would be home late, due to a possible call for a natural gas leak at his work. My past experiences have taught me that it would be a few hours before he would be home. I decided to go for a walk down to the gym, get my run in for the day and then start dinner. I began cooking, turned on the television and saw the image on the next page.

My heart sank, fear tried to overtake me, and I remember grasping for my phone. I fell to my knees in front of the television. My heart felt like it stopped. I began trembling and my worry for my husband was overtaking me. Instead of worrying, I decided to start praying for him and his coworkers. I couldn't even speak and I did not know exactly what to pray for but after praying I felt at peace. A scripture came to me that I had learned as a little girl. "Peace I leave with you, my peace I give unto you, let not your heart be troubled, neither let it be afraid" (John 14:27). I then remembered, from years of being a CALFIRE wife, "No news is good news." And I just kept praying.

I wanted to reach out to another fire wife. I picked up the phone and called my husband's Battalion Chief's wife. She was hysterical on the other end of the phone. I remember praying with her and reassuring her with stories of Christopher being on big fires with CALFIRE and not hearing from him for days and how this was a good sign. I know from past experiences, that if we did receive a phone call from his work, that wouldn't have been a good sign. I tried to be light hearted and not to let her sense my gut fear and helplessness. Then we prayed again, I asked her if she had the numbers of any of the other fire wives of the husbands that were on duty during this incident. She said she did and we kept calling each other checking on how we were holding up and if anyone had heard any news. Finally, after what seemed like an eternity, I received a small text message from my husband.

"I am ok, I got burned, I will be home tonight." My heart was relieved, but sank again. I was faced with another great fear of mine. My husband got burned; I began to wonder how bad was this burn? From my previous experience from working in the emergency department at the local hospital it caused my imagination to run wild. Then I prayed again and remembered "he is coming home, he is safe, thank you God for answering my prayers."

I immediately texted Christopher's Battalion Chief's wife and told her I had heard from Christopher. She said that her husband was ok as well and she had not heard any details yet but all they could tell us was that they were safe. Now I waited again, feeling helpless and I sat at the window waiting to see his car. I began praying that he had enough energy to drive home and enough strength after such a huge incident. He made it home safely but I will never forget the expression, I saw in his eyes. I remember crying and just grabbing him disregarding the soot that he had tried to shower off at the station but still remained. My heart panicked and I ordered him to get into the shower so I could check him for any Injuries. Now the bathtub was now black from soot and the bathroom filled with the odor that we, as fire wives are so familiar with. I remember checking him franticly for any injuries and praising God that he only had a few minor burns. After I dressed his wounds, I could see He was exhausted and still in shock from this "near death" experience.

Now my job was to set aside my emotions and care for him because he was physically exhausted and also emotionally exhausted as well. My husband is a strong and confident man, but I could see in his eyes that I would never truly understand what he had just gone through. So I got him to bed and just curled up next to him. I kept my tears in check until he was finally asleep. Then I cried tears of thankfulness that he was ok. Though I had worried myself to the point of exhaustion I was thankful that we had another night to hold each other. I was extremely grateful that God protected him and brought him home to me. As I reflect back on this incident, I can see how my faith was tested to my limit. This incident not only tested my faith but how easy it is to become callused. I hate to admit that I had become callused but I had took for granted that my husband would return home after each shift. I began to question myself and asked:

Do I truly set him up for success before he returns to work? Or do I dump everything on him while he is home, because I'm exhausted from taking care of everything on the days he is gone?

What did I learn from this?

This incident has taught me that the future of my husband is out of my hands. However, what is in my hands is this: I must set him up for success at home in order for him to have success at work. The last thing he needs to worry about, are my emotions and needs while his life is on the line. Thankfully, my husband's training, quick thinking, and our Heavenly Father brought him back home to me. The reality is, he shouldn't have made it out of that fire.

■ ■ ■ ■ ■ ■ ■ ■ ■ ■ ■ ■ ■

The greatest advice I can give to another fire wife is 'you have to get to the point where you do ultimately trust that God is in control.'"

■ ■ ■ ■ ■ ■ ■ ■ ■ ■ ■ ■ ■

What can others learn from us?

My advice to new fire families is to trust your loved one. Please do not get mad at all the training they are required to attend on their days off duty; for it may save their life one day. Also, it is wise to have a plan with other fire wives if there is a big event that you can contact each other so you can support each other through it. The greatest advice I can give to another fire wife is "you have to get to the point where you do ultimately trust that God is in control." I know, that if I didn't trust in God, I would've gone crazy worrying about my husband. Please, do not ever take your husband's shift for granted, always kiss him before each tour, and set him up for success.

•

– for discussion –

For Discussion Together

- What thoughts related to the fire service induce more than acceptable amounts of fear and worry?

- Discuss in depth the training and educational experiences that firefighters complete on an ongoing basis.

- How do you want your spouse to react when you are experiencing anxiety and vice versa? Establish an understanding of what the feelings are like and how each of you can help each other through these moments with the best words and actions.

RESOURCES

All resources mentioned in this chapter can be found at HonorAndCommitment.com/Chapter3

- Fire Wife Academy eBook: *Firestrong Thinking: The End of Fear, Worry and Sleepless Nights* available at 247commitment.org

- If your anxiety symptoms are overwhelming you in any way, seek a local counselor or therapist for personal counseling sessions. Churches often offer low cost, affordable private counseling.

4 Committed to Mastering
Those Scheduling Logistics

It's a Monday through Friday world and we're a 24/48 or 72/96 (or pick your shift) schedule life. Then add in the unexpected overtimes, long calls, trainings and more; while the spouse is left to manage the family/household solo. How can you own this lifestyle, rationalize it, and make the best of it? Because there are a lot of perks to this as well.

We all know that we've had those silly little tiffs about:

"You said it was on the calendar."

"Well I didn't put it on the calendar?"

"But you told me you put it on the calendar."

"Well, do you ever read the calendar?"

A schedule like the fire service schedule isn't one to be just memorized and retained in your brain. It takes some communication and planning. And not everyone around you will understand.

Have you ever been at a family event or a neighborhood gathering or church and someone says "That was fun. We should all get together for again." and your insides start to squirm and your brain starts thinking of polite excuses?

So these are super nice people and it was really fun. You and the wife get along. Your husband and her husband get along. Your kids play together nicely. But all you can think about is your husband being gone the upcoming week for training and then working a trade resulting in a 48 and then the family boyscout camp. And. And. And.

■ ■ ■ ■ ■ ■ ■ ■ ■ ■ ■ ■ ■

"It can be a gut wrenching feeling if you let it. Or it can be a very freeing opportunity to hold tight to your values and know what is best for your family."

■ ■ ■ ■ ■ ■ ■ ■ ■ ■ ■ ■ ■

It all adds up to the fact that there are literally only 2 evenings in the next 14 days without any events that your husband is home. And you want him all to yourself. (Well, you'll share him with the kids too!) It can be a gut wrenching feeling if you let it. Or it can be a very freeing opportunity to hold tight to your values and know what is best for your family.

I know personally that when we have tried to squeeze in more events and activities to stay in touch with everyone who wants to socialize with you, it just adds more stress to your family. If you don't have enough time for each other, don't stress yourself out trying to fit in more social engagements.

I can remember feeling stress over groups of couples who wanted to have a monthly euchre night for 5 couples. One of the other couples was a police officer and they also had 4 children. While we so appreciated everyone's efforts to find a date to make it work, just having those conversations made me cringe. I'm sure my facial expressions and body language gave me away.

■ ■ ■ ■ ■ ■ ■ ■ ■ ■ ■ ■ ■

"I give you permission to be selfish with your family time. He doesn't get to tuck them in every night. So it's ok to say no just to be home for that routine."

■ ■ ■ ■ ■ ■ ■ ■ ■ ■ ■ ■ ■

My mind was silently screaming and willing them. "Please don't pick that Saturday night. It's the only night my son is with us and all 6 of us can be home together." (Ah yes, the blended family factor further complicates this.)

I give you permission to be selfish with your family time. Feel the freedom of that statement? This is one of those unique issues with the fire family schedule. He doesn't get to tuck them in every night. So it's ok to say no just to be home for that routine.

You don't have to be rude. There are other ways to stay connected with these friends. Texting. Emails. Send cards. Facebook of course. As these people interact with you more, they'll start realizing how much your husband is gone at times their husband is home. I finally found a neighborhood mom who is a runner and realizes why 2 out of 3 mornings, my husband is gone so I can't slip out of the house at 6 am for a jog. And on that 3rd morning, I really prefer to wake up next to him.

You can find other families that connect with your kind of schedule. Other fire or police or medical employee families seem to get this. We recently connected with a family where Dad is in the reserves and works at a hospital. Our kids play hockey together. The wife and I really connected over the weekend work challenges....we get to be the only mom's on the weekend hanging in the boys locker room getting the kids laced up in their skates and pads. And when we try to get together at other times, we now just laugh at our crazy schedules. Once we were 6 weeks out on our calendars before we gave up. We've come to the conclusion that we'll just plan it even if only 2 or 3 of the 4 adults can make it.

There is so much awesomeness about the Fire Life schedule that we must start there lest we sound like a grumbling group of ungrateful Israelites (reference to the story of Moses).

What to Love About the Fire Life Schedule

It's always better to look at the bright side. While we all may complain about long times apart in the fire life, the benefits of this schedule stand out as a primary reason many people are drawn to it. When you are frustrated with the fire life, come back and read this list.

- **Weekdays at home**, multiple in a row sometimes. This alone allows more projects to be done around the house and more kids to have time with their parent than many others who work 50-60 prime hours during the Monday—Friday week.

- **Waking up at home with the family more often.** True a 24 on / 48 off schedule means only 1 out of 3 days is this possible but a Monday—Friday work week allows this only on Saturday and Sunday if they're lucky and if you don't have to travel for your job.

- **One day off = Five days off**. This is true if you are on a 24 on / 48 off schedule but other fire schedules have even better variations. One shift off = Ten days off in some.

- **You always know when you work.** It's a perpetual calendar. There's no waiting for the schedule to be posted. Ask me what's happening for Thanksgiving in 2037. I can probably predict.

- **Kelly Days.** Not everyone has this kind of schedule but a Kelly Day is that one day of the week you always have off. So if you work 24/48 but have a Tuesday Kelly Day, you'd never work any Tuesday, even if it was your normal shift day. This is fabulous. You know that infant swim lesson you've been trying to schedule? Or the weekly date night? Now you always know Tuesdays are available. Personally we've never had a Kelly Day at my husband's departments but when other fire families talk about this you hear a little bit of excitement in your voice when they say "that's your Kelly day! It's perfect!"

- **Possibly avoiding childcare costs**. For a while, I worked part time around my husband's fire schedule and he watched the kids while I was at work. We had to be extra intentional about our time together as a couple but it definitely gave the kids lots of mommy and daddy time and was a lot less expensive than childcare. Personally, I'm pretty envious of those nurse schedules where three 12 hour shifts rake in some nice cash and all happen around the firefighting schedule leaving much family time in between. That's a good gig for those of you who've landed it!

- **Trades**. At some departments, trading shifts is a fabulous way to get that one day off you need for an important family event, when there isn't a vacation slot available on the schedule and without burning vacation time. Policies are different everywhere but when you do trade, be sure to be the kind of guy who pays it back! Building up a couple of solid trade relationships with people on other crews at your department provides so much more flexibility in your fire family schedule. It's a big relief to know we aren't locked into the vacation days we have to pick a year in advance.

- **Allows for a second job.** Most firefighters I know also work a second job partially because 48 hours is a long time to kill when you are off shift and partially because not all firefighters make a large salary. There are many firefighting related jobs that take skilled firefighters such as training, ambulance or ER services or filling in part time for other fire departments which works nicely around the firefighter schedule. For families wanting to have a parent stay home full time with the children, this means a lot of time away for the firefighter but the possibility to provide well for the family. That's a pretty fabulous list when you look around at so many others struggling to make ends meet, in jobs they don't like, that keep them away from home for so many of the prime daytime hours with their families.

■ ■ ■ ■ ■ ■ ■ ■ ■ ■ ■ ■

"The key to making the schedule work for you is to do what works for you without guilt, shame, worry or regret."

■ ■ ■ ■ ■ ■ ■ ■ ■ ■ ■ ■

The Solution to Mastering Fire Family Schedules

Before we even cover the challenges, I'm going to give you the solution. There is no cute printable schedule with little fire trucks on it to go along with this. In fact, many people have asked me to create a fire family planner and it never materializes for me purely because every fire family has different ways they make it work for them. The key to making the schedule work for you is to do what works for you without guilt, shame, worry or regret.

Give up the vision that you can plan your way to a picture perfect family schedule per the standard American family with 2.4 children and 21 vacation days per year. That's not your life and because it isn't, you get all the bonuses we listed above.

When the Monday—Friday schedule was a burden to fit into, I temporarily thought to myself, let's try to run our family by shift days. Here's what we do on one unit, two unit and three unit days. Yeah, well, that wasn't so brilliant either because the soccer coach has no clue what I'm talking about. In case you get that bright idea, well, try it out and test it for yourself.

The answer is in the moment. Just as many wise sages suggest we should be living our lives, my suggestion is to live in the moment while not failing to ignore and prepare for the future. Here's our plan for now but we understand the variables that may change it. I'm not going to grumble or fight those variables. I'm going to embrace them and trust that it's exactly right for our family in this moment. Flexibility and adaptability, especially to unplanned situations, are essential to firefighting and as a family you can honor that by making the commitment to the same. The alternative is to fight it and complain your way through which only adds negative energy and emotional exhaustion to the moments.

Logistically I do this:

- Put the shift calendar on my schedule (now both online and written)

- Put all the kids' activities and my work on the schedule.

- At the beginning of the month, block out family time and activities and guard them from being invaded as much as possible.

- On a weekly basis, figure out who is going to be home on what day and call in the support troops to help with carpool sharing. Determine where each of us parents is going to be either together or separately. Anticipate potential overtimes and have a plan B in mind.

- Be sure our weekly routines are scheduled in—when will I exercise, grocery shop, run errands, clean house, do laundry, etc. I know how many days we can go without a grocery stop or laundry (like none there!) before everything comes off the rails and be sure those activities are planned in. I even have "short grocery trip" and "long grocery trip" routines. For example, I know that I can go 2 weeks between long grocery routines if needed.

This all takes trial and error and some adjustment when the seasons change. With 4 kids who are all sporty, I typically have a good cry when I lay out the spring sports / end of school year schedule and then get over it and dive into living the moments. It's ok to grieve that you or dad won't make every event. It's ok to have a little moment of desperation and reassessment of your family priorities as you come up for the 10,000-foot view on your family's schedule. It's not ok to be trapped in that negative swirl of emotions because you have the choice. The choice with how you will respond and the choice regarding what you will say yes and no to on your calendar.

How do you make this mental shift? Try these thoughts:

- It's only for a season. For a season of medic school. For a season of terrible two's (which are really worse when they are three). For a season of teenage drama. For a season of working under this difficult Captain.

- If I complain, will it get better?

- Get good at preparing. Being unprepared has a way to really make you feel bad about yourself and your abilities. Denial is an evil demon that sometimes keeps us from preparing well.

- Trust that you know what's most important for your family and have made those choices. When we swim around in self-doubt and let the critics (both internal and external) get into our minds, it's like standing on shifting sand. But when you've discussed together, prayed over and decided on what you will do together as a family for this season, letting doubt creep into that constantly is going to steal both joy and energy. Trust your decision. Note the issues that come up but don't dwell there and when changes are needed, have the conversation and promptly act on them.

- We do have the power to make changes. We are never stuck. If this is too much, I'm going to talk to my spouse and we will make a change. A crew transfer. A move to a 40-hour position. Dropping a second job. Changing hours for your non-firefighting spouse's career. No one is stuck. Especially in this grand old country we live in called America.

When You and Your Spouse Have Different Planning Styles

Here's my marriage advice on this topic, know your spouse's preferences and try to adapt to them, in both directions. It's that whole meet in the middle thing. I know that my husband is not really good at getting things into the electronic calendar. He wants to be but when he's on duty, he doesn't always have his smartphone handy to drop an appointment into. I get it. It's way different than my work mode which is in front of the calendar.

Here's the difference, he knows that I need that. He knows our family needs that. He wants to be good at it, so I love that even though it's not the best, I know he's trying. That helps me to be a little more reminding of, "Hey did you to check this," "I want to remind you that I put this in the calendar." He knows that I don't like last minute stuff to be dropped on me because it doesn't fit well in our life.

We also want to be able to do things, and when we're free we are very spontaneous. We want to be. We might go to the Blue Jackets game tonight just because there's nothing on the calendar, and there are a lot of cheap tickets because the Blue Jackets haven't won a single game yet. And it's a weeknight. Most of the rest of the city is preparing for work tomorrow but we have the fire family benefit of the weekday date night.

A Few Notes on Technology and Calendar Sharing

Tis the way of our world now with smartphones and computers everywhere. I am a technology nut and was gifted in these ways since I got my first computer in 1981 (a VIC 20 for those other geeks out there like me) so I'd be remiss to leave out a small section on how we can use technology to help us with scheduling, even though whatever I write here will be outdated in 6 months when the next great apps are available. Nevertheless, here's how to leverage technology to help you manage these calendaring logistics, even when your spouse is anti-techie.

Shared Google Calendars are currently the best invention of all time for managing multiple calendars. They are free. You can have as many as you want. You can share them, color code them, set reminders and view them from any type of device or computer at any time with complete accuracy. Here are some quick tips for mastering google calendars for your family.

- Create a calendar for each person, yes even the wee ones, so you can see each person with a different color code.

- Share those calendars to at least your spouse so you both have full access to each other's agenda

- Use the features to view just one, a few, or all calendars at the same time depending on your need.

- Use a smartphone app that gives you the best view of your calendars for quick access. I currently use one that I prefer the way it shows a color coded weekly view of everything at once.

- Use locations to include driving directions and addresses.

- Invite your spouse to key events you both need to attend

- Set reminders on key events

- Once your kids are about 10 years old and have their own electronic device access of some sort, teach them to use and manage their own calendars. It teaches them great skills as well as saves time for you and gives them ownership of their activities and responsibilities.

- Create calendars to block out chores, family time or anything you want to leave space for in your calendar. I have one that lays out my work and writing schedules so I can visually see them and honor them as I plan other activities.

- The key is for everyone to use these calendars consistently and for all activities to go on the calendars. As soon as you have some activities somewhere else, your system is complicated and possibly broken.

- If you have a work meeting calendar that is integrated to a work system such as Outlook, there are tools where you can one way synchronize that to your google calendar so your life is referenced in one place only. So convenient!

Now that you know you aren't missing the best-ever-pinterest-answer-for-fire-families-everywhere-solution, let's take this frame of reference for flexibility, preparation, adaptability and commitment and look at some specific challenges in fire life schedules.

The Challenges of the Fire Life Schedule We Can All Master

This book is here to inspire and encourage but we won't deny the challenges. You've made a commitment and you can honor the fire life and make it work for your family. Let's look at some of the challenges you may encounter and how other fire families addressed them in a healthy manner.

It's a Monday–Friday World

The most unobvious part of the fire life schedule which took me some time and frustration cycles to adapt to is how to fit into the "rest of the world." I was a scheduling genius (i.e. control freak about scheduling) before I met my husband. My schedules revolved around efficient planning systems time blocking events on a weekly basis in my printed planner I carried everywhere. I called it my brain in a book. Bear in mind this was 2002, long before we all carried our calendars in our phones. That's all good and fine as you need a solid system to track everything. There's a difference between being good at planning and being a control freak. I used to be in "control freak mode," but now I'm just in "good planning mode."

Where I ran into issues was trying to schedule "every other Tuesday night" kind of events into our fire life schedule. It just doesn't work like that. I knew it and did everything I could to draw it neatly into my planner but it was the non-firefighting world that gave me angst. The sighs, grunts and shifting eyes of my friends, the church volunteer team, doctor's office receptionists and my colleagues at work as I shuffled through my planner trying to find the right days we could meet up were majorly annoying to me. Even when I would say "he works every third day" they would say something back like "What about Tuesdays? Does he work Tuesdays?" I possibly shot daggers through them with my eyes. Oops! Not so honorable but I was trying to do the impossible and there's nothing more frustrating.

Truthfully I wasn't annoyed with them, and their annoyances were probably just a reflection of my frustrations as I flipped through the planner. I wanted my husband to be there for some of the kids' doctor's appointments. That's one of the perks of the schedule right? And we wanted to get together with our life group for pizza when I didn't have to show up solo with the kids. I wanted to get together with my girl-friends once a month but never if it was a night my husband was home. Praises to those few people in our life who understood and were flexible meeting Tuesday night one week and Thursday the next.

Flexible and adaptable solutions to the Monday—Friday world:

- Don't take it out on the traditional Monday—Friday crowd. Get used to answering honorably with patience and a smile how your spouse's schedule works.

- Don't carry around guilt when you can't make an event fit. What is meant to be is meant to be.

- Do not be afraid to attend events solo without your spouse, including weddings or other couples oriented events. If these are true friends and family, and they will see your commitment and support you in the fire lifestyle.

Exercise Schedules and Other Cyclically Scheduled Events

Another challenging example are any cyclically scheduled events in your calendar. Perhaps you are doing the "17 days to six pack abs" challenge, which of course starts with grocery and meal prep on the weekend and a Monday kick off. But that weekend is your spouse's only full weekend off so you spent it on a fabulous hiking trip and your Monday will be all about reset and recovery. Do you lose a week and wait until the next week to start it or just try to adapt the schedule so that their Monday is your Tuesday? See how annoying that can be? Ok, annoying but it's the small stuff in life, truly. I just want you to know you aren't alone in those crazy annoying thoughts.

If you've ever trained for a marathon or any kind of fitness chal-lenge, you know that scheduling is key and working out with a buddy is a super effective way to achieve those goals. There was a neighborhood friend of mine who knew I liked to run and would constantly invite me on her morning runs. I tried my best to fit it in because you want to be social and connect with those around you and I really like her. Every time I looked at my schedule for a week or two, I'd be lucky to find one morning we could run together and usually that morning my husband would text me and say he got held over. She politely gave up on relying on me and we laughed it off together.

Flexible and adaptable solutions to cyclically scheduled activities:

- This is one area where it may make sense to follow the shift schedule, especially if you and your spouse are doing a fitness challenge together. Create your schedule for the next month or even just the next week to fit around that fire schedule.

- Don't let yourself be frustrated or compare against others who announce they did 5 days in a row of a workout when you are going to make up 2 days on your spouse's next shift off.

Lack of Seniority and Vacation Scheduling

Don't hate me but I have to say that we've not experienced this challenge as a family but boy do I hear horrific stories about this. In most departments, vacation days are picked by seniority. So if you are the new guy, your vacation is likely to be during some off season time like first week of December or March or November and most definitely not including any major holidays. For some fire families this poses challenges with taking kids out of school for a trip or corresponding with your spouse's vacation window. Our best advice for this issue is to find those trade buddies and treat them well. Then make the most of discounted travel and missing the crowds during those off season dates.

Flexible and adaptable solutions to vacation scheduling:

- Go ahead and brag up those crowd free discounted travel seasons. It's a bonus of the fire life.

- Trade, trade, trade. It's just one way fire families show the love to each other.

Overtime—Planned, Unplanned and Overdone

Overtime is such a mixed blessing for fire families. Yes, the money is good but boy that 24- or 48-hour shift was already a long time to be apart. When our kids were little, overtime would just CRUSH my heart, even when I knew full well that he didn't pick it intentionally and we totally needed the money.

The worst overtime call for a spouse who works outside the home Monday—Friday is the Saturday or Sunday morning call. Those weekend days are sacred (on many levels) for family time. For our family's 24 on / 48 off schedule, this already means that we sacrifice 2 our 6 weekend days every 3 week, without even counting Friday night as part of the weekend. There were seasons when I LIVED for weekend family time to reconnect and recharge. Inevitably when it happened, we'd find ways to make it special and throw in a visit to the fire station. Daddy missed us and dreaded the overtime too, and actually got the tough part of that deal—another sleepless 24 hours at the firehouse.

Here's an excerpt from our real life fire life world last year:

My husband finished a 48 this morning (Wednesday). 24 on his full time department followed immediately by 24 on his part time where they've been running low on staff lately. Of course he got home after I had already left for the office and the kids were on the bus. Around 4 PM, everyone (except the high schooler) converged in the kitchen for 10 minutes of quick conversation before we piled in the van to run the soccer carpool and then split ways for same time soccer and hockey games. 2 hours later we're all back in the van and then finally home and back in that same kitchen. Only it's now nearly 8 pm. I whip up a quick batch of tacos and set out some paper plates for everyone to serve themselves buffet style. We're soaking in family time at home since he's back on shift tomorrow, home on Friday (which I've successfully blocked out a couple hour midday date for us!) and then Friday evening it's divide and conquer again. The girls are off for an out of state soccer tournament while the boys manage sports on the home turf.

Then, just as we were rejoicing that the iPhone wasn't broken and simply needed some extra charge time, it rang with an unknown number. Which he unfortunately chose to answer. Yep. Overtime. They called him in for the night. I pretended not to really hear the conversation hoping it wasn't really going down. But someone had to go home sick. And if it was my husband who wasn't feeling well, or my child was very sick and I needed my husband home, then I'd for sure want another firefighter to return the favor with a gracious heart.

He made the rounds saying goodbye. All went well except for baby girl, who was already in a meltdown about using ink, not pencil, on her homework and upset about the ugly scratch mark she couldn't erase. Realizing that Daddy would be gone for 2 more nights sent her into fits of sobs that brought tears to both of our eyes. I tried to deflect with the homework and tell her it's ok. Lots of people make mistakes and have to cross them off. But no go. She climbed up in my lap sobbing about Daddy leaving. I consoled her with the chance to sleep in bed with me tonight while he quietly snuck out the front door.

■ ■ ■ ■ ■ ■ ■ ■ ■ ■ ■ ■ ■

"Realizing that Daddy would be gone for 2 more nights sent her into fits of sobs that brought tears to both of our eyes."

■ ■ ■ ■ ■ ■ ■ ■ ■ ■ ■ ■ ■

It wasn't until after he left that I realized it would make 7 straight nights that we would not be sleeping together. And all day long I was so looking forward to just a short neck and scalp massage. Just to be touched by someone who wanted to love on me, not another child needing me for another task. Guess that will have to wait.

This isn't a complaint, just a healthy understanding vent session. It's my life. My heart is full. We are blessed with his job (and mine). Our life is very busy with 4 active kids but thank the Lord they are healthy enough to play all these sports and it's fun to enjoy them together as a family. And in 4 short years, we're only left with 3 at home. Then 2. Then 1. and 10 years go by in the blink of an eye. Quick tacos are still delicious and require less cleanup. And facetime keeps us all closer than ever.

Flexible and adaptable solutions to overtime:

- Get really good at communicating clearly with each other how you will decide when and when not to take overtime as best meets the needs of your family.

- Have a plan B. Just in case.

- When possible, look ahead on the overtime schedule and know the probability of overtime coming the next shift. Just knowing it's a possibility can really help lessen the emotional outburst we want to have when it happens.

- Don't get mad at your firefighter. It's not like they planned for it to happen. Adding anger to the annoyance and frustration doesn't help anything.

- Discuss and have a plan together for how you will handle unplanned OT. Is there an opportunity to decline? In what circumstances would you? Can you agree to button up the task at hand before making a mad dash out the door? (i.e. tucking a child into bed, washing a couple dishes, checking the online account)

- Think about how the kids perceive it and consider ways to make the exit transition easier on them.

- Don't lie. Just take the OT. It's the right thing to do. Most of the time it's legit and someone sincerely needs help. (And I'm sorry for those of you at stations where the brotherhood isn't so thick and OT is manipulated in either direction. You know what they say about taking the high road.)

- When the OT happens while the firefighter is already at the station, be sure to agree on how you will discuss taking it or not (when given that option). Will you call and discuss? Are there certain absolute no's? What if you can't be reached? Is there a list of "good days to take OT" that you could create?

- Look at the positives—the reward of the extra OT money. Thank goodness for this extra cash that will help us cover the cost of those new tires we need on the car. Some families actually name that OT by what the money will cover. That's soccer camp, or we can finally get the deck finished.

- Stay positive for the firefighter. It's not easy on them either to have to suck it up and take on an extra shift but to do so when their family is home crying and upset about it is even worse. Control what you can—yourself and your emotions.

Long Times Apart

I'll put this out there for you to process and remember for perspective. Military wives trump us all with the 3-6-9 month deployments. If you feel like crying a bit, think of those strong ladies. Next up is wildland firefighting season. It's a beast of its own and my apologies for not addressing it here. Pray for that in a future resource we can release with some more funding support perhaps?

Now don't let those scenarios make you deny the fact that sometimes it's just a long freaking time to be apart in the fire life. Most notably for me are those moments when you realize that you just agreed to an extra trade shift or an overtime which will keep you apart from each other for the next 7 nights. Ugh!! Yes, have a healthy little vent and then put your big kid panties back on because you are committed.

Flexible and adaptable solutions to long times apart:

- Immediately try to block your schedule for the first day you are back together to just be together and reconnect as a family. Don't add anymore additional stressors like visits to the in laws or home projects if at all possible.

- Be intentional about your talk times during this long stretch. Don't multitask while you are on the phone but intentionally stop and listen and converse.

- Ask for help. Especially if it's unplanned don't be afraid to ask for more help from the community around you.

- Lower your expectations of what will be done at home with only one spouse there. Go easy on yourself and each other.

- Send some surprises to the firefighter who is enduring this long shift of work and missing on the family time.

Kids Routines

This scheduling challenge carried over into the routines for our kids as well. As I attempted to make chore system after chore system, we failed to get into a rhythm. Ever. With this statement, I give all of you families struggling with this permission to just abandon it entirely. Your kids can still learn responsibilities I promise. Our challenge was that all the 7-day week chore charts were perfect, but on any given Tuesday or Friday or Sunday, there was a different adult running the household. On some days it was me, on other days our babysitter and then sometimes my husband. To top it off, my oldest went to his Dad's every other weekend.

To get 3 adults on the same page with how to run the chore system with "fairness" and effectiveness was a struggle.

If it was a morning for one child to take out the trash, but that morning happened to be a day Dad was home, everyone wanted to savor the Dad time and it didn't seem fair for trash duty to interrupt that. Or if Dad wasn't home and I was struggling just to get the basics under control, like teeth brushing and a healthy breakfast, chores never happened.

Let me interrupt this for a second with this thought. How we raise our children is so much a reflection of our own upbringing. I can hear one of you saying right now that you married a drill sergeant dad and he'd be all over the child with trash duty that morning which is how love is shown in your home. That's totally fine. Our family has taken a very relaxed approach to parenting, possibly because we are engulfed by enough helicopter parents in our community our rebellious selves just run rapidly in the other direction, but also because after 4 kids, one child going back and forth to his biological dad's, and the fire schedule, we cried uncle. It works for us. Remember that you need to find what works for your family. Families with fewer or more children at different ages may find different solutions for them.

Flexible and adaptable solutions to routines with kids:

- Stop reading Mommy Blogs and being influenced by your play-group parents and do what works for your family. No one walks in your shoes or knows your children as well as you. Yes, it's good to research and listen but may we suggest finding other fire families to connect with so you don't feel like the pagan alien mom suggesting alternative torture methods when you try to explain to people how this fire life affects your family.

- Kids do love and thrive in routine but no one said that routine had to be Monday-Friday. In fact, most kids aren't able to long term plan and all they know is what's now and what's next. So addressing the next day's events is usually sufficient for their little minds. Is tomorrow a shift day or not? This is sufficient routine for young children to understand.

- Incorporate some of the fire life into their routines to make it relatable. If dad's doing truck checks and house chores right when he gets on shift each morning, assign your little ones their own 'truck checks' on shift days.

- As best as you can, get onto the same page with your spouse on how you will do this as a family. Remember that by the time you get a routine, the kids will change and need to adapt again. So don't break out World War III over a "small thing" parenting topic.

- Decide what your "non-negotiables" will be. For us it's things like always brush your teeth, no lying and to give a helping hand when asked even if it isn't your turn. Having a clear simple set of foundational principles allows you to manage an adaptable schedule within a set of criteria. Here's a profound thought as you plan this for your family: Principles and boundaries are way more important than routines.

- Do put a family calendar on the wall somewhere prominent, typically the kitchen, where kids can see what days are shift days and not. It helps for them to have a visual reference at a high level to know what's coming.

Bedtimes

I'm going to set somebody free with this paragraph I just know it. It happened to me already when I was chatting with a bunch of hockey moms, one of whom is married to a police officer. We were discussing kids' bedtimes and the room seemed to be in agreement that early bedtimes in the 8 o'clock hour were necessary and mandatory for the sanity of their personal lives and marriages. They all have this perception that since I have 4 kids and run my own business and volunteer here and there as well, that I must really have this down. I'm glad that the appearance is that the Mercer's have got it together because most of the time I do feel like we are living on the ragged edges which could unravel with the next phone call. So what does our bedtime routine look like? Sometimes we don't get the kids to bed until 10:30 PM! On a school night! I know. Gasps and jaw dropping everywhere. But the adaptability and flexibility and knowing our boundaries is what guides us. If Dad's been gone for a few days and we had a busy night, the bedtime routine is going to linger with conversation and giggles and perhaps some tickling and that's the good stuff. We never want the kids to grow up feeling like Daddy worked all the time. With those words, my fellow hockey mom and police wife felt such relief. Both of them work shift schedules and finding a routine in that lifestyle is nearly impossible. But no one said routines are what makes for a good childhood. Put down those strict parenting books if they aren't sitting right with you and observe what's happening in families like yours. There are many ways to be a good parent.

We also teach the kids to guide themselves a bit in learning when they are tired and ready for bed and how to make good choices about that. Perhaps this has been a forced learning as four kids outnumbered our ability to keep the rank and order in our home and teaching self-sufficiency has been our answer. Clearly the younger kids need more prompting than the big and we all deal with the consequences of bad choices. But if Dad needs some snuggle time, we compensate for that by running the "quick prep" routine the next morning as we get out the door for school. It's all about your family priorities.

■ ■ ■ ■ ■ ■ ■ ■ ■ ■ ■ ■ ■ ■

"Don't make a schedule so tight and inflexible that the firefighter parent feels like they are missing out on some of their time as a parent."

■ ■ ■ ■ ■ ■ ■ ■ ■ ■ ■ ■ ■ ■

Flexible and adaptable solutions to bedtime:

- Get on the same page your spouse as to what your guidelines and principles will be without involving the kids input.
- Don't make a schedule so tight and inflexible that the firefighter parent feels like they are missing out on some of their time as a parent.

Firefighters Rely on Routine in the Midst of Chaos

I want to close with this thought. Emergencies are chaotic. First responders are able to manage those scenes with a set of routines and protocols that keep them safe and help them to best serve those in need. When life gets all out of hand, some firefighters cling o systems and routines to give them a sense of sanity and control over rather out of control scenarios. "Smoke is showing. My next step is......" is how they think their way through. Be aware of the situation. Know what's going on around them then be able to rapidly decide and implement the next step for that moment. The routines to keep their gear and equipment in service and functioning well allow them to make better rapid fire decisions. Tools are always in the same place. The people around them are hopefully doing what's expected next.

At the risk of generalizing, I see firefighters fall into two camps with how this carries over into the home life. Some firefighters cling to routine and consistency. They pack the night before and lay out their meals and uniform and whatever they need for their day away. It truly is like packing for an overnight stay, except it's all the time. If you have never done this, imagine what it's like to be in a perpetual state of having overnight stays for your work. As John Dixon points out, "When you don't have a permanent assignment but float to various firehouses, this becomes a much more demanding and time consuming task in your schedule as you prepare the night before." You must pack up your routine and consistency and adapt it to where you will be serving the next day. It's how you stay safe and able to execute those routines flawlessly when the call comes in.

So if your family routine that evening is extra busy or even happens to be the day after a vacation or you are staying overnight somewhere, plan for this. It's just going to take some prep and adjusting.

On the other hand, some firefighters fall completely out of routine when they are off duty. This allows them some freedom and relaxation and to add anything scheduled into their day becomes an annoyance. Then before shift, they transition into a "ready" mode as they prepare.

These two approaches are really different personality types so it helps to know your spouse's tendencies in dealing with chaos and how that carries over into your home life. Here's a hint from our mistake book: rigid and structured organization techniques and toddlers haven't typically mixed well in fire families.

Grace for Things that Throw Your Schedule out of Whack

Sickness. Emergencies. Bad weather. The list goes on and on. And that is in your home life, not at the firehouse. Remember it's about adaptability. Here are some thoughts for you as you ponder your fire family schedules:

- What is our Plan B in case of weather emergency?

- Have we left enough margin and space in our schedule to adapt to closed roads, unexpected phone calls and just moments to breath and arrive on time? Or are we constantly dashing from one moment to the next in a precariously stacked game of scheduling jenga?

- Are you emotionally prepared for disappointments that will wreck your neatly planned schedule?

It's About Energy Management, Not Time Management

I am often asked how I "do it all." First, let's get things straight. There are lots of things that don't happen in my life and it's all a matter of prioritization of what matters to you. Our house is not a showcase. We don't even have landscaping and that's an intentional choice as I don't want to spend hours maintaining it. For some people that's a joy and stress release but for me it's an exercise in futility as I don't have a green thumb.

I have always been a very driven person by nature, blessed and cursed with a naturally hyperthyroid that gives me energy even in moments and places I don't want energy. Then I crash. I know my limits. I can ride sky high on energy for a few days of a big event but immediately following that event, I know I need to schedule lightly to let my body properly recover. If I didn't recognize this, I'd schedule the days that follow like any other day only to disappoint myself when I can't accomplish it all.

After a big emotional event, I know I need to make space in my calendar to recover. This could be a scary parenting moment with a sick child, one of those epic fights that are mile markers in your marriage, or the loss of a job or worse, a loved one.

I believe you are given the right amount of time and resources to do what you need to do in each moment, but you do have to be good stewards of those resources and use them wisely. Recently, while writing this book, my kids caught that 12-hour stomach bug. I didn't escape as a victim except that it put me down for 6 days. It's probably been a decade since I've been that sick but looking back, I know why. I've been driving myself hard to complete this book and my body and immunities were weak. I depleted my energy and it took me out. Even though I had enough hours in the day, my energy was low.

If you have a big event, give yourself recovery space for your energy. If you have a workday stacked with 8 meetings on the hour, every hour, you aren't going to come home with a lot of energy for your family. (This was me when I worked a full time corporate job).

As a fire family, don't have big expectations for the day after a shift day if your firefighter works at a busy department. Chances are there needs to be some recovery time built in and if not, then you've just found some bonus time together. As you read further in this book and see the chapter on line of duty deaths you will see that those events require a lot of energy cycles for long seasons. Even September 11th remembrance events can really zap my energy in ways that others around me don't understand.

■ ■ ■ ■ ■ ■ ■ ■ ■ ■ ■ ■ ■

"As a fire family, don't have big expectations for the day after a shift day if your firefighter works at a busy department."

■ ■ ■ ■ ■ ■ ■ ■ ■ ■ ■ ■ ■

Never forget that your family was made for this role. It is honorable and a commitment you are equipped to keep, especially if you're reading this book and connecting with the fire families around you.

HONOR GUARD

~ for the firefighter ~
Committed to Mastering
Those Scheduling Logistics

Firefighters it's tough for you to live in that world of shifts and then bounce out to the Monday—Friday week your family is most likely subjected to. Here are some things to understand about that shift that will help you and your family make this fire life commitment work:

- Communicate as soon as possible about schedules / changes to schedules so there is awareness and the ability to adapt as needed. It may not make sense to you from your shoes but having an extra hour to call someone to cover for a carpool is super helpful.

- Talk and learn about each other's time management styles and preferred methods of compromising. I know it's not the most exciting date night conversation but when it's not said, you may keep annoying each other while there's an easy fix.

- It's a big transition from coming off shift and back into your family environment (in fact, we wrote a whole chapter about just that). Learning what you can do to help with the schedules and routines at home will make your fire life routines run more smoothly.

- We're beating a dead horse with this trade topic but be that guy! The good guy. The one who can cover for trades back and forth for other firefighters. It pays off in dividends when you don't have to miss the championship t-ball game.

- Don't hesitate to participate in "every other Tuesday night" kinds of activities (coaching, clubs, church, etc). Just be clear to those in attendance when to expect you.

- Before committing to a second job or off shift responsibilities, be sure you have played out what that does to your family schedule and have enthusiastic agreement from your spouse that you are ready to take on this next season together.

~ for the spouse ~
Committed to Mastering
Those Scheduling Logistics

Spouses, this is an exercise in patience and understanding. Instead of petty, dishonorable fights about the "little stuff" like schedules, which are really masking the big stuff like "does he even want to be here?", learn about the fire service scheduling and learn to be adaptable. This is your family. You were made for these moments and you can make them work well.

- Know and understand all the time commitments of the fire service job. Before shift, after shift meetings, additional training and the informal networking required.

- Have a system that works for both you and your spouse, keeping in mind that a firefighter is often not with their phone or computer when schedules need to be checked or adjusted.

- Try to avoid being a schedule freak kind of person. The only way to truly embrace the fire life is to understand there will be adjustments necessary. Not just scheduling changes but adapting based on what kind of sleep your spouse got on shift the night before. Learning to embrace that and not let the emotions sweep you away is essential.

- There are friends who aren't in the fire life but who get it. These may be friends whose parents were in police or fire or did shift work. Perhaps their brother or sister-in-law is a first responder. These friends are precious and priceless in your life.

- Don't forget all the benefits. The grass is never greener.

- Ask for help. Ask for help. Ask for help. Did you hear that? It's totally ok to ask for help.

– for discussion –

- Share the best methods and practices you've used in your family to stay connected despite scheduling challenges. Celebrate what's working well for you.

- What's the best perk this schedule has allowed you and your family?

- How well have you handled the exceptions and emergencies? Think about that for each person in your family. Not every personality adapts well to change.

- What are your families "must dos"—your principles and boundaries for what must happen that keeps your train on the tracks? Note that a long list is impossible to achieve so be practical here, not idealistic.

- Talk about the "hot spots" in your schedule that drive each other crazy and equipped with this knowledge that you aren't the only fire family facing this, make a plan to eliminate those frustrations.

RESOURCES

All resources mentioned in this chapter can be found at
HonorAndCommitment.com/Chapter4

- Watch our video on how we track schedules in our firefighter marriage
- Article "Choosing Vacation Days As A Fire Family"

5 *A Test of Commitment*
The Transition To / From Home

Families adapt to operating without one parent and firefighters adapt to the firehouse environment. This happens on a cyclical basis every few days. When you are always in a state of coming and going, how do you minimize the transition impact and make the most of your time at home together as a family? We like to call home the "soft place to land" after a long shift dealing with the wide world of everything thrown at the fire department. After 24 or 48 hours of being "on," coming home should feel like the firefighter's place to let down, just be yourself and be ready to recharge. For the family who has missed them, the reunion brings peace and a sense of wholeness.

Pre-kids the routine was so sweet. If it was a weekend, he'd just slip into bed next to me. We'd talk about his day or he'd just want to forget it and talk about our plans for fun ahead. If I was off to work, he'd grab a coffee and the newspaper and enjoy a day ahead with no plans, decompressing, and not having to jump up when the next unpredictable emergency struck.

Now with children, it starts with that race to the door when Dad's car pulls up or someone hears the turn of the key in the doorknob. Years have passed since I was the first one to get a hug and kiss, but I don't mind waiting. That will be over in the blink of an eye, and soon I'll be the only one at home to greet him. But we make it a point to never skip that welcoming hug and kiss. I can usually tell how bad the night was when I see it in his eyes, in the depth of his furrowed brow, and the thickness of the smell of coffee on his breath. Sometimes I ask that question right away and other times it waits until after we discuss a thousand other details of the school day ahead and events that happened since Dad was last home. "How was your night?"

My favorite responses come with smiles and heroic tales tinged with the giddiness of a school boy as he recounts working fires and those you-won't-believe-this stories that keep his love of the job burning strong. Then there are the hysterical tales of firehouse pranks that build up the happy memories and friendships of the fire department brotherhood. And stories of sadness that remind me why I fell in love with his gigantic, caring heart for serving others as he spent final moments with grandparents and tragically young victims alike.

■ ■ ■ ■ ■ ■ ■ ■ ■ ■ ■ ■ ■

"For a family who is not accustomed to this off shift transition, they may be thinking 'was it something I said?'"

■ ■ ■ ■ ■ ■ ■ ■ ■ ■ ■ ■ ■

That sounds so beautiful written out like that. Dreamy firefighter marries beautiful girl and rushes home to her side. Then there's the reality view we all have or will experience. I love the days that are like that Norman Rockwell view on being married to a firefighter, but the decompression zone can appear in many shades of emotion from anger to discouragement to depression to apathy. For a family who is not accustomed to this off shift transition, they may be thinking "was it something I said?" For too many years I stood at the kitchen sink furiously scrubbing dishes and biting my tongue wondering what in the heck I did to deserve the treatment I was getting when he walked in the door. It was so unexplainable and so off. Spouses listen close. This is a gem of information to tuck away and practice often. When we project our spouse's emotions on ourselves we complicate the problem. Suddenly we've made their bad mood, in a moment when they are needing compassion and empathy, into a moment about US.

Here is another key point I learned early on from a child psychologist. Do you know why children act out more at home than anywhere else? Because you are their safe place of love that never ends, no matter how they behave. The same is true for spouses. Although we'd all like to be at a point of emotional maturity where we can handle our grumpies and not take them out on our spouse, there are moments when we just want to be in the feeling we are feeling. I do it to my husband too. Can you just let me have a good cry session about this please? There's no one else I can tell it to who understands me like you do, and I don't need it to be fixed I just need to vent.

So as I'm biting my tongue, I remind myself that he's this way because he loves me. I won't run when his emotions boil over. That's our commitment and why we were made for each other.

It's not just the firefighter who walks in the door needing a safe place to land. The family is eager to pounce on him before he's even entered and share happy stories, worries, woes and wisecracks. Maybe they weren't fighting literal fires, but their 24 or 48 hour "shift" may have been just as stressful and require a big comforting hug and a safe, protective place to land as well. Two worlds collide and re-adjustment begins. You're so grateful to see those boots kicked off by the front door and their bag in that familiar place. And ultimately that's what matters most. They came home safe and sound again.

When the Firehouse Environment Leaks Over into Your Home

It should be obvious that language and tone used amongst a group of men who've served side-by-side using primal acts of survival is going to be different than that used within a home environment amongst women and children. I've even found myself having to adjust my language when transitioning from my corporate day job to our dinner table. Adjourning meetings is a bit more formal than inviting family to break bread together. It's human nature to adapt to what's around you. When you spend a lot of time in that other environment, it's easy to pick up the habits, like inappropriate language for instance. While my husband does an awesome job around the kids, occasionally the tone he uses to vent to me about work leaves me feeling like I need to wash my ears out with soap, and I run away like frightened puppy. The other complaint I've heard from wives is when the snippy, command-barking mode used effectively with firefighters is applied to you and your children. Let's be honest. They are good at this and it's natural for them. We truly want them to be good at this skill on the fireground. Not so much in your kitchen.

If you're new to this fire life you may think "Who is this man and what did he do with my husband?" I've learned to find a subtle, non-chastising and humorous clue to drop him when he gets into this mode as a gentle reminder that I'm not "one of the guys". Right away Chief usually does the trick.

Walking on Eggshells

Sometimes the transition is more serious. The moods of the adults in the household set the mood for the whole household. So if the bad mood is walking in the door after every shift, or is what the firefighter faces when coming home after each shift, then it's time to have a conversation about some strategies to deal with those frustrations and some methods that will have less impact on the household.

As our kids get older, they know and ask me, "What kind of mood is dad in?" I know my husband never wants our kids walking on eggshells, fearing that he's in a bad mood and their next annoying childlike question is going to invoke anger. As the adults, we must do the courageous thing and find the right moment and words to talk about this and make some adjustments. Walking on eggshells is not a healthy and safe place to land and the last thing we want in our homes. Let me share this excerpt from our life.

Disarming Your Irritable Sleep-Deprived Firefighter

The sun is rising. You're freshly showered. The little ones are all rumpled and still warm to the touch after climbing out of bed. Your cell phone rings and it's your firefighter. Your smile grows bigger because this means he's made it safely through another night on shift and you're eager to talk to him.

But then you hear his voice. And you immediately know what kind of night he had. You can hear the wrongness of life in every word. That bad night has spilled over into our normal day. Traffic stinks. Someone looked at him the wrong way getting off shift. I didn't answer the phone with my full attention. Patience runs thin and little irritants become big problems for a sleep-deprived firefighter.

This week it was a rough night on the medic. One that started with a midnight run on a 70-something woman in cardiac arrest but who was too far gone for them to save. And from there 2–3 more ups and downs for runs that just don't seem worthy of being woken up in the middle of the night as an emergency. A woman with diarrhea whose paid home health caretaker is just exhausted from caring for her and wants them to take her to the hospital instead. Someone who has had a toothache for 3 days and decides 4 am is the time they NEED to go to the hospital for it. (Who goes to the hospital for a toothache? I know. People do this. The fire department can solve anything right?).

I can get angry just thinking of these people who are stealing my husband's sleeping hours for their needs in exchange for his awake daylight hours with our family. Then my heart softens thinking of people who have no one. No family. Living on limited incomes. Sometimes medical providers are their only human touch. And my hubby is good at it. Even in the middle of the night I can imagine him sweetly serving a little old lady in need. (Ok....if he's really a grump, no one tell me. I want to keep that sweet vision in my head!) Once my head cycles through these thoughts in like 3 seconds, I immediately go into nurturing role. What can I say? How can I help him? What are the right words for this moment? Lord give me the words. I rehearse the 293 other times we've had this exchange for what worked and what didn't.

Sometimes he comes around and his groggy voice tells me he loves me. Can't wait to get home and see the kids before the bus comes. And reminds us both out loud how blessed we are for his job and the life and health we have.

■ ■ ■ ■ ■ ■ ■ ■ ■ ■ ■ ■ ■

"It's at this point we have a choice on how we are going to react."

■ ■ ■ ■ ■ ■ ■ ■ ■ ■ ■ ■ ■

Sometimes he says irrational things that sleep deprived people say. I know, I've said them in those early weeks with a newborn being up at all hours of the night. They usually start with "I swear on my grandmother's grave I will NEVER EVER EVER AGAIN _____ (fill in the blank)____. I am done with it. That's the last time."

Sometimes we hang up and he's still in a major fog and negative funk. And I need to put on my happy face and get into the office to start my day (because often these conversations happen while I'm driving to work.) An office where everyone slept through the night and none of us are ever going to review enough charts and data to compete with a task like saving someone from cardiac arrest.

It's at this point we have a choice on how we are going to react. Yes, it hurts like mad when someone we love so much is hurting. And I have had days when after conversations like this I'd have an ugly feeling in my gut that I just couldn't shake. Something good would happen and I'd laugh but then I'd have this dark shadow feeling and remind myself, oh yeah, my husband is hurting today. I wonder what he's doing. Is he ok? Are the kids ok with Daddy in this mood? I need to get home so I can talk to him. I need to get home. My head is not in this game at the office. I need to talk to him.

When we marry the love of our life, two do become one. His pains become your pains. Your joys become his joys. And we carry those emotions with us. But it's a tricky walk to take with compassion. It likes to lead us down the "woe are we" path together. I'm telling you now if you go down the doom and gloom path with him, you're never going to help him out of that funk. I can't tell you exactly what to say. Honestly, I still don't know. 11 years together and it seems like there's always a new situation in our marriage I need to learn to communicate through. But I can tell you that things got a whole lot better when I dealt with my own junk and stayed strong.

#1 Don't mistake his tired grumpiness for being irritated at you and get all defensive or worried about what you are not doing right in your marriage. Nothing is worse than one out-of-whack person trying to communicate with someone else who has turned it into their problem. Follow that? Just because he's grumpy and projecting it at you, doesn't mean the sky is falling and he wants to divorce you. Call a spade a spade. He's tired. Later when he's more alert, you can keep working through that never ending list of things you both need to do to improve your marriage.

#2 He's projecting it at you because he loves you. You're his safe zone. And you're his first contact outside the firehouse. He can't project it there because all those guys feel that way. Suck it up partner. I just had the same night you did.

#3 We have an obligation to our employer and to our family to serve them at our best. When I'm in a slump, that doesn't happen so well. Me being also in a negative slump with icky feelings of worry and sadness for my hubby..... well, those feelings don't help anyone feel better. Me or my hubby.

#4 Your compassionate broken heart can burst with even more love and respect for you hubby when you don't fall into a slump but intentionally take action. I'm not saying to be a fixer. Read the "Just Act Natural" contribution from my hubby for more details on that. I'm saying to take an intentional action in your mind to stay positive and move forward with your responsibilities. Just being around someone who is a shining light and who finds the silver lining can be enough to rub off a little bit on your hubby and even your kids as they observe your reaction.

Warning on #4: This can backfire depending on your husband's personality. I'll just put it out there that my husband can get irritated with me at times when I push through the tough stuff while he's sidelined really struggling with a slump. It helps to always reset their expectation that no one should be expected to function normally after little sleep and horrific traumas. It's ok. You love him right where he is.

And just a couple hints to our firefighters, when you come home in these funks, these tiny little things will help your wife stay on track:

- Text or call her again as soon as you can muster the strength to speak a little sunshine into her life. It's tough work receiving all the tired negative junk and just a tiny little pick me up goes a long way.
- Did I mention text or call as soon as possible? Yep. She's a woman and she just might get stuck obsessively worrying about you. A quick, short "I'm ok. I still love you. I'm getting some sleep." will go a LONG way.
- Just try to end the conversation with "I love you and I'm going to be ok. Don't worry about me."

Trust me when I say, those simple words go a LONG, LONG way. Sleep it off Sweetheart <3.

There Might Be an Easy Fix. Honey, Take an Ibuprofen.

Sometimes the root of my husband's mood is based in his selflessness. He goes so long taking care of others I do believe he gets used to ignoring his own hurts. This can manifest in a grouchy attitude simply because he has a headache or bodyache of some sort and sits at the table looking like an ogre grumbling under his breath. I don't know what he just experienced the last 24 hours. Perhaps a ladder fell on his foot and he's in pain. He walked in the door 5 minutes ago and unlike me, who has a list of things in my mind I'm eager to share with him, those details spill out in his time, when he's ready, and he's not intentionally doing that to tick me off. It's just his style of communication. I've learned over the years to not assume he's grumpy at me and to first check the obvious and ask, "Do you need an ibuprofen?"

Compartmentalizing. It Works for Some.

Some firefighters compartmentalize. You'll hear that term a lot. What happens at work stays at work. What happens at home stays at home. No need for one to affect another. While I don't have a man's brain to draw conclusions here, I have heard admirable firefighters say it can work and others say no way. (In case you skipped Chapter 1, there's a great account of this way to balance fire life and family life by Ret. Chief John Salka, FDNY.)

■ ■ ■ ■ ■ ■ ■ ■ ■ ■ ■ ■ ■

"In short, be flexible.
One of the key quality traits of any fire family."

■ ■ ■ ■ ■ ■ ■ ■ ■ ■ ■ ■ ■

What Will Work for Your Family?

There's no formulaic solution. There is a complicated formula. It's a combination of each of your pasts and upbringings and life experiences and emotional maturity and major events and current season and probably a hundred other things that will lead you to the method that will work for you and your family in this moment. In short, be flexible. One of the key quality traits of any fire family.

My husband has a super valuable view on this topic of the re-entry into our home. To be quite frank, I didn't even realize it until he wrote this piece. There's a hint. Get your husband to write and you might learn something. I'll let him take it from here.

◆◆◆◆◆◆◆◆ "Just Act Natural" By Dan Mercer ◆◆◆◆◆◆◆◆

I struggle with what I have to offer in writing to an audience of wives. The practice initially sets me back as I don't want to appear as though I have all the answers. (Trust me, at least in the fire community I work in, nothing is less welcomed than a know it all.) But my wife insists I have valuable input. And there does seem to be a question or two that many of you ask in different ways that bears addressing. Today I'd like to offer insight into the "what does he expect when he gets back from a rough call/duty day/shift" query. At least, my perspective as a career firefighter at a busy urban house. Which may be one more than you have today.

The job that we've chosen is wonderfully rewarding. The opportunities to impact people's lives in a positive way drives most of us to efforts far greater than we would most likely put forth were we say sitting in a cubicle, answering the phone and entering data,etc. (You get what I'm saying) These efforts and the usual outcomes of the effort can usually keep us motivated, sustained and generally not pissed off at our job. There are however times when despite our best efforts there is nothing we can do to be "excited" about the job. Whether this is precipitated by a bad call, an extremely busy shift, an extremely looooong shift or a less than pleasant fellow fire house inhabitant being, well, less than pleasant. Any one of these situations can cause a guy to suddenly shift from "this is the best job in the world" mode to "can I really do this for another 10, 15, 20 years" mode.

My belief is that this is perfectly natural. I'm not a mental health professional but something about my interactions with people in general tell me that the guy who runs around with the "rainbows and unicorns" attitude 24 / 7 is usually masking some pretty painful stuff and not being honest with himself or those around him. You know who I'm talking about here? I don't mean that super nice guy who always seems to have a positive attitude, is friendly, genuine, and understanding. I'm referring to that robot who's always pouring his sunshine on ya just a little too thick. Yeah.....that guy. So, since we've established that it's perfectly natural for even the best of us to get a little dragged down with the potential circumstances of the job we need to answer the question.

What Can You as a Wife / Girlfriend Do, or Avoid Doing to Help?

I find the best thing Lori can do is act natural. Since what's going on in my head is natural, I find the easiest way for me to adjust back is for there not to be a bunch of adjusting to this circumstance or that situation. I'm probably honked off that something at the firehouse went contrary to how it usually goes for me or the crew and the last thing I want is to return to "tranquility base" (home) and have something be different there. Let me give you an example of a conversation I don't want to have standing in the kitchen of my home with the person I love the most.

Lori: Hi honey, how was your shift?

Me: Not so good, but I'll be cool. What time does Luke have practice tonight?

Lori: No honey, something's bothering you, tell me what it is.

Me: Well I had to take a 4 month old baby girl out of a pillowcase and pronounce her dead this morning. You see her father put her in it and slammed her around the room beating her to death inside it, anything else you want to know about it cause I have details if you need them?

I just did all the adjusting I want to do for the moment surviving the challenging crap I just went through on shift. I don't want to "adjust" where I find my comfort and strength. I want to gather strength and be comforted. For me and a lot of men, that lies in knowing that there is sanity in the world of tragedy and pain that we witness. You guys are that assurance of sanity and normalcy. Please don't mistake what I'm saying here for "don't say anything to him at all," or "don't ask me questions about my day." That's not at all what I'm saying. If Lori asks, I tell her. What I appreciate is when she listens, maybe even discusses an aspect or two of the situation and then we go about our business. If I want to process things further we talk more later when I bring it up or after I've had a little time to bask in that normalcy and sanity I was talking about. I'm not advocating walking around on eggshells here either. All I'm saying is that this is one of those areas where the firefighter has to be the gauge on how it's handled. It's not healthy to have things unspoken in a marriage. After I've got my head back on straight and I've had lots of hugs and kisses from our youngest daughter I'm totally open to Lori giving me the "what was stuck in your butt when you got home the other morning?" line of questioning. That's my obligation to her (and my mental health in general) to share with her what's going on in the space between my ears. If things are overly cluttered or I don't think I can get the pressure relief needed from a pleasant conversation with Lori then it's also my obligation to seek a professional to "thought and word vomit" on. They get paid to clean that stuff up.

So there you go. Act natural ladies. The pressure's off. No major obligations on your part.

Go about your business and let the process be the process. There's nothing to fix that is going to get fixed unless the dude doing the job wants to admit it might need fixin. And even then, he has to be the one to start the fixin if need be. (Hard to swallow I know if you're in a relationship with someone who needs fixed but ain't admitting it, hence my admission earlier that I am not a mental health professional). I hope this lends some insight, That'll be a $15 co-pay. Oh, and I see we're out of time, please see the receptionist to make another appointment on your way out......

Daniel Mercer, Husband, Father, Firefighter. In that order.

■ ■ ■ ■ ■ ■ ■ ■ ■ ■ ■ ■ ■

Can I Say This Out Loud? Sometimes It's Easier When He's at the Firehouse.

Ok I said it. I know I'm not the only to feel this but I'm all about transparency and speaking the truth. Being the wife of a firefighter, we find ways to deal and get into our routines and keep the home life running effectively when our husbands are away. It takes a strong, capable woman to do that job, often the kind of woman who might be sort of set in her ways. So when the firefighter comes home, tired, groggy and not having witnessed the efficient flow of life for the past couple of days, and with children who are willing to test mom and dad against each other, it can get a bit rocky.

■ ■ ■ ■ ■ ■ ■ ■ ■ ■ ■ ■ ■

"Throw in the differences of firehouse environment compared to your household environment and there could be quite a lot of adjustment to take place."

■ ■ ■ ■ ■ ■ ■ ■ ■ ■ ■ ■

We each bring our own styles of household management into our marriages which do not always mesh neatly. Picture drill sergeant style versus the free spirit, creative type. Or single mom family vs the Ward and June Cleaver model. Perhaps the transient, move-a-lot, only child family compared to the 5 children orchestra that was stationary for 40 years in their family home. Just merging those two philosophies together is challenging enough and now you must learn to operate in a couple of different modes—when one spouse is home and when both of you are home. Throw in the differences of firehouse environment compared to your household environment and there could be quite a lot of adjustment to take place.

For our family, I know that if we have a super busy couple of days coming up and certain events to attend that aren't my husband's favorite, it's sometimes easier for all of us to just knock that out while he's at the firehouse. Why subject him to events he considers torturous like birthday parties at bounceland for sticky-fingered talkative neighbor kids? When the fire schedule neatly coincides, we take full advantage. Another example is certain home projects. I'm much more of a DIYer than my husband. So if I can knock out a home improvement project without his grit and muscles, I'm so glad to do that while he is on shift and save our time together for something we both enjoy. Honestly, he's never admitted this to me but I imagine there were seasons of whiney 2 and 3 year olds not sleeping through the night which made him grateful to be at the firehouse instead of home.

Now don't look at these feelings as if you are glad to be apart from each other. This is simply a bonus of the fire life. Who else can navigate schedules to where your time together is optimized for your most favorite activities together? No it doesn't always work out that way but what a bonus.

Superstitions, Routines and Traditions—How You Say Goodbye

For many, it's not the transition back into the home which is the struggle, but surprisingly the transition out of the home. As a firefighter, you might be in a season where work is really hard and the environment at your station is currently a little toxic. Changes in leadership, call volume, new policies or lack of policies can all contribute to not looking forward to heading into the job you love the next morning. So the night before shift brings shortness and a mood shift that isn't pleasant. As a spouse, you just want to do whatever you can to make it better. You can feel so hopeless watching your spouse struggle with frustrations like that affecting their peace and calmness. No one wants to say goodbye on a bad note, yet gearing up to face a toxic environment takes a whole lot of positive self-talk and motivation. The family may also slip into a foul mood realizing their spouse/parent are going to be gone for the next day or longer.

We never want to let future worries steal present joys. Focusing on the present moment where you are right there together can improve the mood. Fun and memorable night time routines (for those who head to shift in the mornings) make long lasting traditions.

■ ■ ■ ■ ■ ■ ■ ■ ■ ■ ■ ■ ■

Always kiss goodnight. Never go to bed angry. Those phrases have a new meaning when one of you is heading off to a job with more obvious danger than most people face in their day. Our family has adapted some goodbye traditions over the years to help stay connected.

For our kids, good night times with Dad are lengthy and important. I finally learned to allocate a good 45 minutes for him to make his rounds to 4 bedrooms. The most popular question ever is always asked "Will you be here tomorrow?" (it never fails to shoot daggers through a parent's heart despite fully understanding the responsibility to be a provider for our family.) Our littlest one likes to send a different stuffed animal to ride along at the firehouse for the next shift day. Dad sends reports back to homebase with the whereabouts of this little critter and frequently they are found doing some sort of mischief along the way. (Whatever did we do before texting photos was possible?)

For us as a couple, we try to avoid any fear-inducing, superstitious goodbye routine. That's like setting yourself up for worry and heartbreak because it's nearly impossible to do the same thing every third day for a 30-year career. He always kisses me goodbye and says he loves me, even when he is mad and does so with a cold shoulder and mumbled words. I try to intentionally wake up enough to receive them and give some encouragement to him for his day. I applaud loudly the wives who always wake up and help their husband's prepare for the day whether it's laying out clothes, packing a lunch or making coffee. I'm not so much a morning person for that 5:30 am wake up call. Sometimes I'll have my act together the night before and sneak some sweet nothings into his bag such as notes, small gifts and well, unmentionable surprises.

And then I hear our security system beep and the front door close, and there's always a wee bit of sadness that washes over me before my game face is on to take the reins fully for our household until he returns. Teamwork feels so good. I know he's always there for us, but when he's physically here and part of our team, life just seems so much more complete.

One Last Important Detail Regarding the Transition— Why Does My Firefighter Leave for the Station So Early?

There is a vivid memory I have, a day in my life when I felt very alone and so incredibly abandoned. We all have these memories, days we never forget, feelings that were so deep they're etched in our memories forever. One of mine is me standing in our front doorway, watching my husband leave for work at 6:00am even though his start time was an hour later, and the ten-mile drive to his station took only minutes. I still remember the faded grey t-shirt, stained with our infant's spit up, the sticky hand of our four-year-old clutching mine, and the weight of our new baby heavy in my arms. Tears streamed down my face blurring his form. The form of him walking to his truck; walking away from his family before he had to. At that time, I struggled to understand why. Why did he want to leave us? Why didn't he want to have breakfast with his little girl, grab one last snuggle with a smiling baby, give me more love? Why did he love the fire department more than me?

I didn't know what he was seeing; a hormonal new mother, an irrational mess, a crazy person who wouldn't listen to a word he said. So, why bother? When we talk about it now, he tells me, "Of course I told you what was going on, didn't I? I mean, what else could I say?" Well he didn't. Trust me. But therein lied our issues. He had no idea what to say to talk me off the ledge. He didn't have the words. He felt like he was explaining it all as clearly as he could, and I felt like he was saying nothing at all.

■ ■ ■ ■ ■ ■ ■ ■ ■ ■ ■ ■ ■

"There are a multitude of reasons that our husbands leave much earlier than they need to in order to be there at the official 'start time' of a shift."

■ ■ ■ ■ ■ ■ ■ ■ ■ ■ ■ ■ ■

What I really needed to hear was why this was a part of his job, and that it wasn't about me. I understand now a few things I didn't then; a few things I wish someone had explained to me. You see, I saw it as a direct representation of how he felt about our family. I felt like he meant to hurt me each time he took away an hour that, in my opinion, still belonged to us. If someone had explained to me that this was a part of his job, and that it was important for not only his reputation, but his health and safety, it would have spared me a lot of these days spent crying in the doorway. What I didn't know then was most days he needed an extra thirty minutes to arrange his gear, to make sure everything was ready to go in case those tones went off at 7:01am. Or that a lot of times he wanted to be there in case a call came in at 6:55am, so that someone else wouldn't have to spend an extra hour or two on shift because he didn't come in early. I didn't know that the reason he was home so often on time was because everyone else was leaving their family an hour early too. I just didn't know. But I also never asked. I simply cried and stood there. I took it personally and made him feel horrible for performing a part of his job that is just as important as the rest.

I know now that sending him off with the last sight of me being devastated with tears streaming down my face also set the tone for his day as much as it did mine. It made me mopey and grumpy, and it took him out of the frame of mind he needed to be in to do his job and do it well. I should have sent him off happy, smiling and content in his marriage and family; not feeling guilty for doing his job.

There are a multitude of reasons that our husbands leave much earlier than they need to in order to be there at the official "start time" of a shift. While you and I can run out the door ten minutes before we're supposed to be in the office, they simply cannot. For the majority of firefighters, they simply want to be there for their brothers in case someone needs to duck out early or a "late call" comes in. Some wives have mentioned that it's just a courtesy. How many times have we wives breathed a sigh of relief that our husband wasn't "held over?" Well, it was likely because someone else's husband came in and took the call that came in ten minutes before our husband was off shift. There are other wives that say their husbands need time to grocery shop for the meals they're going to eat on shift. Some of us believe that they simply want time to shoot the breeze with the shift who's coming off, or discuss a new protocol or procedure. For some of us wives, we have those firefighters who simply need to check the boxes: gear in place, everything where it's supposed to be and ready to go. And don't we want that for them? Don't we want them to feel secure and confident before say, running into a burning building? I think so. While some of us wives know this, imagine how it must be for a new firewife, or a new mom with an infant. It doesn't always seem so clear.

For me, it took a lot of crying, a lot of self-reflection, and a lot of wasted time to realize that it wasn't about me. I sure wish someone had spared me all that heartache and explained the reality of the situation. I wish someone had given my fireman the words. Take note firefighters: I needed to hear that it wasn't about me, that he didn't love the fire department more than me. I needed to be told that it's just another part of the job. I could have used an ear that understood too.

Our family has done a few things over the years to lessen the "early shift day" struggle. We make new traditions. Dad may not have breakfast with us, but he wakes each kid up with a kiss and hug before he's off, he's their own "love alarm." On days he comes off shift he picks the kids up from school, this gives them something to look forward to all day and lessens the difficulty of him not seeing them off the day before. We've started to realize that even though that stolen hour can sting sometimes, those extra hours we get can be pretty great.

Sometimes my fireman and I have lunch together on a random week day, just us two, something we'd never be able to do if we both worked a nine to five. Often there are long stretches of days in the summer when Dad is home, the place is a complete madhouse, and the laughing never stops. What other kind of job affords those stretches of days off? Sometimes I don't have to leave work midday when the school nurse calls because one of our kids redeposited their breakfast on the desk. Dad's not on shift, he's got it. Just this week my Firefighter got off shift early (and thank you to the husband who went in much earlier than normal to make it happen) and took our youngest to her first day of school in his uniform. She was totally surprised, and excited would be an understatement! So to the mom in the doorway, with sticky hands and wet cheeks: I get it, we all do. We are here for you. And one last thing: he doesn't love the Fire Department more than you, we promise.

■ ■ ■ ■ ■ ■ ■ ■ ■ ■ ■ ■ ■

Firefighters listen up to this next contributing authors story as it just might save a life, possibly yours. John Dixon is a career Fire Officer with an urban Fire Department in New Jersey and has over 20 years in the fire service. John has a passion for the fire service and for training, mentoring and inspiring up and coming officers and firefighters. He also serves as an Instructor with the Bergen County Fire Academy (NJ) and is an Advocate for the National Fallen Firefighters Foundation.

John has served as a US Marine and during that time he believes, the traits and principles such as discipline, education and servant leadership among many others are the cornerstones of great company officers and firefighters alike. He is passionate about helping others in seeking continuous improvement, while providing cutting edge training and education, spreading the message to others about the important role it plays in developing and refining great leaders within the fire service.

Success for John is seeing those that he has trained, mentored and inspired become great leaders that lead and inspire other firefighters and then duplicate themselves into more great leaders, thus having a positive ripple effect on the fire service and those we all serve. John has been married for 13 years to his wife Lynda and together they have 2 girls.

"The Commute" *By John Dixon*

How My Hour Long Commute Allows Me to Prepare and Decompress

As a fire officer I value my responsibilities very seriously. What would be great for families and loved ones to understand is that the level of preparation before our shifts does not begin the moment we walk into the fire station. There is a level of anxiety, routine, and mental preparedness that must be addressed. This is where my hour long commute to work may at times seem as a pain but I have made the conscious decision to use this time wisely. Let's discuss what actions we can take to best maximize and prepare for the transition to work.

Shift Planning

Currently my platoon assignment is the roving officer and I'm stationed at headquarters. This brings a level of anxiety onto itself. I have very little idea of what station I will be assigned to for the next twenty-four hours. This is sometimes troubling to plan my day as I have to wonder about what meal arrangements have been made or do I pack three meals for myself and be that guy! Of course there will be company training which may or may not be scheduled from the department training officer so we as a company will have to decide what to do. Often times as I read through the trade magazines and websites, I will use current events to dictate the content of our company drills. Often times, we as a company decide what to do as a team so there is buy-in from the entire crew. A great resource that I utilize during the commute are podcasts.

Podcasts

There is no shortage of fire service podcasts to listen to during a commute. Some episodes are better than others and most will discuss training and how to become better at our profession which can even become audio drills for the company. I have found great content with the help of podcasts. There are also great podcasts that are not fire serviced centered that can prepare me for the next twenty-four hours of unknown chaos or relative boredom.

Audiobooks

Most firefighters spend a bunch of time in our mobile offices. This leaves a considerable amount of time to audibly read. Whether it may be promotional materials, college course work, or leisurely reading. The hour can be spent wisely listening to books that we would otherwise not read because we are too busy on the home front.

There is a considerable amount of preparation for us to go to work. Physically and most importantly mentally. The commute for me is a way that I can set aside issues that are at home such as family schedules, soccer or basketball practices and games, and even the honey do list. This is a major part of how I prepare for my home life to my fire officer transition.

■ ■ ■ ■ ■ ■ ■ ■ ■ ■ ■ ■ ■ ■

The transition for me begins the moment I step foot off of the fire station grounds. Like a switch, I take off my fire officer hat off.

■ ■ ■ ■ ■ ■ ■ ■ ■ ■ ■ ■ ■

Now on the opposite hand is the ride home. This is where we can utilize our commutes as a decompression time. We are faced with major decisions, personalities, and stressors while we are at work and are now driving home for the same set of circumstances just with our families instead of coworkers. This is extremely vital for me to unwind and prepare for my home life.

Sounds crazy right? Having to prepare to go home.

The place of respite and comfort. Consider this, how many times while we were on shift has a broken water pipe pushed our significant others over the edge? How many double booked athletic events wreaked havoc on the family taxi? Most assuredly, there were phone calls and texts from our loved ones reaching out for comfort while we try to hold the line from far away.

The transition for me begins the moment I step foot off of the fire station grounds. Like a switch, I take off my fire officer hat off and begin the process of becoming the husband and father that my family needs and expects. Thank God that I have an hour. Sometimes I feel that I may need more time!

During the week my two girls are off to school before I get home which means that my wife is home. One way to decompress is to stop at the bagel store and bring peace offerings. The honey-do list items seem to grow exponentially bigger overnight, and maybe I can check off a few during my ride home by stopping at the home improvement store. Often times a "good morning beautiful" text or encouraging words to "get some" as my wife heads to her workout session sets the tone for the rest of the day.

The commute home for me is a way to stop thinking about the fire service and start thinking of how I can better serve my family. Just as in hazardous materials responses where time, distance, and shielding are ways to keep safe so too will they work for the transition home. The better that we can learn to compartmentalize our work lives from our home lives will most certainly help with stress management.

One way that I have found to be extremely helpful for our marriage is to have regular lunch dates. There is so little time devoted to just the two of us that we find at least an hour or so to go and grab a bite together. This time together has proven to become a must for us every day. This allows us to be selfish with our time and not take away time from the children once they get home from school and athletics.

I find that this is the best decompression method. My wife and I stop what we are doing, get in the truck and simply enjoy our alone time. It makes a significant difference!

In closing, our significant others may not see the need for us to prepare for work much less having to prepare to return home but this is a staple to a healthy and happy home life. Utilizing the time, distance, and shielding method has helped me and my family to stay happy and strong. I hope that a small glimpse into my daily life will help some of you as you read this very valuable resource that I wish was available when I first started out in my fire service career. From my family to you and yours, stay safe out there, love one another selfishly and may God continue to bless you and your families.

Instructor John Dixon

■ ■ ■ ■ ■ ■ ■ ■ ■ ■ ■ ■ ■

Remember we're trying to cover so many scenarios in this book and not all may match to your marriage and family. Truly your fire life needs to look like what works best for you. Perhaps we've sparked some inspirations. Let's close this chapter with our best tips for surviving the test of the transition commitment.

~ *for the firefighter* ~
A Test of Commitment
The Transition To / From Home

- Do figure out what works best for you to decompress after a shift. Communicate that to your spouse and make a game plan to allow you that healthy transition.

- Listen to your spouse and family's needs for that transition as well. Compromises can work to meet everyone's needs.

- You may have faced a day with life or death circumstances and feel that your spouse's stories pale in comparison. There's no comparing. Marriage is give and take and your spouse's needs are no less important than yours even if it did involve a tragedy. Love is being present for your spouse right where they are.

- If leaving for the firehouse is bringing anxiety and stress before a shift, commit to routines that minimize this joy stealer and involve your spouse.

- Remember that feelings are real and allowed but can set the tone in your entire home. Learning to use a few words to let your spouse know "I love you. I just need some time to deal with _____" can prevent unnecessary hurts in your marriage.

~ *for the spouse* ~
A Test of Commitment
The Transition To / From Home

- Your home should be the safest most comfortable place for your firefighter to rest and recover from a tough shift. It helps me to remember good old Proverb 21:19: "It's better to live alone in the desert than with a quarrelsome, complaining wife." You want your husband to seek home as a shelter and not avoid it for alternatives that are not as helpful such as alcohol.

- This does not mean to forego your needs. Marriage is give and take. After a long shift, you may need a similar break from the household duties. Be clear about communicating your needs and working together to find decompression routines that work for both of you.

- Realize that transitioning from a firehouse environment to home may not be as easy as flipping a switch.

- Understand that time before and after shift is critical for the job of firefighting and your husband may leave early and arrive home late due to transition time, training and simply being helpful to the off going and oncoming crews.

- for discussion -

- Are you both satisfied with your transition routines to / from the firehouse?

- What one thing could you add to your routines to bring more joy and understanding and build a long lasting fire family tradition in your marriage and family?

- How do you as a couple want to handle that transition back into the home after a rough shift? What words or signs will you use to indicate it's been a difficult night? And what works best to help both spouses decompress and best support each other's needs?

RESOURCES

All resources mentioned in this chapter can be found at HonorAndCommitment.com/Chapter5

Honor Your Mothering and Fathering
Raising Kids of Firefighters

No matter what you do for a living, becoming a parent redefines nearly everything about your life; and I'm talking way more than sleepless nights and empty wallets. Suddenly your perspective on everything includes this little person we are solely responsible for feeding and keeping healthy and safe and raising into a moral, successful adult." And you thought firefighting was a tough gig!

Parenthood changes your outlook on your career priorities, financial game, and especially how you spend your time. That whole adaptability and flexibility thing you've already learned as a fire couple will be taken to an entirely new level. If you don't have kids yet, don't let this scare you. To answer the age old question: There is never a good time to have kids. There's never enough money, or the right time in your career, or when you're at the optimal health.

You can call my husband and I somewhat authorities in this category; at least through age 16, since we have 4 kids and that's how far we've made it on this journey. I'll start with one of those tearjerker stories. Here's your warning.

Warning: This is a roller coaster emotional heartbreaker happy ending kind of story

It's been a fun season in our household. We survived promotional testing process and guess what? My husband ended up first on the list! I couldn't be prouder. It's been a long 12 year wait. Of course there are no current openings but this was still a big milestone. Of course this also means everyone's favorite word in the fire service: training. Queue the long hours and fewer phone calls home.

Last night was one of the first bedtime tuck ins in a long time and at that moment there was a fresh clean Friday slate in front of us and promises of a school lunch date with Daddy. Then we picked up that phone call that is the only one that comes after 10 PM. You're needed at the department.

■ ■ ■ ■ ■ ■ ■ ■ ■ ■ ■ ■ ■ ■

"I searched for the words and the look on my face that would soften the blow. I have some sad news. Daddy got overtime."

■ ■ ■ ■ ■ ■ ■ ■ ■ ■ ■ ■ ■ ■

He was torn. Once I convinced him we would all certainly survive another day, I still wasn't sure his heart could bear this. But duty called and he was off before sun up.

I heard her bare feet coming down the hallway first and then her steel-trap of a 7-year-old mind instantly remembered.

Where's Dad? He's coming to my lunch at school today.

I searched for the words and the look on my face that would soften the blow. I have some sad news. Daddy got overtime.

And the tears flowed.

I hugged her and pulled her hair out of her face and kissed her wet cheeks and thought up a great new approach to make her feel better about all of this. The kind of logic I use all the time on myself but wasn't sure would work for a brokenhearted 7-year-old.

Hey! Did you know about Daddy's new important job at the fire station? The tears slowed and she looked up with anticipation and a momentary break from the tears. He is learning to be a Lieutenant. He'll get to ride in the front seat of the fire truck and be the one in charge when there is a fire.

Her eyes lit up and her mouth burst open a genuine smile. "Really?"

I could see the pride in her daddy glowing in her eyes. She couldn't control the smile.

I went on about how important that is and he needs to learn new things and there aren't as many people who do that job so he has to be ready to go help people when it's his turn a little more often. She enthusiastically shook her head in agreement. My daddy is super important.

I thought we were good but the moment passed as quickly as it arrived. "But he promised he would go have lunch with me today!" Even stronger tears flowed. Sobs really. Gut wrenching sobs that made me question whether I should even tell him. And sobs that reminded me there are days I feel the exact same way. They are of course fewer and farther in between. But some days you do wish the fire department could give family time just a little break from the routine.

We snuggled longer, calmed down and looked to the bright side of seeing Daddy and all our friends at the firehouse for family pizza night the next night. A promise of a visit to the firehouse, especially when her little trio of 6-7-8-year-old firefighter's daughters is going to be there, is heavy ammo I pull out in negotiations sometimes. The morning routine progressed, the school day passed, the bus brought them safely back home to me and not another word was mentioned of this missed lunch date.

But Daddy. That man's heart will be crushed to hear this.

He called over lunch and of course he wanted to know how she took it. Because we share EVERYTHING in our marriage, I told him the truth, along with truck fulls of encouragement that we are all fine. Really. And again how proud we are that his hard work is paying off. And while disappointing, there are many other moments she gets to spend with him. And we've got a few days together coming up this week on our Spring Break Stay-cation.

■ ■ ■ ■ ■ ■ ■ ■ ■ ■ ■ ■ ■ ■

Another fire family crisis averted. {Pat myself on the back and move along.} It's not the first, won't be the last and doesn't make me extra special to anyone but my sweet husband and kiddos. Let's talk about other nuances of the fire life as they impact children.

Handling a Crisis Well Comes in Handy as a Parent

If you're going to have kids, you're going to have some crises. They develop into the fabulous and sometimes hilarious stories of your family history. A crisis may start as early as premature labor and abrupted placentas, and a firefighter who knows far too well how near death the experience his wife just went through was. These crises continue through smashed fingers, broken bones, fever-induced seizures, playground bullies, and pre-teen daughters receiving inappropriate text messages from boys who are lucky to be miles away from your family home.

Those family crises are just a few of our personal experiences. My personal favorite was the "caught on video" moment as I conducted a Skype interview with another fire wife across the country. My children ran frantically behind me and then busted into my office screaming, no words, my son's hand on his forehead removed to reveal massive gash and a lot of blood. Gotta go! Be sure to check out our resources at the end of this chapter if you want to relive that now comical moment with us.

One of the beautiful aspects of the fire life is the somewhat "small town" feel of your area fire family. For example, our local fire department knows my husband is also a firefighter (not in our district) and tends to keep a little closer eye on us. During the gashing of the head on live video incident, before I could even get in touch with my husband, the guys at that station were texting him to say they were on the way. They even knew it was his unit day and he wasn't home. I hope you all have taken the time to introduce yourself to your local fire department. It's truly an asset to your community to have the awareness and understanding of what fire families go through. And if you are like our family, neighbors will sometimes call on your firefighter to check on a cut or bump and see if it's emergency room visit worthy. They are always serving.

About those crises, if you're married to a firefighter and you're in the medical profession, this may all seem like no big deal. But for someone like me who could never handle the medical profession, being married to a firefighter is especially handy for those bodily fluid explosions. Personally, I used to pray the vomit would come when he wasn't on shift, and he graciously accepted that awful duty in our household.

There are really two different approaches to parenting that I've seen taken by first responders.

One is this style as shared by instructor and Lieutenant John Dixon of New Jersey. John shared that handling the stress of the job has allowed him to be a better stress handler and crisis manager at home. He doesn't sweat the small stuff at home because he recognizes how blessed he is to have happy, dancing, noisy, active, bickering children, compared to the victim of the car accident he helped on the last shift day. Hanging upside down on the playground doesn't worry him. He's not a helicopter parent for those "small things" because he has a real life comparison to what are truly the "big things." High stress situations at home are nothing compared to the high stress situations at work.

That approach can sometimes backfire when the wife and kids feel that something is uber critical and he has disengaged. It's critical to watch for those signs and cues from your family members to be sure that as a firefighter, your sensitivity radar is where it should be for your family's needs.

■ ■ ■ ■ ■ ■ ■ ■ ■ ■ ■ ■ ■

"If you are a firefighter, and you are annoyed with the 'small stuff' in your own home, it's a sign that the stress of the job may be getting to you a little too much."

■ ■ ■ ■ ■ ■ ■ ■ ■ ■ ■ ■ ■

I love John's example as it demonstrates a healthy outlook and adjustment between the firehouse and the home environments. Some firefighter dads really struggle with this though. If you are a firefighter, and you are annoyed with the "small stuff" in your own home, it's a sign that the stress of the job may be getting to you a little too much. Yes, those seasons when the kids are little and loud and messy and can't tie their own shoes or pour their own cereal are exhausting and challenging sometimes. Exploding in a fit of rage over one of their tantrums is never going to be the right response, and a sure sign that something is bothering you. Check out the Stress First Aid free training from National Fallen Firefighters Foundation's Everyone Goes Home program mentioned in the resource section of this chapter. Your family will thank you. It's very true that the death you pronounced at 3 am that morning is the 'big stuff' in life. But to your family who hasn't been exposed to that, the big stuff is daddy walking through the door as the tickle monster and wrestling them to the floor in their PJs.

Children can sense a parent's mood and adapt to it. The worst feeling for a spouse or child is learning to "walk on eggshells" because dad had a bad night, bad shift or a bad call. Awareness of the effects of the job helps everyone adjust and adapt. Spouses can make the home a "safe place to land," but kids may not quite understand what's got daddy all worked up. Bottom line: Firefighters be sure you are taking care of you so that you can be the best parent/spouse possible. With a schedule such as firefighting which limits your time at home, you want to be sure those are the best family hours possible.

Schedules and Families

We already talked a lot of handling the crazy schedules of the firefighting world and even shared another real life example above but let's spend a moment on the effect on kids. The most popular question for me in our house is "will Dad be home tomorrow?" And for my husband it's, "do you have to work tomorrow?" I'm sorry to say that the crushed looks on their faces don't dissipate with age nor sting any less over the years. We soothe and explain with phrases like, "it's Daddy's turn to go help others," and "Daddy took this overtime so Joey's Daddy could be home for his birthday." Or when you are anxiously awaiting Daddy's arrival home only to get that phone call—forced overtime—breaking the news to 6-year-old girls who are already excited about their lunch date with daddy will break all hearts. The ultimate parenting question for all situations is this: are we doing the right thing for our kids? I'm not going to answer that for you as it's a very personal topic but I will share some thoughts we've wrestled with over the years.

Kids are resilient and flexible, usually way more than us adults. Your parenting influential years can feel like centuries when they are in the stage of screaming in their carseat incessantly, and they can suddenly feel fleeting when they enter middle or high school, and you can count on one hand how many more summers they'll be under your roof. There were seasons when no amount of money was worth the overtime away and seasons when we needed that extra overtime check to cover the special camp one child was invited to. Most of all, we want to look back and minimize the statement, "Daddy was always at the firehouse." If your heart is struggling with this, the best people to talk to are adults who grew up with a parent as a firefighter in a healthy, balanced home. They turned out alright and have great perspectives to share on handling this.

Shielding Your Kids from the Fire Service. Yes or No?

If you've ever spent time on any mommy blogs, you know why I keep saying "it's up to you." There are way too many people out there ready to judge your parenting choices. Consider this as another area to think about as parents.

The fire service can be harsh, bitter and tragic. I remember when one of our littles was about four years old, asking daddy when he got home "did you save any kittens today daddy?" Aw. How adorable! But the conversation went on down a predictable path as their imaginations followed along what it must be like to be stuck in a burning building. What it must be like for Daddy to be in there with his gear that protects him; and the sad reality that some people do not make it out alive, including some firefighters. It also allowed us the opportunity to reinforce his training and safety and to stave off worries little ones sometimes face.

■ ■ ■ ■ ■ ■ ■ ■ ■ ■ ■ ■

"Our family has chosen to be very open and real about what Dad sees on the job, with rules and limits about grossness around the dinner table."

■ ■ ■ ■ ■ ■ ■ ■ ■ ■ ■ ■

Our family has chosen to be very open and real about what Dad sees on the job, with rules and limits about grossness around the dinner table. It's clear who got the "ok for the medical profession" gene and who did not in our family. There are of course limits; topics Daddy isn't even ready to discuss and topics Daddy knows Mommy doesn't need all the details about. But yes, we have discussed what it must be like for your car to roll on the side and your arm to be trapped underneath and the amazing technologies and tools that allow firefighters to help people in those scary situations. It's a moment-by-moment decision as the conversations develop. You must be aware of how everyone in the conversation is feeling, watch their body language, listen to their words (or lack of words), and be sure you button it up with a healthy ending. Even still, there might be some follow up at bedtime tuck in. Kids need to know they are safe and secure in a place that they can grow and learn, and be loved no matter what. These fire life stories introduce them to moments that aren't so safe and secure; and at the proper age with the proper approach can give your fire family a perspective on life others may not experience until tragedy strikes them personally.

Know that some firefighters take a completely different route and do not share much about the job at home with their families. It's a way for them to keep their home safe and sacred and protected from some of the nastiness in the world. It truly depends on your family choices and reactions what will work best for you.

Moms Must Ask for Help

The *only* way I've survived four kids and the fire schedule is by asking for help with carpooling and ridesharing. It is so not in my nature and I cringe a little bit when I miss one activity for another but there's simply no way for you to be on both sides of town at the same time nor to fairly choose dance over hockey or vice versa. This is my plea to women everywhere to just get over it, make friends with the other moms that you trust and ask for help. Now the one interesting twist on this being married to a firefighter is this; my husband will overly scrutinize the other parents that we send our kids off with. Having seen far too many tragedies on the job, there is no need to be embarrassed about getting to know these families and their values, habits and lifestyles. There are definitely families we have chosen to not let our kids hang out with due to use of alcohol, pot and older teenage brothers and sisters who are a bad influence on the younger ones.

Mr. Mom FF's

After our first child (together) was born, I changed my work schedule to part time. The hours were flexible so the grand plan was for me to work on my husband's non-duty days and he'd keep the kids. After a lengthy four-month maternity leave, I began day one of driving 25 minutes to my office. By the time I got there, he was already calling me on my desk phone with that inconsolable frantic newborn cry in the background. I turned around and drove home, walked in the door, she smelled mama and instantly stopped crying. He shook his hands in disgust claiming defeat. The Firefighter Mr. Mom gig appears to be an awesome cash saving option *if* Mr. Mom is up for the task. My husband *loves* his children and is a mega awesome dad, but much better by the time they are three or four. Those infant and toddler years really stressed him out and in turn our children as well. When the kids got older, I was so envious of the daytime fun he and the kids shared together. Yes, he made a trade-off to not pursue his fire career as intensely during this season and looking back he still claims he wouldn't trade that decision, despite many other firefighters his age passing him up to officer positions. But it's truly a decision you need to make as it fits the needs of your family.

Planning Child Care

Speaking of Mr. Moms, childcare arrangements can be most challenging in a fire family. In order of most ideal situations ever, let me list some options:

1. Nearby family whom you love and adore and will take in your little ones nearly any hour of the day. If you have this option, it's one of the most amazing blessings.

2. A local drop-in childcare provider, typically in someone's home, who offers flexibility and schedule changes that are different almost every week. Ask around your local community and get references.

3. Someone who comes to your home with similar flexibility. Because there were seasons when my job was more flexible, we used college girls and I made my work hours around their school schedule. It's great money for them and very convenient for you and your family.

4. Just paying for full-time Monday through Friday daycare even if you don't need all the days. For the firefighter in your family to have a weekday with no kids to get house chores done, or catch

up on sleep, is really handy as well. This, however, is one of the most expensive options.

5. Live in nannies/au pairs. Our family was blessed with this option for 5 years. The guys at the firehouse called us millionaires because we took this route. It's far from the truth. An au pair was way cheaper than daycare once we had 3+ kids. It was also the most convenient scenario for the kids and myself as we didn't have to get everyone up and out the door every day. However, you do have to be comfortable with hosting a semi-grown up "daughter" in your home and introducing them to American traditions. We were very blessed for that season of our life that I had a job allowing us to afford this option (and no it didn't make us millionaires for anything but our love for each other).

Missing Mom / Dad at the Firehouse

It's going to happen. You're going to face an age where a child is weepy and sad when their parent cannot tuck them in or possibly attend a school function. Without sounding harsh and unsympathetic, this is inevitable and you might as well gear up and get across the bridge of that season. One of the hardest things as a parent is watching your innocent sweet little ones experience the first stages of painful adult emotions—hurt, heartache, loneliness and grief to name a few.

Missing a parent who is at the firehouse can start as young as the toddler age, which can be tough to negotiate since there aren't really good words for negotiating with a toddler. Redirect, redirect, redirect. As they hit the 4—6 age range, facetime bedtime calls, special stuffed animals and the storybooks or videos where the mom / dad who is away has recorded the story are great methods to let me feel connected when apart.

■ ■ ■ ■ ■ ■ ■ ■ ■ ■ ■ ■

"Being realistic but reassuring about the dangers of the job is one approach. Be sure the firefighter parent leads much of this conversation for the most effective results."

■ ■ ■ ■ ■ ■ ■ ■ ■ ■ ■ ■

As you approach the older ages, there may be new awareness of the dangers of the job. Anxieties very frequently show up starting around this age. Teaching kids healthy ways to manage anxieties early on provides a solid foundation for life. Being realistic but reassuring about the dangers of the job is one approach. Be sure the firefighter parent leads much of this conversation for the most effective results. Taking the child to the station and showing them hands on the equipment and safety measures in place is a good step at this age. And we all know there are endless videos on YouTube, not all dramatic and scary, where you can teach your children some basics about fire attack and observe great safety standards that are in place to protect all the firefighters.

These days there are many more dangers besides fire that can harm a first responder. Kids are practicing active shooter lockdown drills at school. Their minds are exposed to much more at a younger age—or at least it feels that way. Depending on what your child asks, addressing the active shooter scenarios with them may be necessary as well. My husband wears a bulletproof vest very often while on the scene and the kids see these at the station when we visit. However, we do try to shield them from news stories which can be sensationalistic and intentionally driving fear in the viewers. Learning to discern what is a reputable news source versus hype is the next level of conversation as the kids approach tween and teen years.

You know your children best and can decide when and how much to introduce them to these more challenging life topics.

The Locker: The Firefighters Gateway to Their Heart for Family

Before kids, I sent cute photos of myself and us together as a couple with my husband to hang in his locker at the station. After kids, the level of "art" (loosely defined for various ages) and letters and photos we sent in drastically escalated to the point that my husband purchased a small storage container for all of it and began a rotational cycle for displaying it. When we visit the station, viewing the locker is an essential stop. Everyone wants to know that Dad put their art up in his locker right away. When said artwork is forgotten on the kitchen counter, this mom must act fast, distract and remove the evidence to prevent heart breakage. I wish we had an awesome piece of writing to insert here from a firefighter describing their feelings about this locker memorabilia because even the most stoic firefighters soften a bit when revealing what's in their locker, their wallet or tucked up inside their helmets. Nothing more to say here except make this your family's unique signature for your firefighter to carry with them on shift.

The Most Special Treat in This Fire Family— Who Gets to Sleep with Mom?

Before you get all upset by this, we aren't condoning any unsafe or unhealthy bed sharing habit. Take your argument to the mommy blogs for that. And if this isn't for your family, kindly move on. Some couples decide that their bedroom is their own sanctuary and not for children to spend time in. I think especially in blended families this could be very effective. In our family, the kids are welcome into our bedroom and the practicality of letting them sleep with us on some nights has outweighed the challenge of keeping them always in their own room and minimizing sleep deprivation in us parents. If you know anything about love languages, we have a couple kiddos that are very keen on physical touch as a mechanism to calm them down and this has been effective for us.

Then there is this rational thought. None of them have done it forever. Our 16-year-old no longer wants to sleep in mom's bed while dad is at the firehouse. If he did, we might begin to wonder if we need to give him a little extra nudge out of that nest.

While this has become a much loved tradition in our family, it also comes with responsibility. Earning the treat of who gets to sleep with mom is a big leverage point for good behavior in our household. You are one misstep away from not being able to snuggle with mom on a shift night.

Minus the octopus-legged, anvil-forehead toddlers, I really enjoy the nights we fall asleep together and the conversations that lead us there. Honestly, I am starting to be a little sad as the kids get older and do not want to do this as often. I clearly see a dog in our future to take up that cold empty space next to me in the bed.

Blended Families

Many firefighters (and their wives) have been divorced and remarried. It's a tough life with many ups and downs and not all marriages survive this, but you are reading this book and we are rooting for you to make that commitment truly last a lifetime. These remarriages bring one of the biggest challenges to fire families—the blended family. Now not only are you juggling a firefighter schedule, but you're doing so with one or two child sharing schedules with ex-spouses. You've got multiple styles of parenting and a lot of family dynamics moving in and out of your home on a regular basis. Happy, successful blended families are achievable but take much effort. While our favorite message is to avoid divorce if at all possible, here's just one reminder that even after divorce, your ex may always be a part of your life.

Our family is a blended family. My oldest had just turned 2 when he first met Dan and they were fast buddies. This blended life is all he and Dan have known as a family. Correspondingly our biggest marriage battles have been about parenting topics with my oldest. As common as it is, sadly there are few blended family resources available. We don't have space to dive into this complex subject in this book however we do have a "Blended Fire Families" small group over at 247commitment.org ready to empathize and strategize the best ways to address blended family topics in a fire family.

When Your Kids Want to Become Firefighters

Would you dissuade them or encourage them? We have a joke/truth in our house that we've told the kids since they were toddlers. You can be a firefighter *after* you go to college. Truthfully, when our kids grow into young adulthood, we just want them to make good life choices. We realize that may or may not include college, but finishing a degree later in adulthood is not the easiest. Having four children, we semi-joke that chances are one of them gets a scholarship, one of them joins the military, one of them joins the peace corps and one of them flakes out entirely (whatever that looks like in the 2020's).

The face of the fire service is changing rapidly like many professions, as baby boomers retire, younger leaders step in, government changes and the economy changes; it's just hard to predict what will the fire service look like then.

Certainly the desire to serve the public in any capacity is an admirable trait. How will you handle the thought of your child putting themselves in danger? It's a long way off and no need to make any hasty decisions. But as you're dressing that little baby up in firefighter booties and onesies and snapping those adorable photos of him fitting in the pocket of bunker gear, it's already crossing your mind. I have no wise advice here aside from these just being some of the "things you never thought you'd think before you were a parent" thoughts.

Choose Another Firefighting Responsibility or More Time with Your Kids?

I can never ever understand the sacrifice my husband made in choosing to not work a second job, to delay his firefighting career pursuits, and spend more time at home with our kids when they were ages 2, 3, 4 and 5. For my husband, a lot of that decision was a no-brainer as he did not want a repeat of his childhood with well-intentioned but absent parents. While he was making this choice, his peers were traveling the countryside becoming certified in the pre-eminent rescue training techniques that were just heating up at that time. Others had their heads down working hard on additional committees and projects to make their way up the promotional ladder. My husband was hanging out at the park pushing the kids in swings over and over and over, soaking in their giggles. That makes it sound very easy but I know it has not been easy for him to see firefighters who started after him already earn their Captain bugles. It's a pain that rears its head in marital arguments every once in a while when we're in a really low place. It can also be a source of wisdom as he coaches other firefighters in priority setting for the "right things" in life. Either way, it's worth considering as you enter and survive this parenting season.

Contributing author Ben Martin shared this on "Impact versus Legacy" at our blog:

> I've confused legacy with impact. Impact is the ability to literally collide ideas and values benefiting the here and now, with an eye towards the future. As leaders, we should all strive to have a positive impact at work. Legacy, is an opportunity to create a gift—an inheritance of our values about the world and how to navigate within it—that we can leave to the ones we love.

The mistake leaders make is thinking the place to create this is at work. Avoid confusing the two and realizing neither. My passion for the fire service has blinded me to my shortcomings as a husband and father and this is creating a conflict within myself. My wife and little girls will remember the memories we make together. I hope to pass on my values and best attributes while raising them. Hopefully they will go on to have great impact in the world and create their own families and legacy. We will sit around one day and watch home videos and joke about how much more hair Daddy had back then. We won't sit around and talk about the project that Daddy worked on for 16 months. And the reality is that in another 10 years, no one else in my organization will either. It will more than likely be redrafted and improved upon by the next "go-getters" of the organization.

■ ■ ■ ■ ■ ■ ■ ■ ■ ■ ■ ■ ■ ■

"My wife and little girls will remember the memories we make together. I hope to pass on my values and best attributes while raising them."

■ ■ ■ ■ ■ ■ ■ ■ ■ ■ ■ ■ ■ ■

My role in the fire service is to have a positive impact at work—do a great job, have fun, and empower the next generation of firefighters and leaders. My legacy is always growing at home with my wife and children and ultimately is determined by their success. They should receive the bulk of my time, attention, and investment. We sink a ton of time into developing our teams and ourselves at work, but are we doing the same at home? If you read a fire service book, do you read one on marriage or parenting? If you travel for a fire conference, do you attend a marriage retreat or take a family vacation? Like a see-saw, it is difficult to maintain balance, and we will have ups and downs in the process.

Out of the mouths of firefighter dads, you may be surprised at the power children have over the choices you make in life.

HONOR GUARD

~ *for the firefighter* ~
Honor Your Mothering and Fathering
Raising Kids of Firefighters

What's the right way to be a firefighter who is a parent? Anyway that comes from your healthy loving heart. Here are some thoughts as you decide what works for your family:

- There is no more important role than mom/dad. You will experience that perspective shift once you are a parent so don't be alarmed. It may be the first time in your career you realize, there is more to my life than being a firefighter.

- Off time begins to look so different but yet you crave it to be that way. You value time with kids on off days. (And it's ok to say you're ready for a break and to head back to the station as well!)

- Talk with your spouse about discussing the risks of what you do—at what age is what topic appropriate?

- If you decided to become a firefighter after you are a parent, it may look a little different. The kids will notice the difference in schedules plus it's a big sacrifice on a family for those early years of getting on with the fire department.

- Get on the same page for discipline when one or the other parent is gone.

- Be prepared for the prospect that they follow in your footsteps as a junior firefighter first even.

- Make an effort to call and check in, especially when it was unplanned. This brings consistency and reassurance to the child who may be thinking "Daddy is gone forever"—because that's what time feels like to them sometimes

- Be patient and understanding when talking to the kids on the phone

- Tell your spouse at home how much you appreciate them for handling the kid crises and home front while you are away

- Make a specific plan for what to do right when you get off duty and KEEP IT

- Special treats on the way home the next day can never hurt (i.e. bring the "hot now" Krispy Kremes when you drive by and your spouse's special Starbucks)

~ for the spouse ~

Honor Your Mothering and Fathering
Raising Kids of Firefighters

I'm not so keen on that phrase "if you think it's hard being a firefighter, try being a firefighter's wife." Simply because I'm not looking for any sympathy nor accolades but if there is one topic that is harder than others for me, it's choking back tears and putting on my brave face when talking with our kids about fire family life. Those kids can really pull on the heart strings! To be ready as a spouse of a firefighter who has now introduced kids to the equation, try these tips:

- Be ready and calm and reassuring when the bedtime tears and anxieties start to flow. How you respond has a very direct impact on how your kids will react as well.

- You play the primary role in helping the kids adapt to the fire life when your firefighter is away.

- Keep your fire family connected to family time with frequent messages, photos, phone calls and by sending little surprises to the firehouse. Drawing pictures to hang in Mom / Dad's locker is a great family tradition.

- Do speak highly of the firefighter's work and how important it is to the community. Speak positively to them and around them. Kids pick up on everything. So while venting to our favorite fire wife who totally gets it is healthy, little ears cannot process that in the same way.

- Be sure they know that just because they are away, doesn't mean they aren't thinking of them and missing them too. Tell them and show them how much they are missed. Have the firefighter who is away call home and ask about how events went while they are away.

- Take them to visit the station or show them photos of their locker with photos and pictures from home so they see they are still close to their parent when they are at the station.

- Have them create something for their parent to keep at the station (my husband has a collection of saved artwork in his locker thicker than all the school papers I've saved over the past 3 years).

- Redirection is still a great tool at young ages but can be used with more logic and reason as they get older since they do understand time better. Redirect them to a more positive outlook for the future. This is lifelong skill to learn. (Ages 5-7 by the way is when you start to see broken hearts because they can grasp more emotions and time.)

- Give them something of their parents to keep as a reminder they are still close to their heart. A teddy bear, a t-shirt, a photo.

- for discussion -

If you do not yet have children, this chapter can leave a scary impression. We insure you firefighters procreate often and with success and there's nothing the world needs more than another honorable, committed little firefighter. Discuss how this chapter impacted your thoughts on children.

If you do have children, consider these topics for discussion:

- Are your children ready for more detailed discussions of the risks of the job? How will you approach this?

- In what ways can you show each other appreciation and support as you parent from home vs the firehouse?

- What are your family's love languages and how can you best meet them via the fire life nuances? I.e. Quality time, physical touch, conversation, etc.

- Child Care: Do you have the conditions viable for a Mr. Mom setup? What are your back up plans?

RESOURCES

All resources mentioned in this chapter can be found at
HonorAndCommitment.com/Chapter6

Some articles and videos you will find:

- When Your Fire Family Calls 9-1-1
- Choosing Childcare for Fire Families
- Disappointing Daughters and Overtime
- "The Love Languages of Kids" Book

Family Visits
To the Firehouse

When you talk to any fire family about how they deal with long stretches of time apart, there is one common cure to ease that pain: family visits to the firehouse. Now, some of you immediately jump to that scene from Ladder 49. You know which one I'm thinking about? It involves a bit of "naughty time" in the station. That's not where we are going to go with this topic, and officially would not condone "conjugal visits" for 24 or 48 hour shifts. Just had to be clear for the record. We're talking about face time in real life—your family seeing each other face to face for a little bit of love tank filling up for mom, dad and the kids.

Our family lives about 25-30 minutes away from the firehouse, which happens to be in a district that moms in minivans shouldn't really be hanging out in after dark. So we don't visit too often, but enough that it has become a well-loved tradition in our family. Our go-to time for a firehouse visit can be triggered by a number of circumstances:

- Someone is celebrating a birthday;
- Dad was forced on an unexpected 48 and our family plans were ruined (everyone just needs a hug, including Dad!);
- We've gone a couple months with busy weekends and finally a day matches up that we can make a visit;
- It's family pizza night for the crew;

- Or, the classic "forgot something important at home and need to drop it off" (sometimes this is legitimate and others times it's a "convenient and because I have the time and need a hug" moment).

Rarely have I been able to drop by during the week, mid-day without kids, just because I was in the neighborhood. And when I did, I most definitely showed up with treats and enjoyed cookies and a cup of coffee with the crew and the chief (who typically isn't there during our normal weekend visits).

We have been blessed to have a firehouse that, for the most part and within reason, welcomes family visits. Over the years, some crews have been more tolerant of them than others, and who can blame them? When I was a postpartum, stretchy pants wearing, ponytail mama with a 7, 4, and 2-year-old, *and* a newborn who was collicky, that trip was an epic journey for us. It was also a major disruption of the peace for the crew who tolerated us. But, it sustained us just a little bit over the course of those two days.

■ ■ ■ ■ ■ ■ ■ ■ ■ ■ ■ ■ ■

"The kids on this crew made fast friends, and recently we've encountered the inevitable sadness of one firefighter being transferred to a different unit."

■ ■ ■ ■ ■ ■ ■ ■ ■ ■ ■ ■

The past few years, we've been with a crew who keeps to a tradition of Saturday pizza night with the families. There is homemade pizza flying out of the oven and many hands in the kitchen, typically those of the firefighters who won't let the wives lift a finger. The wives tend to reciprocate with a combination of delicious and healthy accompaniments. The kids on this crew made fast friends, and recently we've encountered the inevitable sadness of one firefighter being transferred to a different unit. While it's a devastating blow to the pack of three little girls who became fast friends at the firehouse, it's a lesson fire families learn to roll with. Nothing stays the same forever in the fire service.

For those of you for whom the firehouse is within the same community your family lives in, this scenario probably looks very different. As kids get older into the teen years, crews may be open to teens stopping by to visit in the evenings "just because" and the "drop something off" excuse probably happens quite often. For those of you who live very far from the firehouse (we're talking hours away), visiting has to be very intentionally planned and coordinated, and is likely due to a special event.

Why does all this matter? Think about the other firefighters and their families. They are all in different seasons with different needs in their life. Maybe they live closer or farther and see the firehouse visit differently from you. It's good to put yourself in their shoes and understand that perspective.

Seasons of "Need"

There are times when firehouse visits are more frequent. We all go through seasons where we are craving or need more time with our spouse or our children. Perhaps it's after a stressful event, you're working through some tough issues together, you're newlyweds or just entering a new chapter of life—as new parents or maybe even empty nesters. There were definitely seasons in our life where we *needed* to visit the firehouse more than others; so we did! When our babies got out of the NICU and dad had to go back to work, he fiercely missed them and worried about us. When we were up to it, we visited much more frequently.

General Guidelines for a Firehouse Visit

So, that's a whole lot of warm fuzzies about firehouse family visits, but let's be sure you are all educated and wise with how you go about these visits and what to expect.

First and foremost, you must remember that a firehouse is both a public building and a "home" to the firefighters who work out of that station. Generally, there are a set of guidelines in place about who visitors can be and where and when they can come. As a new firefighter and family, you will want to familiarize yourself with this. I highly recommend both privately asking the firefighters on your crew and reading the official guidelines so you are not caught by surprise if someone raises a red flag. Some individuals may be very relaxed and appreciative of family visits while others have made a very clear separation of home and work, and feel that a bit of their privacy is invaded by family visits.

~ *for the firefighter* ~
Family Visits
To the Firehouse

You Are the One Responsible for Knowing the Guidelines for Family Visits

As a courtesy and to show respect, we recommend that as a firefighter (not as a spouse) you are clear with your crew and officers about the expectations and guidelines for visits to the station. It's your job to know what they are and to take the lead there. It's pretty awkward if they show up and the officer has to address you in front of them, in the way that officers sometimes awkwardly handle relational topics, that something about the visit is out of the guidelines.

Invite Your Family (And Keep Those Communication Lines Open!)

When it's acceptable, invite your family to the firehouse. They should feel that you want them there, at least occasionally, and are not trying to keep the firehouse a "secret" from them. Speaking as a woman here, I can give you an insider tip: that may have nothing to do with what you are feeling, but it can be twisted so easily in your spouse's mind. To them, it's the fear of the unknown. If I don't know what it's like there, and he doesn't want me to visit, what possibly is happening? The worst of the worst thoughts start percolating, and suddenly your firehouse has become a brothel of scantily clad women where she is not welcome. This may seem far-fetched to you, but I've had girlfriends my whole life and know how far women can take these thoughts. Family visits to the firehouse eliminates that fear of the unknown and helps the family to personally connect with where their firefighter is eating, sleeping, working, and hanging out for so many hours each week.

A classic way to start a marital disagreement is to not tell your spouse about a family event held at the station to which they were not invited.

True, you may have good reasons to not tell your spouse about an event. Perhaps you are in what we will call a "grumpy season" with your crew and you don't want your family in that "grumpy" environment. We've all been there. It's a 25-or-more year career and sometimes called a dysfunctional family for a reason. Be clear and direct with your spouse about this event and your perspective. Talking it out together may either soften your heart about the situation or help your spouse to understand why it may not be a good idea. If you are new to the fire service and can't possibly understand why this might be uncomfortable here's one example: A series of promotional tests just finished. There was animosity about the selection process, and your firefighter ended up taking the brunt of the fall. The last thing your firefighter may want is for his family to show up and have cold shoulders turned on them. Sometimes it's just best to let some time pass and heal those wounds.

■ ■ ■ ■ ■ ■ ■ ■ ■ ■ ■ ■ ■

"Always assume positive intent. Ask your firefighter. Don't bottle up emotion and unfairly hold against them something that they aren't even aware of."

■ ■ ■ ■ ■ ■ ■ ■ ■ ■ ■ ■

Sometimes fire wives get a reputation for introducing some drama and gossip.

There. It's admitted and out in the open. First, if you are reading this as a fire wife, I challenge you to hold yourself up to the "honor and commitment" of the fire service, your personal character and your marriage, and to avoid those situations at all cost. But I know how easily you can slide down that slippery slope mentally. Women are tough on each other, brutal actually. And there's this old adage for how word spreads: tell a friend, telephone, tell a firefighter. In this case, when one wife hears from another about a firehouse family event, say Thanksgiving dinner at the station, and her husband hasn't told her yet, it could start World War 3 (I may or may not be speaking from personal experience here). You know how communication changes up after it's passed through a couple hands. Always assume positive intent. Ask your firefighter. Don't bottle up the emotion and unfairly hold against them something that they aren't even aware of. A common answer from my husband when we've had this happen is, "we briefly mentioned it at breakfast but I don't know what was decided." In the meantime, Firefighter Smith has told Mrs. Firefighter Smith who posts it on Mrs. Firefighter Miller's Facebook page and you are left feeling excluded; possibly by both your firefighter and these other wives. Don't go there, get the facts. Assume positive intent and poor communication practices on the guys' part. It's not like they were preparing formal Martha Stewart invites and guest lists. If you were left out by the other fire wives, still take the high road and uphold that honor and commitment we keep talking about. Husbands, a good clear rule of thumb here is to mention any small discussion about events and your thoughts about attending as quickly as possible so it doesn't get out of hand in the communication cycles. A good example, tell your wife "the guys mentioned possibly doing a family camping trip in April, but with our little one and the possibly cold weather then, I didn't think our family would be up for it. I just wanted you to know in case Joe's wife mentions it." See how easy that is?

Always Introduce and Welcome Your Family When They Visit

When your family does visit, introduce them so they feel welcomed. It can be a bit awkward and uncomfortable for them, especially the first time. As the firefighter you are comfortable and familiar with everyone there but your family may not have met everyone. And speaking from personal experience, I find myself trying to discretely read the name on their shirt if I haven't seen them for a while and don't recognize them. People change, ya know?

Prepare for that First Visit to the Firehouse

If at all possible, make that first visit at a time when there doesn't have to be a grand entrance into the kitchen / TV room. If you're reading this, chances are you already have a "first time they visited the firehouse" story but keep this in mind in case you get transferred to a new firehouse.

I'll share a story of my first visit with some classic firehouse humor. The first time I visited my husband (at that time boyfriend) at his permanent full time firehouse, I walked up the stairs that bring you around a corner and surprise, you are smack dab in a kitchen full of firefighters. No way around that entrance. On your first time there, you're going to get the once over. Immediately someone may lay their sarcastic humor into you and if you're lucky, you escape from that first visit without a nickname. A firefighter who will go unnamed, who is now retired and I have grown to learn truly does have a kind heart, said to me "So, you're the woman that has Dan all worked up in a frenzy. He's all mine. I'm going to scratch your eyes out." I'm not a funny girl by nature, pretty serious actually, and had no quippy comeback. I'm sure the look on my face was the topic of much jabbing after I left. It continued, every time I visited and bumped into this firefighter, "I'll scratch your eyes out," with a big smile on his face. Truth is, that's one way they look out for each other. Ladies, this is some man humor we may never fully understand. In girl speak he's saying, don't mess with his head and rip his heart out, we need this guy focused on firefighting. As our relationship grew, it became a sort of term of endearment (although he'd never admit it) that I'm all right and they're glad their brother is happy in love.

So yeah: the lesson is to be prepared to be sized up on that first visit. To the firefighters: please make that as painless as possible.

~ for the spouse ~
Family Visits
To the Firehouse

Things You Must Understand About Firehouse Visits...

It's not always a good time to visit. There are some very busy days at the firehouse with training or a lot of calls that just make it not right for a family visit; and sometimes you don't know that until moments before the visit. Like firefighters, families must be prepared for anything. Also, Monday through Friday during the daytime hours are typically set aside for traditional business, paperwork, admin and training. Those are not good times for a family to descend on the firehouse. Late evenings are also not always suggested, the firefighters are wrapping up their night and hoping for a good night's sleep, so understand that dropping by around 10pm is going to be an inconvenience to their schedule. Good visit times are generally weekends and evenings and only after all other chores or trainings have been completed.

■ ■ ■ ■ ■ ■ ■ ■ ■ ■ ■ ■

*"You are a representation of your firefighter when you visit.
What you say and do and how you act is a reflection
on him, no matter how independent you are."*

■ ■ ■ ■ ■ ■ ■ ■ ■ ■ ■ ■

Expect interruptions. Visits can very easily be interrupted by calls. In fact, sometimes you may feel it's a curse that they head out on a run everytime you show up. Again, not their fault and it's time to be flexible once again. A peck on the check is better than not seeing them at all. Be sure to know and follow the guidelines if the station empties out for a call and you are left there solo. Depending on the station, it may not be acceptable for a non-employee to be in the building unaccompanied.

Honor and Commitment. Represent well. You are a representation of your firefighter when you visit. What you say and do and how you act is a reflection on him, no matter how independent you are. The message is to be respectful and polite, and interact in a positive manner with all others on the crew and other families.

When the firehouse isn't family friendly, don't blame your firefighter for that. Your firefighter shouldn't be unfairly punished when rules or guidelines, formal or not, were set by others. What should you do instead? Set the best example in your outside family and marriage and pray for some positive changes. There could be very good reasons why a firehouse is not a good one for family visits: space limitations, rough neighborhoods, on government property with security regulations, just to name a few.

Always try to visit when they ask. When your firefighter asks, and wants you to come visit, do everything in your power to make it happen. It could be that they just finished with a bad run and all they want to do is hug their babies and kiss their spouse.

Watch your words. Don't share those cute little anecdotes about your firefighter. There are things about your firefighter you may not want to share around the dinner table at the firehouse. Things that might be "used against him" in ways that only a good hearted crew of firefighters can drag out for a 25-year career. Early on, I spilled the news that my husband hated to eat sausage of any kind: kielbasa, bratwurst, etc., (I know, weird right?). Wouldn't you know it, they attempted to cook some form of sausage for dinner just to press that button. Now, when I'm about to divulge a little gem like that about my husband, I look around the room at the company and decide how long he might pay for my innocent remark. All in good fun. It's a fraternity of fun (when they aren't all serious fighting fires and saving lives).

■ ■ ■ ■ ■ ■ ■ ■ ■ ■ ■ ■ ■

"The firehouse is their second home.
They have to 'live' there for a lot of hours.
Walking around and complaining is a bit disrespectful."

■ ■ ■ ■ ■ ■ ■ ■ ■ ■ ■ ■ ■

Talk positively about your firefighter's firehouse. The firehouse is their second home. They have to "live" there for a lot of hours. Walking around and complaining about cleanliness or uncomfortable furniture, or how things are done is a bit disrespectful. It is not yours to judge. If you see some small way you could make it easier on them, offer to do so. One great example is within your firefighter's bunk space. Send photos, kids art, special mementos, small holiday decorations seasonally and most importantly, good bedding! For as much time that is spent there, even with interrupted sleep, laying down on a nice sheets and a warm soft blanket may be just the reminder of home your firefighter needs before trying to rest for the night. It's a small way you can add your personal touch for your firefighter while they're away from their bedroom at home.

It Only Takes One Bad Apple

Family visits to the firehouse may be going great and then, suddenly, there's a new policy in place. New policies show up often when there's something that hasn't been thought of yet.

ATTENTION: No outside visitors are allowed in the weight room effective immediately.

Perhaps one of those reckless toddlers smashed a tiny finger in the weight room. Or worse, family nights are ended indefinitely. You may have seen some awful news stories about domestic violence at or within a firehouse. Yes, that's extreme, but it happens. Sure you may not get along with every other firefighter family there but again, it's public property and you are a visitor. Respect their policies. Speaking of policies: **Your opinion about anything firehouse related is not relevant and should not be shared.** Yes, there are many things about the fire service which affect your life, but you are not an employee of that department and anything you say could be damaging to your firefighters career. Zipping your mouth is going to be the best approach, always. The union president, the next in line for captain, nor the newest rookie firefighter care to know the spouses view on the vacation selection policy. It's hard enough for them to get all the firefighters on the same page. While yes, everyone is entitled to opinions, voicing them at the firehouse is the firefighter's job. Again, anything you say is a reflection on your firefighter; don't be that bad apple.

Unconditional Commitments You Must Make as a Couple

Vow to be open and honest about the firehouse life. Secrets in a marriage are already a tough topic (see Chapter 11 on trust) so sharing even day to day tidbits about the firehouse is a way to share life together. Even just saying there was new carpet or paint let's a spouse know what's going on in the "other home."

Get on the same page about the guidelines for family visits and how you will navigate them. Your agreement may look different than other families'. It's fine, make it your own and communicate clearly about it.

Be an example of honor and commitment during family visits. So many fire families struggle with their relationships. The best thing you can do is to not bring your issues into the firehouse and to set an example for other couples you have no idea are struggling.

— for discussion —

- Share your views on the good and the bad of having families visit the firehouse and how your family will approach visits. What do you need to be especially sensitive to and respectful of? Do you both know the guidelines for family visits to your firehouse?

- What are your favorite stories of your family visiting the firehouse?

- What can you do to help both your family and your department in bridging a healthy family visit policy?

- What is the frequency of visits, stay time and areas of the firehouse acceptable to visit?

- What traditions and character do you hope to establish in your family through firehouse visits?

RESOURCES

All resources mentioned in this chapter can be found at HonorAndCommitment.com/Chapter7

8 *Honoring Holidays Apart*
with New Traditions

If there's any one thing a seasoned fire wife has figured out, it's how to make holidays special no matter what day you are celebrating and with whom. But any seasoned fire wife will also tell you it's hard to escape even a little pang of sadness on the actual holiday itself.

The first few years of our marriage, I spent fighting and resisting the fire family system. I literally grieved the holiday traditions I shared growing up with my family. I struggled to find a rhythm when one year it was Christmas on the 23rd and another on the 26th and every 3rd year we could actually travel together. I craved our own set of family traditions for the holidays and took the control freak approach to planning perfect family memories for those 12-hour periods he was home and awake on a December weekend. Putting up the tree. Driving around to see the lights at night. Baking and decorating cut out cookies with the kids.

It became forceful and stressful as I tried to fit my family traditions into the new fire lifestyle.

Firefighters if your spouse is exhibiting this extra stress, here's the clue. She might be GRIEVING this holiday, which explains the grinch-like spirit.

She might know only her family life traditions and yearns for sharing that with you. But like everything else in marriage, it's new and different, and really weird with this wacky fire service schedule. And you only get one chance a year to test it out. Then next year, it's different again. And some crappy years, she loses you for Thanksgiving AND Christmas AND New Year's. And some really, really crappy years it's Leap Year and happens twice in a row.

Some comments from some spouses of firefighters to demonstrate the intensity of these emotions:

"We got so lucky this year and he had all Christmas Vacation with the kids. Most likely not gonna happen again in 2016."

We catch ourselves marking time by counting the years since our firefighter was home for a particular holiday. It can be years between being able to celebrate Christmas on the actual day all together. I know how frustrating it can be. This is due largely in part to the senior firefighters getting first pick and choosing to be off for specific holidays—Memorial Day and Labor Day Weekends for example. Great times to travel for weekend getaways.

■ ■ ■ ■ ■ ■ ■ ■ ■ ■ ■ ■ ■

"Emergencies don't take holidays and neither does public safety."

■ ■ ■ ■ ■ ■ ■ ■ ■ ■ ■ ■ ■

Jessica Jackson shares this:

"I know how it feels, my heart sinks a little every time I see the coming holidays and which ones my fireman is working. It just so happens that this year he is on shift every holiday from 4th of July until New Year's Eve. Sometimes it just doesn't feel fair, I get that little twinge of being angry and sad but I suggest pushing those emotions out as quickly as possible. It doesn't do anyone any good to let those feelings come out. They are irrational because loving men who are in the profession of being a firefighter means that they often work hours and days that are far less than desirable. Emergencies don't take holidays and neither does public safety. It's to be expected, so plan ahead and make the most of it all.

I'm not new to the fire world but I am new to missing both of these days and to be honest, I'm trying my best to not let it steal my Christmas Spirit. We're happy, healthy and have so much to be thankful for. Christmas has been rescheduled, so I must adjust.

My advice for anyone struggling with their fireman working on holidays…

THROW THE CALENDAR IN THE TRASH

…make your own calendars. If you have to move a holiday to a regular day, do it. That doesn't take anything away from the special occasions, only your attitude about it does. The traditional calendar does not work for the fire service."

Sound advice and the positive outlook we need to spin out of our pity party. We get it. On to those honorable solutions that make this all work for committed fire families.

Make Your Own Traditions

Bringing a new tradition into play can be something that will set the tone for coming years, whether your firefighters are working or are lucky enough to have the holiday off.

■ ■ ■ ■ ■ ■ ■ ■ ■ ■ ■ ■

"I understand that there are departments across the country that aren't exactly family friendly. Give it time and see what kind of seeds you can plant for future gatherings."

■ ■ ■ ■ ■ ■ ■ ■ ■ ■ ■ ■

Pick-Your-Own-Holiday Date

Plan a Thanksgiving meal on an off day before or after Thanksgiving Day according to your fireman's schedule. Even if you have to celebrate with your families on the day alone, make a special day to share with your fireman.

Organize a Fire Department Holiday Meal

If your fireman's department doesn't host a Shift Thanksgiving, check into taking them a meal. Coordinate with other spouses. Have your fireman check into having a family friendly meal with all of the fireman and their families where everyone brings a dish. Of course, be prepared from someone's fried turkey fiasco to interrupt your Fire Family meal.

Send Something to the Station for the Crew

Enjoy your own family functions and have a meal catered to the station or help them plan a meal to fix themselves if it isn't allowed to have families there. I understand that there are departments across the country that aren't exactly family friendly. Give it time and put that on your list to test the waters and see what kind of seeds you can plant for future gatherings.

Magical Notes for Special Fire Kids

If the kids are struggling with the idea that you won't be celebrating the same day as their friends, there are many ways to make them feel special. A letter in the mail or a phone call from that big guy up north, and these days even a personalized video from Santa, can all let the child know that fire families are on a "special list" and Santa understands their need to celebrate on a different day. He won't forget them.

Ask for Flexibility with Your Families

If your family or his family is willing to be flexible and it works with the fire department schedule, you can plan a whole family Thanksgiving that includes everyone. It is hard for a lot of families to understand the schedules but you could try to convince them to try it out. My Firefighter's family is good about planning our holiday functions around all schedules. Sometimes this means doing Thanksgiving the week before or Christmas on New Year's Day. That totally works for us and never feels any less special.

Distract Yourself with Holiday Fun— Don't Let the "Woe Is Me" Mentality Creep In

The worst part is getting over the feeling of dread and disappointment from sometimes having to celebrate holidays on a day other than what is marked on the calendar. Once you find the truer meaning of each holiday, that will be easier to let go of a calendar and what much of the regular world calls tradition.

■ ■ ■ ■ ■ ■ ■ ■ ■ ■ ■ ■ ■

"The worst part is getting over the feeling of dread and disappointment from sometimes having to celebrate holidays on a day other than what is marked on the calendar."

■ ■ ■ ■ ■ ■ ■ ■ ■ ■ ■ ■

Birthdays, Anniversaries and Personal Celebrations

Birthday celebrations were a big deal for my family growing up. But not for my husband's. This set us off on a challenging foot when my expectations for his behavior on my birthday were not clearly communicated and were 180 degrees different than what he thought was normal. Talk about hurt feelings. Carry this over to the annual State Fire School pilgrimage that left on Mother's Day every year and he was not earning any points with me. Thank goodness we finally got on the same page about that after quite a few years because I had some serious heartache over my husband not acknowledging a bit of celebration on those special days. Now, when he has to be at the firehouse for a family birthday, we do alter by a day or two but sometimes it works out just right to eat cake with his crew and have a little celebration at the firehouse. For the kids especially, this has eliminated a few tears and added an extra element of "special" to their day. We even have a firehouse that's open to an occasional birthday celebration on the back parking lot picnic table. Little ones (and their parents) who don't get to visit the firehouse very often are giddy to climb up in that engine and see what it feels like. One word of advice—ask permission of your chief first! Regarding these personal holidays, everyone is really different in this space and at different ages so be creative and stay in communication on this topic.

Gift Buying—Use it to Your Advantage

The time apart created by the fire schedule makes for ample opportunities to surprise each other with fabulous gifts. Gifts could be delivered to the station for example without one knowing anything. And for firefighters, there is an endless parade of fire related clothing, tools, home decor, and unique hand made collectibles for your shopping list ideas. Just remember this, there is nothing honorable about wearing that firefighter t-shirt if you aren't making the commitment to all aspects of the job—your mental and physical health, your training, and your character. (We're a little serious about commitment around here.)

■ ■ ■ ■ ■ ■ ■ ■ ■ ■ ■

"It's always so heartwarming to see firefighters without little ones take trades on holidays like Christmas or Halloween for families with little ones."

■ ■ ■ ■ ■ ■ ■ ■ ■ ■ ■

Helping Other Fire Families

As kids get older, it's always so heartwarming to see firefighters without little ones take trades on holidays like Christmas or Halloween for families with little ones. Even trading the first few hours on Christmas morning so that little ones can open their Santa presents is a really big deal. Five year olds really struggle with patience and understanding in these moments, and all the rationalizing we are doing in this chapter means nothing to them. Be that guy. The one who gives back.

Give Back as a Family

Not celebrating a holiday on the actual day gives your family the opportunity to give back as well. Serving meals at a soup kitchen on Thanksgiving Day or Christmas Day, or visiting elderly shut ins can make some memories that your family will never forget.

■ ■ ■ ■ ■ ■ ■ ■ ■ ■ ■

"If I catch myself in a pity party there is one thought that slaps me right back into reality, especially on the Christmas holiday."

■ ■ ■ ■ ■ ■ ■ ■ ■ ■ ■

Don't Get Stuck—Be Grateful

It's important in this crazy fire life not to get stuck on the days specified on a calendar. Birthdays, Christmas, Thanksgiving, Anniversaries. You pick a day and make it your own, make it special, create your own traditions. Be happy in celebrating together and don't worry about the rest of the world who get normal hours and holidays off. They might not understand but they don't have to. Oftentimes I find myself just focusing on gratefulness. Gratefulness that there is a job to provide for our family and for my husband's health and ability and willingness to work that job.

The One Thought that Gets Me Through Every Holiday

If I catch myself in a pity party there is one thought that slaps me right back into reality, especially on the Christmas holiday. Imagine what it must feel like to be a family who needs 9-1-1 services on Christmas Eve or Christmas Day. Not only have you had a tragic family event but it is forever scarred by the memory of "that Christmas." Even the firefighters responding on Christmas Day hold longer memories of those tragedies referring to them as "that Christmas fire" or "that Christmas suicide." These are the moments firefighters were made to serve regardless of the calendar date.

When a random acquaintance says something that seems so ridiculous to you such as "Why don't they get Christmas off?", practice the tongue biting before something dishonorable and full of spit and vinegar comes flying out of your mouth. They weren't made for the fire life but you were.

Oh how I wish I could bottle my lessons up in magic fairy dust and send one to every new fire wife out there.

For the holidays, I made a little jingle for you instead. Oh how can the holidays frustrate a fire wife. Let me count the ways.

12 Hours of Overtime

11 times being asked where your husband is while solo-parenting the church Christmas party

10 gifts still left to wrap by yourself on Christmas Eve

9 -to-5ers bragging about 14 days off work with their family

8 little gifts to find for the guys on his crew

7 dozen cookies to bake for the neighborhood cookie exchange

6 text message photos from the store to figure out which gift is best for the father-in-law

5 upset family members because you can't attend family Christmas on the day planned because he's on shift

4 different plans to explain why Santa is arriving the morning of the 24th instead of the 25th

3 hour drive, by yourself, with kids in tow and car packed to the hilt, to celebrate Christmas without him at your parents

2 bickering kids who are missing their Daddy

1 tired firefighter who took a very hurt baby girl out of a mangled car at 1 am and doesn't need to hear you whine about any of these minor annoyances

Cute, but a little stressed out and dark for our encouraging atmosphere around here. How about some more tips from spouses regarding things their firefighter has done to make the holidays more personal for their family:

"Put our lights and decorations on the outside of the house, and set them on timers! Swoon! In past years, the lights were only on on the days he was home because he knew how to plug them all in without blowing a fuse! Last year he connected timers, so there's lights every night! No more depressing nights of deflated decorations on the lawn!"

"He puts up the Christmas lights so that I can turn them on the day after Thanksgiving."

"My FF worked his butt off to get Xmas eve and day off this year. We are very lucky to have found someone willing to work for him on those days. Xmas eve is a BIG deal with his family. Typical Italian seafood night. He does the majority of the cooking, so his parents were stressing out that he wouldn't be there this year. But he pulled it off. He found someone. He has even told his shift partner that he would go in (on his day off) to cover her shift for 4 hours so she could spend some Xmas time with her family. I have the best FF hubby ever!!!!"

"Little things like leaving a book for the kiddo with a video of him reading it, a note acknowledging the role of being lonely during the holidays, helping when he's home, conversations about how to prevent the loneliness (planning dinners with friends, date nights when he has to miss a Christmas party)"

"Text back when I text him. Even if it is just hi…"

■ ■ ■ ■ ■ ■ ■ ■ ■ ■ ■ ■ ■

"Loneliness can be felt by the firefighters too, so be sure you are reciprocating and including them in the activities of the day with phone calls, face times and texts as well."

■ ■ ■ ■ ■ ■ ■ ■ ■ ■ ■ ■ ■

"Text an 'I love you,' or 'How's your day,' or something when he has time. And responding back with at least an 'Ok,' once he sees my messages, even if it's not right away."

"Validate my feelings."

"We talk and text. Then during our celebration, we FaceTime so gets to talk to the rest of the family. Love that we have this technology that helps us stay better connected with our FF. Back 20 years ago a simple phone call was all we had."

"Texting and calling throughout the day. We always make time to go see him at the station."

Loneliness can be felt by the firefighters too, so be sure you are reciprocating and including them in the activities of the day with phone calls, face times and texts as well.

This chapter suddenly feels overwhelming. Like, I can do all this fire life thing but boy the holidays are what just pushed me over the edge. Can I give some hope for those of you who are newer to the fire life and just learning to experience this? Yes, it's kind of weird to know that lots of other families will be off having holiday that day and it will be me and our 4 kids. But we are so much better about that than we used to be. Because we get to have a family day all day on another day. No school and no work. Our kids are older now and can understand and appreciate that. It. Gets. Better. It totally gets better. I promise!

But you may not be there yet. And it's ok. One thing I never used to do early in our marriage was reach out to other fire families. It felt weird and scary. Until my blog with my lonely fire wife thoughts I wondered if anyone was even reading, blew up into this amazing community of other fire wives who felt just like me. Here's one of my favorites from Elaine:

> "My husband heard about FirefighterWife.com when he was on shift one day. He had watched some of the Mercer YouTube videos, and really liked what he saw.
>
> Thanksgiving of 2014 I was home alone with a toddler, my first of many holidays where he would be on shift. I had NO clue he knew about Firefighter Wife until I woke up on that Thanksgiving morning to my husband telling me he signed me up! He wanted me to be surrounded by ladies who "get" the fire life and could pick me up! I was so overwhelmed at first, but the admin team and the ladies in the group made me feel welcome. I shared my emotional feelings in the Fire Wife Sisterhood Facebook Group and had such wonderful feedback. These girls actually knew what I was feeling and helped me figure out a how to make it through that first Thanksgiving. Coming up on my one-year anniversary in the Fire Wife Sisterhood I'm extremely thankful for the friendships I've made.

■ ■ ■ ■ ■ ■ ■ ■ ■ ■ ■ ■ ■

After all of that, I'm in the mood for some turkey and to put up the Christmas tree. Oh wait, it's February and our lights are still strung outside. Too many shifts of work for my husband to take them down. So glad our neighbors understand this life a bit now too.

~ for the firefighter ~
Honoring Holidays Apart with New Traditions

Firefighters if you find your spouse in this grinch-like mood, I have a list of things to NOT say in this delicate state:

- "You know I have to go to the station. Why is this different than any other day?"

- "It's no big deal. I'll be home tomorrow and we'll celebrate then."

- "Go on and enjoy yourself at my family's Christmas without me."

- "Don't wait for me. You can put the tree up with the kids."

- "I'll call/text you a lot." (And then don't. Because firefighters have busy days. But broken promises do more damage than the hope they hold.)

- "When you visit me at the firehouse, it will be just like we're all together for Christmas." (No. It's not just like that. It's like celebrating with you and 8 other prankster boys.)

- "Why don't you cook up a nice dinner for you and the kids at home on Christmas day?"

- "The kids won't even notice what day we open gifts."

So what *should* you do and say?

You've got to be on her team. To join in the cause. Simply recognize her efforts. Be understanding of those feelings. Help her grieve. Ask her how she's feeling and brainstorm ideas for how to make it all work. If you really want to wow her, surprise her with thoughtful new traditions specially designed for your little fire family. Special ornaments. A firehouse recipe you make at home. Be present with her on your off days and enjoy some holiday cheer together.

Basically, remember the Who's in Whoville who loved Christmas a lot. The truth is, it's not about when or where or how you celebrate. Because Mrs. Grinch, Christmas, means a little bit more. You've already got the keys to her heart and only you know best how to make it grow.

~ *for the spouse* ~
Honoring Holidays Apart with New Traditions

Here it comes again, you must embrace this life because resisting it will get you nowhere but with a wedge further driven between you and your spouse. We already covered a lot of great tips above so I want to focus on this. Your firefighter isn't happy about this either. Being apart from family on a big holiday isn't their first choice. Yes, you will see them make the most of it with their crew. Some of the white elephant gifts I've seen surface from the firehouse are hysterical. Remember that humor is often a diffuser of those other uglier emotions no one wants to let loose. Daddy's do shed a tear when they miss that first twinkle of Christmas tree light in their baby's eye.

Do share the memories with them while they are gone. Try to whine a little less to them about the holiday stresses you are under. Do visit the in-laws, if that's what they wish and even if it's super hard to do alone. Get on Pinterest (but don't get lost in a time warp) and find the cutest projects for your fire family and start some new (practical, not Pinterest-perfect) holiday traditions. Perhaps making a family ornament together with the date you celebrated Christmas together that year would be meaningful, and funny actually to look back on.

If the holidays push you over the edge a bit and you get the blues, it's normal. Many people find the holidays to be an extra blue and depression inducing season for them. Seek help for this and don't struggle through it alone.

If you're the praying type, pray a little extra over the holiday season. No one wants a family to experience the tragedy of a house fire or car accident ever but most especially during the holidays. Pray protection over first responders and the communities they serve. Your insights into the fire life do give your prayers a purpose and meaning unlike others.

Oh yeah, one last very important thing. Reach out to other fire families and build your support network. You don't have to do this fire life alone.

- for discussion -

- What were the favorite traditions your family created to get through holidays apart? If you don't have one yet, take this time to come up with your own.

- How do you help the firefighter spouse to feel included when they are working during a holiday?

- What are the best ways the firefighter spouse can help the spouse at home prepare for a holiday apart?

- Make decisions about about trades/vacations/working holidays together with your spouse. What is your plan? When you do this together, it somehow shares the load of the burden. You're a team and you'll get through another thanksgiving apart, just like last year. And perhaps it's in trade for having off the entire week of July 4th. It's your fire life to plan for.

RESOURCES

All resources mentioned in this chapter can be found at HonorAndCommitment.com/Chapter8

Resources listed at the website include:
- @WifeonFire Youtube video—The Thought That Gets Me Through Every Christmas

- Fire Family Gift guide

- Christmas Has Been Rescheduled

- Why Is Your Fire Wife Such A Grinch?

SECTION 2

A Marriage On Fire

I commit to honor my marriage with
my thoughts, my words, and my
actions no matter what the fire life
throws our way.

9 *Honorable Communication*
In a Committed Fire Marriage

I f commitment is the never ending, always-replenished fuel that keeps you in it for the long haul, then healthy communication is the grease the keeps your marriage engine well-oiled and firing on all cylinders.

How many times have we repeated so far "you need to talk about it" or "have open communication on this topic" or "have the courage to address this with your spouse so they know what you are feeling"? I've lost track. Thank you for listening to our repetition on this crucial point. However, it's just not that easy sometimes in the fire life and that's what this chapter is about.

Unfortunately, we don't have space here to unpack a whole dialogue on marriage communication so I'll summarize it in these bullets:

- You're going to disagree. Learn to fight fair.

- He / she can't read your mind. Learn to say exactly what you mean and feel (with truth but kindness).

- Always be honest, always.

- Learn the policy of Enthusiastic Agreement.

- Apologies bring healing.

- The right words, activities, gifts and actions can fill up your spouse like nothing else, even sex. i.e. learn their love language.

The fire life introduces a unique set of challenges for communication in marriage. Time apart, interrupted phone calls, recovering from the stress of the job, and unpredictability all challenge healthy communication. When your firefighter leaves for a shift (typically a minimum of 24 hours in length) and the two of you have your love tanks filled, no issues hanging over your head and lots of quality time together in the past day, communication can flow nice and easy.

Early in our marriage, I had irrational thoughts like "He's working at an easy station today, I'm sure they are just playing basketball after dinner. Why can't he take the time to call me?"

Then when he did call, and didn't have much to add or say, I felt like he was trying to hide things from me. In reality, he had just stepped out of a conversation with someone senior he wanted to get back to, had a house duty he needed to finish, or was just tired and ready for bed.

Both of us made mistakes in those conversations that led to hurt feelings. It would have been just as simple for him to say "I've only got a couple minutes because I need to go finish helping with the dishes." Then expectations would be set and I wouldn't try to dive into anything serious. If a serious conversation needed to be had, I could say, "When do you have more time to talk? I need to tell you what I found out about _____." So then, he would know it was more important for me to hear back from him that night.

Sometimes we would get time to talk and the conversation would be dry. I'd ask questions, he'd give one word answers. Over the years we figured out legitimate contributing factors, like how uncomfortable the chair near the house phone was that made him annoyed to talk on it, or that the phone made his ear hot when we talked for a long time. A true, weird story about my husband. This is pre-cellphone days people, no hands-free devices. You were corded to the wall the phone was hanging on! Despite the physical discomfort, I hadn't heard from him for possibly the whole day, and I just missed knowing what was going on in his life. My conversation was filled with little gems I'd been tucking away in a mental list and was excited to share with him: our daughter's reaction to trying a new food; a bill we got in the mail; what our neighbor told me about the block party; someone from church who called; a friend who was sick. These are all little pieces of a 24- or 48-hour period spent apart from the ones you love, and sharing those stories are what keeps you connected. However, sometimes your communication styles are simply different, and you need to learn that about each other. I craved to hear what he ate for dinner, a funny joke someone shared, or how he felt about training that day; and he was on the other end, just annoyed by a phone cord not realizing how easy it would be to satisfy me in that moment. Clearly my need for quality conversation to stay connected was higher than his.

■ ■ ■ ■ ■ ■ ■ ■ ■ ■ ■ ■ ■

"These are all little pieces of a 24- or 48-hour period spent apart from the ones you love, and sharing those stories are what keeps you connected."

■ ■ ■ ■ ■ ■ ■ ■ ■ ■ ■ ■ ■

A lot of your personal communication preferences come from your family upbringing. My family can be described as "highly informed." Everyone knew (almost) everything about each other, including where we were going, what we did that day and what we planned to do the next day. Other families, like my husbands, were more independent and it might be perfectly natural for the husband/father to be gone all day at work, come home, and not mention a thing about work, and everyone is totally good with that. Keep each other's family styles in mind as you learn to navigate your own style of communication between each other.

You know how you read Chinese fortunes and then for fun at the end of them say "in bed"? Let's apply that logic to this chapter as we dissect some general communication topics but at to the end of them "in the fire life".

Communication Frequency Expectations *In The Fire Life*

One young girlfriend of a firefighter shared this with us:

> I am feeling so let down and emotional right now. I've spoken to my firefighter a total of 14:43 mins today. I'm feeling like he'd rather play blackjack with the fire boys than have an actual convo about my day. I've sent him countless pics and texts and

have gotten very little or no reply. I hate this!!! This is the time I start to question where I stand in this relationship with him…. does he truly care?? I'm so sad disappointed and tired. And when I send him a message about how nice it was for him to take 15 mins out of his 24 hr day to talk to me I get nothing back.

A Wonderful Response from an Experienced Fire Wife:

My firefighter and I are the "old goats" of our firefighter wives group: I'm 45, FF is 55, married 16 yrs, sons are 14 and 11. I have worked out of the house, from home and been a SAHM. firefighter life is all we know.

My firefighter is so busy at work he doesn't have time to get on the phone, if he does he can't give 100% attention. There are times he can get to his phone but can't focus enough to reply to a text w/ anything more than "OK." I asked if he thinks of us while at work and he said, "all the time." At the fire department they talk about spouses/kids, his lockers is like a family shrine, he has pictures in his duffel bag.

My husband and I got together in 1996—no cell phones or texts. We had pagers & landlines. It was common to go an entire shift without speaking much less seeing each other. We, too, lived/live too far from the fire department to visit.

Before you get upset with him and/or your marriage, think about this: What can you do? What can you do to ensure you have others you can call so your firefighter isn't the only adult with whom you have contact? It doesn't have to be someone in the fire service and it doesn't have to be a best friend…just someone you can meet at the library with the kids, or at a McDonald's playground, a park, a mall. You may have to do a few of those things on your own at first and it might be uncomfortable but it gets easier and once you meet another mom/parent it will be worth it. It doesn't mean this other person will get our firefighter wife life but you will be able to get out of the house. I don't eat McDonald's but the air conditioned playground was great when it was raining or 98 degrees outside. The mall was also a great air conditioned place the kids could run around and burn some energy.

I can't tell you this goes away…even after 16 years (with cell phones, texts, e-mail) my firefighter and I still don't get to talk.

He is in the middle of working 56 now and we exchanged one text message and spoke for 3 minutes last night – then I heard the tones and he said, "I have to go."

For my firefighter…just because he is in the station doesn't mean he can or wants to talk. He wants to eat, use the bathroom, take a shower, clear his head. I think about being home with the kids when they were very young. If given the opportunity to shower, nap or sit on the toilet alone….I would take it over anything else. This is no different from our firefighters. Just because they are not on a call doesn't mean their brains aren't churning about the "next" call. Most of the time when not on a call my firefighter is in a class, training, or giving a fire department tour. We are married to firefighters. The only thing you do have control over is your mindset. Don't wait for things to get better, you make them better. In your head say, "My life is falling together." Do that enough and it will happen. This is one of the reasons we firefighter wives are a special breed.

Like all topics in this book, you need to find what works for your relationship. As a general rule, you should not expect to have many personal conversations during daytime "office hours" when training and other official work is getting done. Occasionally you may go for the full shift with nothing but a short text if anything. Even for couples who agree to not talk a lot during a shift, I encourage some sort of communication as it can be easy to become so independent in this fire life which leads to bigger problems. Short sweet nothings keep the love life lit up.

The quick text can be wonderful for moments when you are pulled away quickly, especially for a fire call. Even wives who don't worry normally, don't like to hear "Shooting. Police en route. Proceed to staging" at an abrupt end to a phone call. As soon as everything is clear and under control, it's so good to hear that text that says I LOVE YOU. ALL IS GOOD. BACK IN QUARTERS.

Staying Connected Through Communication *In The Fire Life*

Once your expectations are clear, the first and obvious challenge in the fire life is simply finding time to talk that is not interrupted with "gotta-go-love-you-bye-click." Should you even try to have lengthy in-depth conversations while one of you is at the firehouse? Not really but sometimes it is unavoidable. No matter how well you are navigating that conversation, it can get really old and annoying after the 2nd or 3rd time. Good conversations have entries and warm ups to the meat of the topic. You typically don't dive right into the hard stuff so having to repeat those phases multiple times is not fun.

Next comes those long stretches of time where you've texted but maybe not talked by phone. The firefighter is all wrapped up into firehouse topics while the spouse has some semi-urgent topics at home she'd like to discuss. For some couples, John Dixon shared, it's best to agree to not plan on talking much at all while on shift. The timing is just too unpredictable and it helps him to stay focused on what he is doing on the job. For other couples who may have a higher need for "touch points" in their relationship, this approach could really drive a wedge between them. Guess what? You must talk to talk about how to talk to each other. It drives my husband crazy when I come up with crazy actions like that. Are we seriously talking about how to talk to each other? Yes, dear. Humor me please because I just want to be sure we're on the same page.

Love Languages

If you aren't talking in your spouse's love language you might as well not be talking. *The Five Love Languages* is one of those essential life books and applies to marriage, parenting, friendship and yes even the workplace. Originally it was written for marriages and this concept might set someone free. If your love language is quality conversation and your spouse's love language is acts of service. You are going to both be angry when you try to talk your spouse's ear off when they walk in the door from shift and all they want to do is fix the broken sink disposal. You are both trying to love each other but you might as well be speaking Chinese and Russian to each other.

If this is the root of your issues in communication, put this book on pause right now and pick up *The Five Love Languages*.

What happens when you don't speak each other's love language for a long time? Your love tank gets empty! Speaking your spouse's love language adds deposits to their tank that will last you through long shifts apart and challenging seasons of work.

Sometimes when the shift gets particularly stressful, a firefighter just wants to call home and hear a familiar voice and a reminder of what's most important in their life.

Sometimes the spouse at home is hit particularly hard by Murphy's Law and just wants to share to the person who cares about her the most, fully understanding there is nothing her husband can do from there. If this is a way your spouse likes to cope, be sure you're both on the same page with just needing to hear "Honey, I believe in you and I'm on your team," but not expecting him to run straight home from the firehouse.

When important conversations do need to happen on shift, the crew may even sense something is going on. Pre-cell phone days that might have meant standing in the middle of the living area using the station phone for a call which is not exactly private. Even with cell phones there aren't always quiet places for a call. Here's a great secret. One place no firefighter wants to hang out is the cab of the truck when it's not on a run thereby making it a semi-private place for a personal phone call if needed. Others have shared they may sit in their car in the parking lot to make a call. Just be sure firehouse guidelines are being followed.

Enthusiastic Agreement *In The Fire Life*

There is a core principle from an organization called Marriage Builders and it's called "The Policy of Enthusiastic Agreement." It needs many accolades for helping us through some tough early marriage conversations. The concept is this. When you have a decision to make as a couple, could be anything from what color to paint the kitchen to deciding if it's ok for one spouse to go on a backpacking trip with their friends for the weekend, both spouses must transparently and completely honestly have enthusiastic agreement over the decision.

■ ■ ■ ■ ■ ■ ■ ■ ■ ■ ■ ■

"When you have a decision to make as a couple, both spouses must transparently and completely honestly have enthusiastic agreement over the decision."

■ ■ ■ ■ ■ ■ ■ ■ ■ ■ ■ ■

When there is not enthusiastic agreement, there is a tendency for hurts to leak out during the event in question and for regrets and anger to build up.

Should I take this overtime? Only if your spouse enthusiastically agrees it's the right thing to do for your family. It's ok to sigh and express some frustration and then to come back and say "You know what? This is the right thing. Go ahead and do it. I'm on board with it."

Should I take the promotional exam for the Captain's test?

Should I make this significant purchase for our home while he is at the firehouse?

Should we let our teenager go to Florida with her best friend's family for spring break?

The list can go on and on. Complete transparency and honesty with your feelings is essential to making this policy work. There must be space in your communication for one spouse to say "this makes me uncomfortable because…" without the other spouse blowing up and replying "I'm so sick of you always saying that….." which leads us to the next best practice in marital communication.

Fighting Fair *In The Fire Life*

What is sometimes more damaging than the disagreement itself is the way the disagreement ensues, tearing each other's heart apart with words and body language and low blows. Yes many of us have short fuses, whether or not we are a firefighter. We are all emotionally wounded in some way and those closest to us know how to push those buttons the best.

What does fighting fair look like in the fire life?

- Not stirring the pot and picking a fight while one spouse is on shift

- Not leaving in anger for a shift day. Call a cease fire and kiss good-bye. Your tomorrow is never promised and a firefighter's head must be entirely in the game while on duty. That goes for a spouse who has to hold down the homefront and likely a job as well.

- Don't drag the fire service into it. Most of the time it isn't to blame and is just a symptom of a bigger issue between the two of you.

- Don't pick on old issues that have already been apologized for and put to rest.

- Don't fight the second the firefighter walks back in the door off shift.

- Don't leave unresolved topics hanging out there after a shift day or two has delayed your argument.

- Stop screaming. We're talking the actual act of screaming but according to one of our favorite marriage resources, "Scream-Free Marriage", screaming can also be sarcasm, the silent treatment, passive aggressive behavior or running away amongst other things.

Learning to fight fair is a constant topic for married couples as we grow and change there are new ways to press each other's buttons. In general, wait until the anger has passed to try to resolve the issue but don't ignore it once you feel better. Delaying the resolution just makes it build up with issue on top of issue until one day you explode in what I like to call, the epic marriage fight. There are about 5 distinct epic fights I can recall in our marriage (there are more but I must have blocked them out for my own sanity). You know they are epic when you can reference them by just one word and both of you know exactly what the other means. Remember last November? Remember that San Diego trip? They become milestones in your marriage whose resolutions are giant leaps of growth you take together. Priceless.

Finally, don't be "hangry" (angry because you're hungry). You'll fight good and fair when you are well fed and well rested.

Never Ever Use the "D" Word (in any walk of life)

Never ever throw around the "D" word. It's crossing a sacred threshold in marriage.

When you use the word "Divorce" in arguments with your spouse, you are saying one of the most damaging words possible.

Trust is broken. Hope is deflated. You are saying "I know I made a forever promise at our wedding but I've considered that I never want to be with you again for the rest of my life."

Divorce is not a word to throw around for impact when you are having an argument. You know about the boy who cried wolf. For a while, the word is traumatic and extremely hurtful. Does he/she really mean that? How serious should I take that?

■ ■ ■ ■ ■ ■ ■ ■ ■ ■ ■ ■ ■

"Is that really how you want to make your spouse feel in order to prove your point in an argument?"

■ ■ ■ ■ ■ ■ ■ ■ ■ ■ ■ ■ ■

But a word with the finality of divorce, when used repeatedly, becomes an empty threat and destroys trust in your relationship every single time. Say divorce, trust needle moves back to zero. If you really don't want a divorce and you say the word, you start at zero to rebuild trust in your relationship. The ultimate promise you made in your wedding vows, 'til death do us part, now seems have been a complete lie. All that time building up to that moment of committing yourself to each other forever, is ripped apart with the mention of one word. All those prior good times and seasons and love and special moments…feel like they didn't mean anything. Yes. It's that dramatic.

I've heard this word. I've felt the lump in my throat and the sinking pit in my stomach without any ability to reply. Your entire spirit is crushed.

Is that really how you want to make your spouse feel in order to prove your point in an argument?

Three Things....

1. If you are saying it in the heat of the moment. Just stop.

    Learn to fight in your marriage without throwing around damaging words like divorce.

    Force yourself to think it through and get clarity. Don't use it in the midst of a fight. Perhaps your parents threw this around when they were arguing and it's a leftover lesson from childhood. If so, now you know. It's the least productive way to make things work in your marriage. (This also goes for any name calling. My favorite reference....which has been highly referenced throughout our marriage is Marriage Builders—check out their Guidelines for Successful Negotiation—which includes all the ground rules for discussing ("fighting") fairly.)

2. If you really do think you want a divorce, then what's stopping you? Why keep throwing out the threat if you aren't following through?

    Again, I'm not an advocate of divorce but of marriage healing. Something has hurt you enough to throw out the word but something is preventing you from acting. (This is a good thing! Fight for what's holding you back!) Dig deep and figure that out. There's healing and growth in those thoughts.

3. What to do if your spouse continues to use the word in fights?

    *   Forward him / her this page in the book. Sometimes it's best heard when said by others.

    *   Don't listen to the word. Listen to the fact that there is something painful and hurting in your spouse. No they are not right in throwing that word around. And it's hurtful to you.

    *   If they do it all the time, have the tough conversation and calmly call them out on it. You may say something like. "A divorce is the last thing I want. I want to work on our marriage. But clearly there is something not working here. Can we focus on repairing that and healing these hurts? Can we agree on not using this word when we argue?"

When the Written Word Is More Effective *In The Fire Life*

Sometimes letters, texts, and emails are more appropriate to get your words across more clearly. Writing down all of our jumbled thoughts is a great way to get our head clear and our emotions sorted out. Sometimes it can be good to share this with our spouse but sometimes that's like placing a live bomb in their hands. It should be tucked away neatly in a private journal for your own self-growth and learning.

If you have the urge to send a long, emotional email or text while you are apart, be sure this is something you've agreed on as a couple. It can give you the time and space you need to process it but for some it can create a wind tunnel of whirlwind over thinking and by the time you are together to address it, the whole concept has been run around the block and back again with all the wrong assumptions.

I've seen many wives do this as their husband is heading off to the station. "I sent him a long message and I know he read it but he hasn't replied." Truthfully, while this may not seem fair, I know a lot of firefighters that can block that out while on shift and go about their responsibilities with a clear head and focus on work. If the wife saw him, he'd look happy and normal. However, she's been at home or work stewing and crying and over thinking and expending much energy on this topic which truly won't be addressed until they are back together the next day. (This part is so easy to write because, confession, I've been this girl.) Your brain just can't sit ok when you have a gigantic uneasiness inside you over the unresolved argument. Your wish is to work through it but perhaps he just wants some time to think and reflect. Husbands, if you have a wife who sort of fixates on the issues like this, you can defuse that with a few short words, "I hear you. I want to work through this. I'm going to need a couple days to process and think over it." When you don't say those words do you know what she thinks? He doesn't even care! He isn't even thinking about it. He's off having fun at the firehouse. And enter a whirlwind path of negative talk. A short acknowledgment that you've received a long letter/message is all that's needed.

Apologizing *In The Fire Life*

I went about 8 years in my marriage before my husband said the words "I'm sorry" to me.

Honestly, I don't even think he realized it.

It's not that he didn't show it in some other way eventually but those were words that were hard for him.

We'd have a major blow up fight. Yelling and screaming. Until he'd be so angry he couldn't speak, let alone concentrate on the issue we were focused on. And I'd feel the same. Are we talking in circles? Does he even hear the words coming out of my mouth? Will he just stop interrupting me so I can finish a sentence????

Then he'd leave in a huff. Sometimes he'd be gone for an hour, sometimes for a day. One time for a week. (I knew where he was. He was at a fire training and we had a fight just before leaving and he didn't call me for the entire week. It was Mother's Day by the way. Lovely. And this sentence may be proof that I still harbor some resentment for that painful season.)

I truly felt like I *always* had to be the first one to break down a wall after an argument, soften my heart and say I was sorry for the argument we had.

Yes, it really didn't seem fair but he was working through some major stubborn issues and examples from his past that were not healthy. He just didn't know how to do it nor what it meant to me.

Finally, after that many years and the many times that I told him how important it was to me to hear those words sometimes (as opposed to just re-entering our life as if nothing happened) he got it. I wish I could tell you the secret button I pressed and the magic words that came out of my mouth but it's just not that easy. But hearing him finally say those words was about the sweetest sound ever.

Some of you might be really resonating with this and just pleading for me to show you how we did it. So with a few years of padding to give me more clarity and hindsight, I can give a few suggestions on how to handle this situation.....

1. Don't let it make you more angry. It's not "fair". I totally agree. But what is? And who defines "fair"? Maybe you are the example that was put in their life to explain this. And consider that a blessing that will only bring you closer as a couple. Once you are on the other side, "fair" has an entirely different meaning.

2. Learn the best ways to soften your heart and forgive so your spouse can truly see what this forgiveness looks like. This is different for everyone but for me it's letting go and trusting God's love for me and His ability to change someone's heart. Basically I focused on God's perfect love helping me through, instead of trying to "fix" my husband.

3. Tell them. Tell them you need an apology to bring closure. That you want to know there is nothing still between you. They can't read your mind and although this is obvious to you, you might just need to say "I really need to hear you say you are sorry after situations like this. This is what truly shows me we have closure on the disagreement."

4. Don't be prideful. It doesn't make you "better" than them to be able to do this so. You've got some other major plank in your eye instead. If you have pride that you are able to forgive, you are missing the whole stinking point.

Most of all, remember this......when someone cannot say they are sorry, there is some big giant hurt inside of themselves holding them in that place of torture. It's something going on inside of them, not some evil part of you that is preventing those two simple words. Someone who is that stubborn and defensive and can't soften their heart and apologize, needs to be loved even more to help them through their hurts.

These are some of the toughest battles you will fight in your marriage. But I can tell you that this was a giant milestone and turning point when both of us were able to soften our hearts, let go of fights more quickly and apologize to each other. Sometimes still agreeing to disagree or needing further discussion but always with our affection for each other still intact.

Crucial Conversations *In The Fire Life*

Crucial Conversations is perhaps the number one book on my reading list of all time for any person anywhere. It's a life skill to be applied in marriage, parenting, friendship, work and especially annoying customer service scenarios. In short, this book teaches a communication technique that "creates alignment and agreement by fostering open dialogue around high-stakes topics." In other words, it can be applied to situations such as:

- You've reached the end of your rope with the walking on eggshells moments fearing angry outbursts

- You know something is bothering your spouse but they've clammed up and won't spill their feelings

- You know something is bothering your spouse based on their body language but they won't open up the conversation.

- You know you've done something wrong and need to come to your spouse with an apology and an appeal for another chance.

- There is a topic you disagree on and has kept a wall between you that needs to be removed.

The key to crucial conversations is this. Approach a crucial conversation with clear, healthy, good intentions in your heart, and are able to seek the win-win scenario that preserves the relationship. It's that simple and that hard at the same time.

■ ■ ■ ■ ■ ■ ■ ■ ■ ■ ■ ■ ■

"Approach a crucial conversation with clear, healthy, good intentions in your heart, and are able to seek the win-win scenario that preserves the relationship."

■ ■ ■ ■ ■ ■ ■ ■ ■ ■ ■ ■ ■

A crucial conversation has a lot of elements:
- The right time
- The right place
- The right mood and atmosphere
- The right mindset
- The right facts
- The right words

A frequent prayer I pray over married couples having issues is for them to have these "golden moments" where the stars align and healing can happen through crucial conversations. These are marriage milestones for sure. Moments you put down a marker and can call back on with each other. "Remember when we both agreed that........?"

When Not to Push *In The Fire Life*

Sometimes talking is not the right thing for the moment. Here's a story of success from one of the wives in our Fire Wife Sisterhood.

> I have to share a success story. It may seem minor to some, but I have had to work hard on this for 3 years now.
>
> Early last week my firefighter must have gone on a horrendous call that left him reeling emotionally. He came home short-tempered and quiet. For the 2 days he was off, he talked basically only when spoken to, and didn't initiate much conversation. He was talking in his sleep a bit—enough to lead me to believe the call was a child abuse type call. I didn't pry. I asked him after a few hours the first day if everything was all right and he sort of mumbled something as he headed into the garage to "work"— basically to occupy his mind for a bit on monotonous tasks, like organizing his tools, etc.
>
> For the two days he was home I tried to be there to support him—extra long hugs, patience and a will to wait this out instead of force him to talk. He went to his next shift and I didn't hear from him all shift except a response to a question I had texted him ("yes" was the reply).

■ ■ ■ ■ ■ ■ ■ ■ ■ ■ ■ ■ ■

"When he wasn't ready to talk about it and I'd push, it would lead to an unnecessary argument over something stupid."

■ ■ ■ ■ ■ ■ ■ ■ ■ ■ ■ ■ ■

> Friday morning, he was still quiet and I let him know I knew something was bothering him but I didn't need to know what it was unless he wanted to talk about it, but either way I was there for him. The day passed. That night I got home from work and he had gotten his mom to take the kids for the night, we went

out and met some friends at a country bar and did some line dancing. During a slow song, he pulled me onto the dance floor and during the song, apologized for how he'd been all week, he said I didn't want to know what had been bothering him, but it was a call he had to go on and he was sorry he let it roll into his daily life at home. I told him I knew what he had to deal with had to be very upsetting and I understood that it is human nature to not be able to always shut off those feelings once you are off shift. I explained that I felt a little uneasy not knowing what I could do or say to possibly help but I just needed him to know I was there for him. He hugged me, kissed me and said that was all he needed to hear and from then on, through the weekend, he was back to his normal self.

My struggle for years has been to push and push to know what was wrong.

When he wasn't ready to talk about it and I'd push, it would lead to an unnecessary argument over something stupid. This route was harder for me to do but so worth it. He told me Saturday that he tries really hard to "not bring his work home with him" and apologized again for the past week. Again, I just told him that he's a hero for what he does, I am always there for him whether he wants to talk about it or not and left it at that. He seemed so much better by just having me reaffirm that to him- knowing he didn't need to tell me about it. Prayers for the continued peace he's found after this call and prayers for the people involved in the call too.

Why Do I Have to Make the First Move *In The Fire Life?*

If you're in a real low place, lack of intimacy, fighting, little positive interaction and repeat patterns of triggers and fights, it's exhausting and both of you have likely hardened your heart. The question is, who's going to soften up and make the first move? It's you. Whoever is reading this. Perhaps it's always been you. If it is then that's a pattern and one that can be changed once you are through this storm with some preventive counseling and crucial conversations.

Often marriages in crisis come to us when the person who has always made the first move towards reconciliation is exhausted and tired of the injustice. They are the first to say "All right, let's call a truce," and then give a nice shoulder and neck massage to ease the tension and get back to living right. If this repeats over and over with no resolution, then you do need to make some changes to the pattern. Perhaps your spouse has tried to make moves to reconnect but you haven't noticed because your heart is still too hurt or they aren't speaking your love language. Perhaps your spouse is a little more broken than you realized and these holes are just too much for them to dig out of. Whatever the case, yes, make the first move, and then get to a place where you can openly and lovingly discuss how to prevent that the next time you fight.

We've already mentioned a lot about the right time and place for a conversation to take place. This is a simple prayer I often pray over couples who are in a struggle. I pray for them to have the right moments ordained for them to both show up with soft hearts and open minds and the right words with no interruptions of any kind until they have closure. If you are in the place where you feel you are the one to always have to approach your spouse first for resolution, pray for the time and place to address this important hurt in your life.

Assume Positive Intent *In The Fire Life*

These three little words can be the mental difference maker in how you approach communication. If you enter a conversation with the assumption that someone was out to "get you," they are going to sense that and immediately go on the defensive. Someone who has been hurt a lot in life is likely to take this approach naturally.

When you assume positive intent, before you know the whole version of the story, you are setting your spouse up for praise and positive reinforcement. Let's take a fire life example. Your spouse is late to arrive home and you haven't heard anything from them. You could assume negatively that they don't care, stopped at a bar and are planning to drink their morning away with no interest in coming to kiss you hello. Or, you could assume positive intent that the chief caught them that morning on their way out and was bending their ear about a key fire department initiative. See the difference in that? One doesn't steal your joy nor paint your spouse in a bad light.

At times I must remind my husband when we are in a heated discussion that my heart is in the right place but perhaps I'm just not communicating clearly. Remember that cynical, sometimes bitter and sleep deprived irritable firefighter we've mentioned a few times? In that mode it's tougher to remember positive intent. He can quickly imagine I am a beastly wife set out to do him harm. It would be easy for me to get defensive in these moments. Through much practice together, we've both learned to assume our spouse's heart wants only good things for you. Any mistake or hurt that was inflicted was unintentional and worthy of mercy and forgiveness. If you can short cycle that pattern, you can eliminate truck loads of hurt between each of you in your marriage.

Common Topics of Miscommunication *In The Fire Life*

So, that's a lot. Not going to sugar coat it but it's certainly achievable. If you need proof think about some of those 20, 30, 40 year marriages out there which you admire. Now think of some more of them within the fire service itself. You've got a group of people cheering you through this. Here is one last list of "in the fire life" topics that might trip you up as a couple. Knowing these, you'll know what's coming before it hits you.

- You're going to hang out with/help/socialize with your firefighter friends again? *What does she expect me to do? Work all the time? I need hobbies and relaxation too.*

- I'm exhausted too. Can you help out around the house? *What do you do all day while I'm gone at the firehouse? This place is a pigsty.*

- I'm going to take that overtime/trade. *I can't believe he didn't ask me what's on our calendar before saying yes to that.*

- He didn't tell me he had another training that weekend. *Why does she need to know everything?*

- Why is he carrying on fire topics when he's home on his phone all the time? Doesn't the job end at shift change? *She has no idea what extra I need to do to maximize my potential for promotion in the future.*

- Why does he get mad when I buy our family groceries? *Does she not understand the tight budget we have this month?*

■ ■ ■ ■ ■ ■ ■ ■ ■ ■ ■ ■ ■

"Sometimes you just need to agree to stop. I have reached my limits on occasion and continued my conversations only through prayer."

■ ■ ■ ■ ■ ■ ■ ■ ■ ■ ■ ■

When There Is Nothing More You Can Say *In The Fire Life*

You know that point where you are beating your head against a brick wall and talking in passionate, escalating circles of emotion on a repetitively triggered cycle? Sometimes you just need to agree to stop. I have reached my limits on occasion and continued my conversations only through prayer. I have prayed for the right man to come alongside my husband and speak rational, life giving words to him for the sake of saving our marriage or at least putting an end to this annoying little skirmish we keep using to pick at each other.

Early in our marriage one very wise and mature firefighter said these words to my husband, "No one ever said marriage was going to be easy." Those words helped him to reframe his outlook and stick to it for the long haul. You can imagine how grateful I was for him to hear those words from someone I really didn't know well. If you're reading this as a firefighter, there is likely at least one other firefighter at your house who needs to hear this too. Go be the light in their darkness.

The Use of Humor to Diffuse Situations *In The Fire Life*

Have you ever been in one of those ridiculous arguments and then something silly happens and you bust out laughing? One of the most ridiculous arguments in our marriage was during a stressful season when we were looking for a new house. Now I'm certain we weren't the only couple who has argued in front of a realtor or the custom home builder trying to walk us through a quote. To this day if you bring up the topic of knee walls versus spindles you will see my husband clench his jaw. #firstworldproblems

If you aren't able to get to this humorous point on your own, sometimes the company of other married couples does the trick. I believe there is some yet to be unlocked marriage healing practice that involves getting couples together, creating a safe space for communication and letting them tell stories that start with "Oh yeah? Here's what we are fighting about." There is just something that brings hope to your own situation when you know you aren't the only ones going through it AND you can laugh it out with others at the same time.

Sarcastic humor is not the same thing. Sarcasm tends to hide some underlying hurts and won't have the same effect here. While it may work in the firehouse to cover up hurts and full grief buckets, it may not have the same effect on your spouse. You've been warned.

Let's close out this chapter with this thought. Any talking you can get done while firefighter is on shift is a bonus. You will need to be intentional about making time at home with you are both alert and focused to communicate well together. I understand between the fire schedule, children and possibly the spouse's job, you may only have a 1-hour time block a week to spend together quietly and the last thing you want to do is talk about a prickly topic. Get good at it so it goes faster! And then get onto everyone's favorite post argument activity, make-up sex.

~ for the firefighter ~
Honorable Communication
In a Committed Fire Marriage

There are entire libraries full of books written about the differences in male and female communication patterns. Mars and Venus. Love and Respect. Waffles and Spaghetti. I'm serious. Google that. This right here is the cliff notes version of how to be the best communicator for your spouse *in the fire life.*

- Do text your spouse often and regularly while you are away. It can be done quickly and easily and put their mind to ease especially after a major fire event. Even the most experienced fire wives get a little squirmy when there is the quickest of all good byes because the "working fire" tones drop.

- Do your best to not leave for shift on a negative note. Even if there is a fight, call a cease fire and hug and kiss her before you leave.

- Take ownership of your responsibility to come back to that conversation when you are back together and in a time and space you can address it. In the fire life, this can be a few days even but leaving it up to your spouse to bring it up, is not fair and not representing the 100%—100% role you both should be playing in your marriage.

- Listen. Just listen. Sometimes that's all she needs.

- Use the words "I hear you" and "I'm here for you" often. Yes, we know you feel that way but saying it out loud is so powerful.

- Talk about more things than just firefighting. One day you may not have that topic to discuss anymore. And, she has lots of passions and interests as well.

- Be clear about the rules and expectations of personal phone calls while on shift.

~ *for the spouse* ~
Honorable Communication
In a Committed Fire Marriage

Beyond all the great tips above, here are some specifics for spouses:

- Understand the limitations of communication while on shift

- Keeping the love tanks full is the best way to decrease the intensity of fights in your marriage

- Agree on how you will handle a quick hang up due to a run so that your feelings are not hurt.

■ ■ ■ ■ ■ ■ ■ ■ ■ ■ ■ ■ ■

Andrew Starnes is the creator of "Bringing Back Brotherhood," a resource where he wants to assist the fire service in living out the character of brotherhood in their actions both personally in the firehouse and in their lives at home. We are grateful to have his thoughts from a firefighter's perspective on this topic. Andy talks here about taking off that fire helmet as you become present and communicate with your spouse and family.

◆◆◆◆◆◆◆◆◆ "Communication" *By Andrew Starnes* ◆◆◆◆◆◆◆

Firefighters today are under more stress than ever before. We are asked to do more with less and we will be the first the public calls for any major emergency. Yet the trend of budget cuts, salaries decreasing, and staffing being reduced all points to a heavier load upon our firefighters. Many firefighters already work a second job along with their spouse working full time. Firefighters often work part-time at a neighboring department as their second job. With all of these responsibilities weighing down upon firefighters today, how much stress is carried over into our homes? How much more is the burden upon our wives and children that we see even less due to being overworked?

Consider this:

"On average, a husband and wife spend 37 minutes in conversation with each other each week."

Our marriages are so important that this equates to 5.28 minutes per day of devoted conversation time with one another. Does this sound right to anyone?

When we leave the firehouse and head home have we truly left the firehouse? When we hang our helmet up at the end of the tour, do we truly ever take it off? We preach that we are never off duty but what part of the job are we carrying home that we need to leave at the firehouse? We preach dedication and service over self but how much of our dedication is being given to our families? We should remember our first commitment is to 'always be on duty' for our family. Consider this statement:

"Every marriage is either moving toward oneness or drifting towards isolation." Dennis Rainey

Which direction is your marriage heading?

In many cases the fire service can become an all-consuming fire in our lives rather than our love for God and for our families. We are constantly asked to do more with less and are expected to perform any service at a moment's notice. This leads us to stay focused and continually learning so we may be ready for when the moment of opportunity arises.

But what happens when all our efforts, our energies, and our focus shifts more towards our passion for the fire service. When one area of our lives is over-focused another is diminished. We have often heard the statement "Everyone goes home" but will our families be there for us when we finally do come home? Will they look upon us as the dedicated family member or the stranger who merely visits our house to sleep and return back to work?

Many firefighters will stop reading at this point and state all the ways that they provide for their families. As leaders in our homes we should provide for our families. But what is of greater value to our wives and our children:

Material presents.

-Or-

Our physical presence.

Consider this story for a moment:

You are a firefighter who is on his way home after working a busy 24-hour shift followed by a 12-hour shift at his part time job. You are exhausted mentally, physically, and to top it off you have spent the majority of those hours dealing with personnel conflicts inside both firehouses. You have an hour commute home which is a blessing in disguise as it serves as a version of personal de-fusing. In the middle of your ride home you receive a call from your wife to inform you that your youngest child is sick.

Does this story sound familiar? In many cases this is a minor reflection of what some firefighters are facing when they return home. They have been busy putting out 'fires' in others' lives and have returned home to find a fully involved family who is in desperate need of their attention. Their spouse has been holding the line for two days on her own, working, and taking care of the children. And upon our arrival we have to remember how we approach the calamities of other's lives: with compassion and courtesy.

Many times, I have entered our home feeling overburdened with negative emotions, physically exhausted, and emotionally spent. In my heart what I truly want most when I walk in the door is a great big hug from my wife and daughter. But I enter into the world of a full speed family and take off one helmet and place upon my head another. The helmet of a husband and a father who needs to be just as strong for his wife and daughter as I have been for the citizens that we serve. So many times, I fail and speak in haste or forget to take off the fire helmet. So many times, I have come home in anguish and tears but never spoke a word to my family about it. So many times, I have swallowed this poison of inner torment rather than giving it to God and talking to my wife.

Taking off the Helmet-Communication Breakdown

What are one of the five top reasons that contribute to a Line of Duty Death?

One of the contributing factors identified by the IAFF is poor communication (https://www.iaff.org/tech/PDF/Contributing%20Factors %20to%20FF%20Line-of-Duty%20Death_IAFFand%20USFA.pdf). Perhaps, you have been on the fireground and seen the effects of poor communication? Critical information is lost, tasks are replicated which often induces freelancing, the overall effectiveness of the incident suffers because the message isn't being received therefore the team members cannot execute the strategy as planned. And even more tragic, is to witness or listen in on a Firefighter calling for help and not be heard by their fellow firefighters. Many have been lost because their desperate cries for help were never heard and sadly the help they needed came too late.

The question we should ask ourselves today is how effective are we communicating?

Are we known as proficient tactical fireground communicators but then fail to communicate effectively to our spouse and children?

Are we an expert in our field but our message isn't being received correctly with our loved ones?

Are we failing to hear our loved ones cry for help?

■ ■ ■ ■ ■ ■ ■ ■ ■ ■ ■ ■ ■

"I have found myself falling into the incident commander mindset in my own home and failing miserably with my family."

■ ■ ■ ■ ■ ■ ■ ■ ■ ■ ■ ■ ■

Have we missed our own families May-Day? Whom does the responsibility fall upon?

As in our lives as Incident Commanders, we are ultimately responsible for the outcome of the incident; so it is in our marriages, our loved ones, and children. We are accountable for our communication breakdown and we are accountable for the demise of our own family if we are not careful.

Consider with me for a moment the devastating effect of poor communication in our homes:

I have found myself falling into the incident commander mindset in my own home and failing miserably with my family. I have been brief and to the point, not giving specific details with no emotion towards my wife and daughter. I have listened only momentarily before moving on rather than taking the time to listen with an empathic heart.

Each time that I have failed to take off the fire service helmet and place on the helmet of servant leadership my wife and daughter have suffered. Yet, I am blessed that I have a wife that loves me unconditionally and forgives my errors in communication. She loves me as Jesus does, unconditionally, as I repent and come to her in humility. The very reason that I am writing this is that through my own brokenness I hope that each of you are inspired to be brave and "confess your sins to each other and pray for each other so that you may be healed" (James 5:16).

So, how do we then improve upon our communication in our daily lives?

In marriage ministry, we are taught that men and women communicate differently. Most men are described as "land the plane communicators" which is to be brief and to the point where as many women describe their message in vivid detail. The challenge before us as men and women is knowing our loved ones better than we know ourselves. We practice and preach crew integrity in our fire service lives how much more should we know and be one with our spouse who we committed our very lives to? Our efforts to be effective and loving communicators in our home should be our first priority and this discipline will carry over into all aspects of our lives.

In my own life, I fail to communicate when my focus is all about me. As Saint Francis states so eloquently "We should seek first to understand, then to be understood." Too often, it is the reverse for us in communication. We begin with our viewpoint in a defensive or self-righteous posture rather than listening to our spouse's side first. As leaders, we are taught when dealing with a problem we are to identify it, investigate, and gather all the facts before making a decision. Let us ask ourselves, are we practicing this in our own lives with our loved ones?

Preventing the Death of a Marriage

The Art of Marriage Conference gives us some valuable wisdom to remember in this area:

Priorities: One reason couples drift apart is that they fail to make their marriage the priority it used to be.

Attitude toward our spouse: "The four horseman of the apocalypse in marriage are: criticism, contempt, defensiveness, and withdrawal. Once these behaviors take over, unless a couple makes changes they are likely to find themselves sliding helplessly toward the end of their marriage" (John Gottman).

Is the love of Jesus displayed in our marriage? "The gospel of Christ crucified for our sins is the foundation of our lives. Marriage exists to display it. And when marriage breaks down, the gospel is there to forgive and heal and sustain until He comes, or until He calls" (John Piper).

As we close, consider the analogy we first began with. One of the leading contributors to the death of firefighters is poor communication and in marriage we see the same contributor to our high divorce rate. Let us ask ourselves this each day:

What am I doing to know God and my spouse better today? How much time and effort do I spend on other things instead of my marriage?

Let us all train hard in the work of maintaining healthy and strong marriages. Stay connected and work to communicate effectively by seeking to understand each other and love one another as Christ has loved us.

God Bless,
Andy J. Starnes

– for discussion –

- What are your toughest topics to communicate about while on shift?

- What are the communication agreements that have worked in your marriage?

- Describe your healthy communication environments (i.e. is there privacy in your firehouse?)

- Healthy Conflict resolution when apart—do you touch that topic or put it on hold?

- Do you know each other's love language? Discuss

- What bad patterns of communication have you fallen victim to and how will you break out of those?

- Do either of you "scream" in non-obvious ways?

RESOURCES

All resources mentioned in this chapter can be found at HonorAndCommitment.com/Chapter9

Resources available:

- Handling the crazy texting girlfriend

- Good Night Routines

- Apology Languages and Love Languages Books

10 *Honorable Behavior*
And Female Firefighters

I'm going to come very clean with something I really struggled with when I was a new fire wife—female firefighters. In general, I am a huge supporter of women doing jobs they qualify for no matter what gender roles show us in statistics. I grew up wanting to be an astronaut, earned an engineering degree, and worked in a very male-dominated field. So any jealousy I held towards female firefighters, my husband could have equally held towards all the men I travelled the world with for my engineering job. (Thank goodness I married an awesome man who was supportive of my endeavors.)

The trouble came when I began to learn more about the fire service and the personal experiences I had with the few females I came in contact with. Because the fire service is really "small town" and everyone knows everyone, I'm going to stay a bit vague about the sequence of events because I truly don't want to incriminate anyone with this. It does no good for anyone. That in itself is a prime example of why there are struggles with this topic for some marriages.

Every marriage is different so please don't let this be an example of what you might experience. Our work with fire families over the past few years does indicate that working with female firefighters is roughly one of the top 5 issues in struggling firefighter marriages so it must be addressed.

There is a perfect storm of conditions which build to make the male-female firefighter relationships troublesome for some wives.

The reputation: There is a sad but true history of female firefighters that have interfered with marriages. And an equally sad and true history of male firefighters who not only acquiesced but pursued. There are news stories of females frequenting firehouses for unmentionable acts and plenty of controversial court cases where females and males claim sexual harassment and in which sexual acts were performed in the firehouse.

New marriages: New marriages are already a challenging relationship as you navigate unknown territory and learn to trust each other. Now if there is a female on the crew who has any sort of reputation for these kind of behaviors, it adds a strain.

Physical ability: In some cases, there are firefighters unable to perform the duties of the job but stay on crew for one political reason or another. This goes for both male and female but just due to how our bodies are built, females may tend to fall into this category, especially if they've chosen to not maintain a healthy lifestyle as a firefighter. Bottom line for me is this—can that firefighter pull my husband out of harm's way when he falls through the kitchen floor? If not, I'm going to worry a bit more while he's having to ride with that firefighter.

Living together: 24 hours of living together. Meals, showers (ok not together) and sleeping (again not together but in bunk rooms without doors very often) as a family unit. Life happens and relationships are built. It's natural, yet weird, to have that with a woman who is not your wife, sister or daughter.

Emotional connections: The emotional bond over difficult runs and life or death circumstances. It can be a slippery slope for someone who is not using proper boundaries in their marriage.

■ ■ ■ ■ ■ ■ ■ ■ ■ ■ ■ ■

"I stand before you loudly and shout that there are some amazingly talented and awesome women out there getting the job done in the fire service and I'm so honored to call many of them my friend."

■ ■ ■ ■ ■ ■ ■ ■ ■ ■ ■ ■

There is one massively effective approach in dealing with jealousy and trust issues with firefighters of the opposite sex—be the best darn spouse you could ever be, shore up the foundation of your marriage and give your spouse no reason to look any further. Yes, you may still have annoyances with members of the opposite sex who don't respect that boundary, but when your marriage is strong, it's not going to matter.

The second most effective approach in dealing with this topic is to get to know the female firefighters on your husband's crew. I stand before you loudly and shout that there are some amazingly talented and awesome women out there getting the job done in the fire service, and I'm so honored to call many of them my friend. Girl power. Keep rocking it ladies. As you get to know these women, you will learn quickly the character of the person you are dealing with. And, if their morals and values do not align with yours, it is not your responsibility to put them in line. I often hear wives who have an issue with another female texting their husband ask, "Should I text her back or call her and tell her to knock it off?" I get that instinct. He's yours and you want to protect your relationship. But if there are lines being crossed with texting, your husband needs to put up those boundaries immediately, not you. This is an issue between you and your husband, not between you and this other woman. And we all know what happens when girl fights go viral on the internet. It's not pretty, classy, nor honorable. Take a deep breath and spend your time on what matters. Your husband and your commitment to each other.

Finally, put yourself in your husband's shoes. Would he risk his employment in a job that is likely his dream job over a relationship with someone who works in close proximity to him? Let me tell it to you straight. If he would, then he is already disrespecting your marriage and you have way different problems. If it's clear to him that it's a bad choice, then you've got a winner and that's where you need to focus. On him. What God has put together let no man (or woman) separate.

This is a really hard topic for anyone who has had trust issues in past relationships or who happens to be in a situation where their husband is working with a single female with a dishonorable reputation. Which brings us back to why we are here—honor and commitment. Having been once divorced before this marriage, I hope you hear me speaking from painful heart wrenching experiences.

Do you trust your spouse to do what is honorable in your marriage? Are you committed until death do you part to your marriage? That's where you begin and end with this topic. It is healthy and ok to have transparent conversations about your feelings. "It makes me uncomfortable when you are partners with _____. It's something I need to work through. Here is how you can help me." These are not easy but the way to work through these uncomfortable situations, often with the assistance of a counselor.

Since I have had issues with this topic in my past, I'm always super careful what I say about it as I don't want my brain to play tricks and wrongly influence my view. A major healing point for me has been a dear friendship I've developed with a female firefighter who I greatly admire and respect and who can call me out on my junk. We are both strong women and mothers of daughters who love to see women do tough things regardless of feminine stereotypes. We get each other. This friendship has truly healed some unfair judgments I had in my life for female firefighters based on a few unfortunate circumstances. So I've asked her to bring that healing to some other firefighter marriages as she sees it from both sides—she's also married to a firefighter. My wish is that you read this, believe in the good of the female firefighters who are there for all the right reasons, and strengthen your own confidence and marriage to ward off any others who aren't living up to this standard of honor and commitment for female firefighters.

■ ■ ■ ■ ■ ■ ■ ■ ■ ■ ■ ■ ■

"My wish is that you read this, believe in the good of the female firefighters who are there for all the right reasons."

■ ■ ■ ■ ■ ■ ■ ■ ■ ■ ■ ■ ■

Introducing Sarah Cooksey, 37-year-old with 23 years in EMS/Fire Service and 14 years with the Tallahassee Fire Department currently as an Engineer. Most importantly she's a wife (of a firefighter) and mother of 2, who wrangles a small business as well as being President of the Tallahassee Chapter of Guardians of the Ribbon. See why I love her? We keep our plates full, but more importantly our hearts fulfilled and still make sure we have plenty of time for our friendship. Our husbands probably don't realize how much they need to thank us for the support we give each other. Take that as a good hint, ladies. Girls need girlfriends because your husbands were never meant to understand everything going through your female brain.

◆◆◆ "Females In The Firehouse" By Sarah Cooksey ◆◆◆

Let's talk "Females in the Firehouse." When I was asked to help with this topic I was a bit overwhelmed. I do realize that not everyone has these issues, but I want to address it for those who do or have had them in the past. I mean, I can totally see both sides to this life of a "firefighter/firefighter wife." Like many of you, I have struggled. I have had my ups and downs with just crazy feelings of jealousy and insecurity. Some were justified and some were just my mind running in a direction that just ended up making me look silly. I know this may sound kind of funny, coming from a girl that runs into burning buildings when others are running out, but hey, I am human. With that being said, I am going to try and help you navigate through this chapter and offer you some tips on how to get through this part of the fire service. I want to approach it with love and sympathy, but also with a little bit of reality to calm some fears, both rational and irrational (let's face it, we all have those).

In this case, one bad apple does not spoil the bunch. In fact, over the years, in my career in the fire service, I have been known to get a bit "passionate" (okay, we will call it angry) seeing some women come in like a wrecking ball. That being said, we are not all like that. In fact, the vast majority are not. I am going to remove my firefighter helmet for a moment and as a wife, tell you that I understand those feelings you may be having and it's okay to have them, but let's remember how small the percentage of "badge bunnies," "home wreckers" or whatever you want to call them are. The majority of female firefighters are just like me and I am going to give you an inside view of my heart and mind, in hopes it offers you some healing. In hopes that it opens your mind and maybe even allows you to have wonderful friendships with the ladies in your husband's firehouse.

I won't lie, when I first started working in this field, I did not really understand why some wives were so standoffish. I guess I was ignorant to the fact that people would actually be jealous of me. In my mind, I was living the dream. I was doing a job that I loved. I grew up with my Dad being in the fire service and I started in the fire service as an Explorer (Junior Firefighter) at the age of 14. I was helping people and loved every single minute of it. Why would I even have an issue with a wife or she have an issue with me? About 2 years into my current job, a dear friend of mine, also a firefighter wife said she had something she wanted to tell me. I worked with her husband at one point in my career and she really didn't like it. She said she struggled with the fact that he was at the station sleeping and I was too. We all have separate bedrooms in my Dept, as well as bathrooms. I had never really thought of it as an issue. We had been friends for years and still are, but she did at one time feel upset about it. I do get it though. There have been times where my own husband has worked with other females and the little jealous side comes out. To be honest, I think that is just human nature. We just have to remember to keep it healthy and not let it consume us. After the confession of my friend though, I started really looking at things and making sure I had strong boundaries.

Fast forward 20 years from when I started EMS and then the Fire Service. (What?! Did I really just say 20 years?? No way.) Let's talk about being honorable and setting boundaries. Oh, how I have learned so much, but I think a lot of things come with age. Now remember, not all bad apples spoil the bunch and there are bad apples no matter which career you are in. We are indeed talking about the fire service though, so that is our focus. In this line of work relationships are formed. I mean we spend at least a third of our lives with our "Fire Family." Balancing male and female relationships can be interesting at times and even awkward. It's about boundaries and courtesy. Treating others as you would like to be treated. I have been fortunate to work with some really professional people, especially at the beginning of my career. They were good family men and they never treated me differently or in a disrespectful manner. There have been a few "bad" ones, but the good ones always handled the situations for me and I have never really had to feel alone in these situations. I do realize I have been very fortunate in this area and not all women have had the same treatment. I am also careful in how I carry myself at work. I am always dressed professionally and I do not compromise in this area. Even in the middle of the night, I am fully dressed.

I currently work with a young firefighter who calls himself my "annoying little brother that I never had." (I am an only child.) It truly is just like that. He purposefully picks at me because he thinks it is funny. Truth be told, most times it is, but don't tell him that! My Lt. is a family man with a good head on his shoulders and good morals. He is an example of what a good leader should be like and he sets the tone for his subordinates. When you have a crew like this, it makes things easy. The job is enjoyable. You don't have to draw lines in the sand because everyone has a mutual respect for others and their spouses and families. All of the above being said, no one will ever take the place of my husband. He has been with me through thick and thin and thick again. He is my best friend. So, those boundaries, I set them and carry myself carefully, not to ever send mixed signals when in the work place. Husbands should respectfully set those boundaries as well. Help your wives feel more at ease when you go to work with us ladies. Marriage is hard work! Just a regular marriage is hard work. Fire Service marriages are sometimes overtime. We all know we have a love hate relationship with that "overtime" word.

■ ■ ■ ■ ■ ■ ■ ■ ■ ■ ■ ■

"Husbands should respectfully set those boundaries as well. Help your wives feel more at ease when you go to work with us ladies."

■ ■ ■ ■ ■ ■ ■ ■ ■ ■ ■ ■

There are times that your firefighter's crew will just "get it." They will seem to understand how your firefighter is feeling and it may seem like you don't. You may feel hurt or upset by this, but it's kind of like your firefighter truly not understanding how your stressful day was at home or work because they weren't there to share it with you. This does not mean your firefighter's crew takes your place! Some of you are fortunate like me and can talk about the calls with your spouse and they are comfortable sharing those things with you. Others, may feel like they don't share. There are so many variables to consider in this. When calls are really bad, my husband and I filter them a little for each other to prevent PTSD. There is Primary PTSD (what you see) and Secondary (what you talk about that triggers what you saw). We try to reduce the secondary in our house when we can. Some of these things only a fire-fighter or someone in this line of work will truly understand. Sometimes our men, well they just want to "protect" us ladies, so they may not share all the gory details. It does not mean you are any less important than his co-workers.

Oh, this fire family! I have made some really great friendships with wives from my Dept. I don't approach them as a firefighter, or a coworker of their husbands. I approach them as a fellow female, a wife, a mother. You see, at the end of the day I am all of those things. I have the same worries you do as a wife and mother. I juggle sick kids, child care, school field trips, meal planning, trying to be the best wife I can be and so much more, just like you do! I am truly blessed to see both sides. I have an inside view of this job your husband has, as well as the tough job you have! Let me tell you, that job is important! Remember, you are the soft place he lands. You make the home he lives in his sanctuary. It is so important to do those things. I know it is not always easy, but this fire life is sometimes rough and coming home to his safe place is the best feeling ever. After he sees someone lose a child or a spouse, he really wants to come home and hold his. Sometimes he is tired and comes home and crashes and it feels like all he does is sleep. Oh weary wife and mama, this is where your life is hard and I get it!

I also understand the worry of whether "this female firefighter" can drag your husband out of a burning building. The truth for me here is I often worry about this even with other men. There are some out of shape people in the fire service, so I do not care if the person is male, female, black, white or purple, as long as they can do the job!

■ ■ ■ ■ ■ ■ ■ ■ ■ ■ ■ ■ ■

"If you really have an issue, talk openly with your husband about it. A lot of times the way we approach the situation is more detrimental than the actual female in question."

■ ■ ■ ■ ■ ■ ■ ■ ■ ■ ■ ■ ■

The last thing we will talk about when having an issue with a female firefighter is, when all else fails, mark your territory, pee on your fire hydrant! I am just kidding, in that fashion anyway, but you can always drop off cookies or some other kind of desert at the station. You don't want to stay too long and overstay your welcome, but just make yourself known. If you really have an issue, talk openly with your husband about it. Make sure you are careful with approaching him. Try to do it when you are both rested and in an open mode to communicate. You don't want to put them on the automatic defense. A lot of times the way we approach the situation is more detrimental than the actual female in question. You have to determine if the issue is that female, or just your insecurities, or even a combination of both. If it is the female, make your presence known (in a not crazy way). Keep yourself calm and focus your thoughts and actions on keeping your marriage strong. 9 times out 10 your firefighter isn't going to want to mess with that girl. They are smart enough to know better. They know what they have at home! If they do go there, then there are bigger issues than that female firefighter and those are covered in other chapters. I also want to add, that I do realize this can apply to husbands as well. Some may struggle with their wife working with a bunch of men. I am writing from a FF/Wife perspective, because that is who I am. At the end of the day open and honest communication is the key, but really the same principles apply to any job/workplace.

HONOR GUARD

~ for the firefighter ~
Honorable Behavior
And Female Firefighters

Let's split this particular section up into male and female and keep it short and to the point.

Guys, do the honorable thing for women everywhere. Keep your eyes and your heart on your wife only. If you need a subtle reminder when a temptation with another female presents itself, remember these two things:

1. Every woman is some father's little girl. Would that father be ok with what you are thinking about her, doing to her or saying to her?

2. Would you say, do or think those thoughts about this woman out loud in front of your wife?

When you work with female firefighters, be the kind of guy to protect them from the kinds of guys who don't respect those boundaries. Their husbands and fathers will hugely appreciate that. Dress appropriately, talk appropriately, and act appropriately in the firehouse when in the presence of female firefighters. Yes, I realize this may cramp your style but what if she was your daughter? How should she be treated? That thought should clear things up immediately if you believe in the honor and commitment message of this book.

If there is an issue with a female at your department who is advancing inappropriately, your best move is to take your documented concerns directly to the officer in charge, or the officer above her if it happens to be your own leader. Transparency and honesty will always be the best policy here. Should you tell your wife? That's going to depend entirely on where both of you are on this topic from a trust and emotional maturity perspective. If there have been recent infidelities, this could really do more damage. On the other hand, there may be more damage done by keeping this information from your wife. A good reality check on this is what does your gut say? Is this eating at you? Then finding the right moments and words to get it off your chest and reassure your wife you are all in for her and her only is going to bring much growth and healing to your marriage.

Ladies, for the sake of women everywhere who are fighting to make a name for themselves in a male-dominated profession, the only thing you should be focused on in the workplace is bettering your skills as they pertain to the job. Use of "feminine persuasion" or any other technique to advance "just because you are a woman" is only going to perpetuate the wrong stereotypes about women. When you adhere to that, there's no need for us to even say "keep your eyes, thoughts and hands off of the married men in your department". Steer clear of temptation and be the best firefighter you can be.

Note that everything written here can be reversed ladies. I realize there are probably a larger quantity of disrespectful, inappropriate comments made to you by male firefighters on the job than the other way around. I empathize. I fought this off for years in my corporate job while trying to advance my career. It's not fair but that's the fight us women are in together. Do the honorable thing. My husband likes to say "the work of good men (or women) will always prevail". Believe it and keep fighting the good fight.

~ *for the spouse* ~
Honorable Behavior
And Female Firefighters

We've covered many of the pointers above so let's focus on "honorable behavior."

What honorable behavior is not:

- Going direct to a woman you feel is interfering with your marriage and having ugly shouting matches or text message battles

- Dragging anyone's name through the mud or spreading rumors

- Assuming your husband is not being honorable before having open communication with him. Guilty until proven innocent is never a good way to start a conversation from the heart.

- Keeping your feelings bottled up and hiding them from your husband. He deserves to know the full truth of how you feel (in mature ways)

What is honorable behavior:

- Having mature, open discussions with your husband about your concerns

- Trusting your husband when he has to work with females you have concerns about

- Keeping these concerns between you and your husband

- Staying classy. It's the most attractive thing you can do in this situation.

- Treat everyone at the department with respect, including the females who give you cause for concern

- Growing together and moving through this season until you can look back and laugh at it and never waste a brain cell or conversation on this topic again

- for discussion -

- Talk about the "classy and honorable" way to handle an issue should it arise

- What ground rules would you set for each other if there was / is a member of the opposite sex on crew?

- Come clean with the wrong, immature thoughts you've had about these situations. Give each other time and space to confess and ask forgiveness.

- If there has been a misstep with a firefighter of the opposite sex, decide how you will work through those trust issues together. Consider counseling or some of the resources from the trust chapter in this book.

RESOURCES

All resources mentioned in this chapter can be found at
HonorAndCommitment.com/Chapter10

11 *Commitment to Trust*
In a Fire Marriage

Do you wake up each morning with a nagging feeling your spouse isn't sharing the whole truth with you?

We experienced seasons like that in our marriage and in hindsight, it is sooooooo freeing to never have those thoughts even cross your mind momentarily.

Trust is inarguably a cornerstone value in every marriage. When you lack trust, your thoughts are filled with worry, doubt, and wondering. These spaces that could be filled with love and giving and kindness. Even when you love someone but don't trust them, that doubt is renting space in your head and your heart. I really love you and want to be with your forever, but I worry about what will happen the next time you go away to that training and meet with new suppliers. Will you strike up another "friendship" with that female sales rep? Can I trust that we'll never have that issue again? Can I trust that he'll honor my wishes to not hang out at the bar with the single firefighters on his crew?

The fire life introduces some trust traps that other marriages don't have to face. Not only do you spend a lot of time apart, but firefighters truly have a second "family" they live with. That's a bit different than say a corporate executive who's gone a lot traveling the world solo to a bunch of different places (The grass isn't greener. That's a whole different set of trust traps.)

Firefighters transition between two "homes" with close family-life relationships in both. It could be very easy to feel like you "get along better" with the family at the firehouse (which may include members of the opposite sex) or for a family to feel like their life is "easier when their husband is at the firehouse." That leads to those feelings in reverse. The firefighter may feel their family is happier at home when they are at the firehouse. Perhaps the firefighter isn't hearing about what's happening at home and is left wondering and doubting and losing trust.

Here is an alarming and ugly statistic that isn't often made known. After 9/11, where we lost 363 firefighters in the line of duty, there were many, many widowed spouses and orphaned children. What isn't publicly shared is how many of them also had mistresses and sometimes their children whom they were also financially supporting and were seeking financial support of their own at the loss of their boyfriend. Yeah. You've heard many a scorned woman claim that firefighters are cheaters and I'm afraid to say it isn't exactly a profession to esteem for it's marital values (hence this book and our organization hoping to shift that culture.) Without disgracing anyone's name or reputation simply by associating them with the fire service, we are simply stating that the profession does make opportunities for trust to be broken in many ways by either spouse in the marriage. For those who are choosing to take the honorable path of commitment, it's not always going to be an easy one to follow in the fire life but with the same discipline and obedience with which you enter into this profession, not only as a firefighter but as the family, there is an honorable path to commitment to the fire service and your marriage.

When you have complete trust in a firefighter marriage it might look like this:

Firefighter: I completely trust what my spouse does at home when I'm away at the firehouse. There are no actions, visitors, or activities that I worry about.

Non-Firefighter Spouse: I completely trust what my spouse says, thinks, and does in all their interactions at the firehouse. That's a wonderful feeling. No phone calls or conversations are filled with those questions that try to dig into the doubts in your mind. Like "where did you guys go for coffee when you got off shift?" or "Who was at the gym when you went to work out today?"

Let's talk through some topics that are sensitive but a reality for some firefighter marriages.

Trust Traps In a Firefighter Marriage

Dishonesty About Money

Perhaps we've been exposed to some of the worst firehouse challenges that exist, so take this with a grain of salt. Some firefighters receive bonus checks or overtime pay and deposit them in separate accounts their spouses cannot see, and then make pacts with each other to not discuss this money when the spouses are around. To be fair, there are probably some spouses doing the same thing to their firefighter spouse.

Money is absolutely a fighting word in marriage and takes shape in many arrangements. Some couples are all in, one account, complete transparency with "your money is my money" mentality. Other couples have an agreement for keeping assets separate and agreeing on who pays for what.

When everything is transparent and agreed upon, this may work out ok. When details about finances are hidden, it's an open door to wonder "What else are they hiding from me?"

The worst thing you can do right now is to take this thought we just planted in an accusatory way back to your spouse. If you feel this may be happening, get clear on your thoughts, refer to the communication chapter where we talk about "crucial conversations" and prepare your heart for a healthy discussion to get to the bottom of this. Money habits also follow closely with family upbringing. A spouse who watched their parents divorce and see one parent left with nothing has good reason to feel they may need to "stash some hidden" money away even if their marriage is rock solid. We all have those points we need to heal from in our past. Assume positive intent and get to the root of why the deception is happening.

Dishonesty About Your Actions

Typically we want to lie about something when we know the reaction we receive isn't going to be nice. If you and your spouse have been arguing about how much time you spend hunting, then you might want to not mention to them that you were browsing the Cabela's website while you were on shift. Your spouse may not want to mention she binge watched Netflix instead of getting the closet reorganized as she had planned on a shift day. Yet the energy of keeping these secrets is exhausting. As some say, honesty saves you time from remembering all the lies. The long time periods apart give much freedom for each spouse in the fire life to act independently. Which is all good. We are all individuals first and must love ourselves well which includes doing things we enjoy. However there could be more temptation for actions you want to hide from your spouse as there is less face to face accountability to our partners.

■ ■ ■ ■ ■ ■ ■ ■ ■ ■ ■ ■ ■

"No act you do, nor words you say, whether in the presence of your spouse or not, should need to be hidden from your spouse. This is the honorable way to a committed marriage."

■ ■ ■ ■ ■ ■ ■ ■ ■ ■ ■ ■

Recall from our communication chapter that sharing the even the minor details of our days is a way to stay connected while apart. Suddenly when you can't share every moment because you are hiding some actions you aren't proud of or your spouse wouldn't appreciate, you lose some intimacy and safety in your conversations. No act you do, nor words you say, whether in the presence of your spouse or not, should need to be hidden from your spouse. This is the honorable way to a committed marriage.

When You Trust Your Spouse But Not the Others at the Firehouse
Perhaps you are blessed with a lot of trust and transparency with your spouse but there are firefighters at the firehouse who have not honored their marriages or who have brought mistresses into the station (google this if you dare; sadly stories like this make the headlines). There are also stories of spouses at home who have had "2 unit boyfriends" for a couple of years until the firefighter finally realizes what has been going on and then she leaves him. Yes we've all heard one of those true stories. Not everyone who crosses our paths is going to practice the same values. In fact, some people may cross your path because by some twist of fate, they were meant to see that it's ok to be honorable. They need some role models.

Nevertheless, it's a lot of pressure to be living in an environment with constant suggestions to not honor your marriage. You do have to get along with your co-workers, but you don't have to be friends with all of them. The firehouse environment is one of those workplaces where work / friend lines can become almost indistinguishable. What a strain this adds to marriages already under pressure.

To further compound this problem, a firefighter who is trying to be honorable and committed can be trapped in a situation where a dishonorable firefighter on their crew is putting them in a situation where they will potentially need to cover for them. If you are that guy and by some miraculous chance you are reading this right now, can we encourage you to carry the honorable traits of firefighting into your personal life? Stop the infidelity and stop putting your brotherhood in the middle of your lies. Believe that in a true brotherhood, when you come clean and decide to put an end to these kind of lies, your fellow firefighters will be there to give you grace and accountability to change your ways. Even if there is a small lie you are shielding with the firehouse, a huge weight will be lifted from you when you step into the way of truth and regain trust in your relationship, and your brotherhood.

■ ■ ■ ■ ■ ■ ■ ■ ■ ■ ■ ■ ■

"When you are confident and loving and believing that you are the one loving your spouse in the best way possible, it keeps their love tank filled up."

■ ■ ■ ■ ■ ■ ■ ■ ■ ■ ■ ■

There is one thing you can do to avoid all trust traps: Give your spouse the best of you. Show them your love and respect.

If your spouse feels completely filled up and loved by you, then chances are less likely to be concerned about the "gaps" we all have in our imperfect lives. When you are confident and loving and believing that you are the one loving your spouse in the best way possible, it keeps their love tank filled up. And confidence is so much more appealing than insecurity. And, it doesn't hurt to send them off to shift with all their physical needs met as well. Truly, **we just want our spouses to want to do the right thing most of all.** "Want to" is the key because we all slip up and say dumb things when we are tired and stressed out. When you can recognize that for what it is and it's followed with a heartfelt apology, it's the "want to" that matters.

What rips holes in marriages is the disregard for the others feelings. You've trusted this person with your most intimate feelings of your heart. Saying things like "Why does that even bother you? I'm done having this conversation" is dismissing feelings in your partner. Right or wrong, it's first of all important for feelings to be heard clearly, and then apologies can be made and misunderstandings can be cleared up. I've seen over the years this classic conversation in marriages where the trust is not wholly complete.

"Why did you say that to her?"

"Say what?"

"When you were talking about that camping trip and the way you said you loved sleeping out in a tent and she giggled and grabbed your arm. It was just all way too flirty for me."

"What the heck? I'm not allowed to cross paths with any women? That's impossible. The world is full of women. Are you always going to react this way?"

■ ■ ■ ■ ■ ■ ■ ■ ■ ■ ■ ■ ■

The pattern repeats until both parties make a change that breaks the pattern and find new ways to communicate and reconnect in love."

■ ■ ■ ■ ■ ■ ■ ■ ■ ■ ■ ■

And so the pattern continues. Her words may come from a place of distrust due to past incidents. Or they may come from feelings of insecurity. His words come from a place of not hearing her hurts and need to be reassured. The pattern repeats until both parties make a change that breaks the pattern and find new ways to communicate and reconnect in love.

When trust patterns repeat involving the firehouse, those on the crew at the firehouse or anything related to the profession that allows for lack of transparency, you've suddenly put the fire service in the middle of your marital issues. In actuality, as a couple with these traits, these issues could have cropped up no matter what profession either was carrying out. While the fire service does make unique opportunities for stressors, I'm not a believer that we should blame it on the firehouse. Each individual needs to own their actions no matter where they are or what they are doing. We do want to point out frequent places the fire life can impact this trust issue but please do not mistake this as us saying it's the fault of the profession. Let's own our actions. For as many lying, cheating firefighters you hear about, we also hear about thousands of firefighters married for 20, 30 or 40 years who have survived these stressors. Focus on them and the commitment you made to your spouse to navigate this road.

There is one last very significant trust trap we all fall into in one way or another.

When We Aren't Truthful with Our Feelings

Marriage Builders has another great foundational practice for all marriages and it's called "The Policy of Radical Honesty". Most everyone can get on board with that in a marriage. It includes being honest with how you spent money, where you went and what you did, but many of us have hidden feelings from our spouse because we are afraid of their reaction. The Policy of Radical Honesty says this:

Reveal to your spouse as much information about yourself as you know; your thoughts, feelings, habits, likes, dislikes, personal history, daily activities, and plans for the future

How would you feel if 2 years into your marriage you discover that your spouse had previously dated one of their co-workers but didn't tell you? Or that they didn't really like your cat, your habit of not cleaning up after yourself in the kitchen or worse, your brother, but just ignored that feeling because they love you so much? It's one thing for them to say that and for you to know and appreciate the sacrifice they are making but it's an entirely different thing for that feeling to be hidden.

As soon as a feeling is hidden, you wonder what other feelings they haven't shared with you. Years of hiding feelings will lead to one of those epic blow ups that are damaging to your relationship. It's common for feelings to be hidden in a relationship where one spouse is more dominant or controlling over the other. Marriage isn't about being controlled but willingly entering into a mutually sacrificial relationship with the intention to give of yourself for your spouse who will in turn provide the same for you.

This trap of not being completely honest with your feelings leads to the most dangerous trap for a marriage.

When We Aren't Truthful with Our Feelings and Let Others Fill that Need

Your spouse wants to know that you share your feelings with them completely and do not turn to other confidantes in your life.

■ ■ ■ ■ ■ ■ ■ ■ ■ ■ ■ ■ ■

"To turn to another member of the opposite sex for that emotional support can easily lead to an emotional affair."

■ ■ ■ ■ ■ ■ ■ ■ ■ ■ ■ ■ ■

Girls need girlfriends to fill gaps husbands can't. Guys need guy friends to fill gaps women can't. But for a female to turn to a male friend for emotional support or vice versa, it's a dangerous trap. It's one thing to vent to a coworker about an annoying work thing and something entirely different to feel like "this is something I could never say to my wife because she wouldn't understand." It's true that neither a husband nor a wife may understand the other's job completely but they WANT to be there for you. They want you to share your emotions and struggles there with them. To turn to another member of the opposite sex for that emotional support can easily lead to an emotional affair.

Want to hear a guys view on this? My husband shared his thoughts about men facebook messaging other women. There is a video linked in our resources but also a simple test. If another woman messages you, is this a conversation you would carry on in person with your spouse and this woman both present? If you have any hesitation then this conversation is crossing unsafe boundaries and needs to be eliminated. This age of private messaging, apps that hide communications and chats that erase after being viewed once introduces many opportunities for distrust in a relationship.

Warning signs an emotional affair may be happening are thoughts like this:

She really understands me when I talk about _____.

He responds with so much more care and concern than my husband when we talk about _____.

My wife would never _____.

I can't wait to talk to _____ about this.

If you are feeling this way about someone, the only way to protect your marriage is to cut off all contact. Period. If something is bad for you, you quit right? Same thing goes here. There's no staying friends and still keeping your marriage protected from the temptation.

Chad and Christy are a firefighter and spouse who shared their powerful story of recovery from trust issues and infidelity in their marriage. Here is their story:

Around year 7 in our marriage is what I like to call the dark time in our marriage. Chad had a female firefighter on his truck. We were all very close. Our families were always together. I considered her my friend. **I had been feeling that our marriage was just a little off and decided to ask him how he was feeling about things. This quickly escalated to a full blown argument. He used words like he felt pressured to marry me and then we had our daughter just 9 months after we were married so he felt stuck.** I was devastated at what he was saying. I decided to call our daughter's behavior counselor. He asked us to come into his office right away. He knew that something was up by Chad's actions and some of the key phrases I was using. He began to dig just a little and that is when probably the hardest words I have ever heard came from his mouth." I have been having an affair with the girl at the Fire Department." It had been going on for a few months at this point. I could feel my heart breaking and the wind being sucked out of my body. Sobs do not describe the cry I was having. Our counselor then walked us through our healing. He promised us that day that we would be OK and that we would be stronger because of this trial. And that one day our story would help others. We went that day at the request of of the counselor to go somewhere and just hold hands and that if I had questions I was to ask them and Chad HAD to answer them. I asked them all, how? when? where? I had this morbid need to know. They were not easy words to hear by any means. I wanted to hit him and her. I felt betrayed by them both. At my request he went to his Chief and Battalion chief and put in for a transfer to a new station and shift. We then began praying together, and doing a daily devotion. We also added a regular date night. It was a very long time before we "baked cookies" or even shared a bed really. I needed time to distance him and myself from her and all the visions I had of them together. I then began a time of healing for myself too. I had to forgive them both. I went on what we called a sabbatical. I went to the mountains, alone. I had never been anywhere like that. I prayed, listened to praise music and went for long walks and drives. I came home ready to help Chad mend our marriage. It was not easy to find forgiveness but with lots of prayer and I managed to get the courage to talk to her. This had to be part of our healing as well. Part of what made this easier was she left the Fire department not too long after this all happened. We made sure that we spent more time with God, alone and together. Chad and I have still had our moments of disagreements since, but one thing I never do is throw his indiscretion in his face. He and I realized during the healing process that we were not filling each others love tanks (from *The Five Love Languages*). He was weak and she was able to fill his tank, and because I was not filling his, he was not filling mine. It was a vicious cycle that almost ended our marriage. I am so thankful for Dr Costintino and his help in guiding us on what a Godly marriage was supposed to look like and to God for reminding us that he had put us together for a reason. We know when to say we are sorry and how to forgive. We know when to give the other space when it is needed. We support one another in all that we do. We work at filling each others love tanks and make that a priority in our marriage. I can say that I am more in love with my husband than I was on the day I first married him. And he says the same about me. We chose to work at our marriage and not just give up. We were able to recognize what went wrong and made things right again.

■ ■ ■ ■ ■ ■ ■ ■ ■ ■ ■ ■ ■

"Small difficult discussions can instead be tough but caring conversations where both individuals want to work through to a compromise."

■ ■ ■ ■ ■ ■ ■ ■ ■ ■ ■ ■ ■

Amen! Even if you are not one who believes in God, there are many valuable statements and healing to learn from in this testimony. The most important point I don't want anyone to miss is this:

If your marriage is feeling a little "off", trust your instinct and ask that question. You can both just move forward knowing something is wrong and not address it. That feels easier sometimes I know. Or you can with confidence and compassion dive right in and address things the moment they happen. "Hey, I noticed you got edgy when we started talking about _____. Can we talk about that again and be sure we are on the same page?" The alternative of stuffing feelings one after the other only ends in an epic fight. Epic fights inflict pain and leave scars. Small difficult discussions can instead be tough but caring conversations where both individuals want to work through to a compromise so they stop unintentionally inflicting small hurts on each other. This method means you must be open about your feelings and more importantly, you must be clear in your own mind about how you are feeling exactly. Trying to share a bunch of swirled up emotions and thoughts is pretty messy and difficult for your spouse to interpret. It's totally ok to say "Something is bothering me and I can't put my finger on it. I'm going to sort it out in my head a bit so I can say it more clearly to you."

Speak the Truth But With Love
There is one important disclaimer about being truthful with your feelings. It's not a license to word vomit your frustrations all over your spouse. "You wanted me to be truthful so there. Every time I come home from shift you are on me about one thing or the other and it makes me want to turn around and walk out the door. I'm done with your nagging."

Yes that's truthful. Yes those could be valid feelings, but when delivered with hurtful emotions still attached, it's not going to be effective. Consider this different approach. You know this has been bothering you for some time. You spend that morning driving home from shift softening your heart and finding the clear thoughts to express your feelings and ready to work through a compromise while also hearing and listening to her feelings. You exchange your normal warm greeting and then she may start in on "the list." You can instead say "Hey honey. I know there are a lot of things we have to do around here but can we delay these conversations until after I've had a chance to shower and just be home for a little bit. When you begin with these lists, I do feel pressured a bit and need some time to acclimate."

Alright I admit, that sounds pretty idealistic like some staged "made for TV" movie that runs on Sunday afternoons. But the concept is solid. Get right in your heart. Validate feelings from both sides. Continue with kindness as you work through a compromise.

Demonstrating You Trust Your Spouse

If you are in the midst of this struggle in your marriage, this chapter may feel trite and superficial. It's a really big heavy topic.

■ ■ ■ ■ ■ ■ ■ ■ ■ ■ ■ ■

"The best thing you can do is make sure he leaves the house overflowing with love for you."

■ ■ ■ ■ ■ ■ ■ ■ ■ ■ ■ ■

I often hear wives of firefighters stressing so much about their husband heading into shift when there is another female, notorious for breaking up marriages, working that day. And the husbands are soooooo frustrated because they have zero interest in ruining their career over a woman who's going to jump in bed with the next firefighter that comes along. Yes your husband will need to interact with her for the job. And yes they may ride a medic together all day. But can you imagine the extra pressure you are putting on him by quizzing and doubting his actions? And, do you think it's attractive to be jealous and doubtful like that? No way. The best thing you can do is make sure he leaves the house overflowing with love for you (on all levels—physical, mental, emotional, whatever way he needs his love). And tell him you TRUST him. Display the trust in him. Men thrive when their women admire and respect them at that level.

Defuse These Trust Traps in Your Fire Marriage
Here are a list of classic traps that firefighters and spouses can fall into if you are not being completely open and transparent with each other:

- What the firefighter did after shift when they did not get home at a normal time

- Bonus money and money hiding

- Distrustful activities occurring within the firehouse

- Lack of transparency from the spouse regarding activities at home

- Hiding feelings for fear of the unhappy reaction of the spouse

- How you handle working with the opposite sex

- How you handle working with other firefighters who are not honorable and committed

- Hanging around friends without the same level of integrity and commitment that you demand of each other

Aye! This chapter is prickly and bound to cause some sensitive discussions between couples who read this book, especially if you've been down the path of distrust and healing or are anywhere still walking that journey. Just go slow if needed. Trust topics are marathons for healing, not sprints, and they take much repetition to relearn how to trust each other. Knowing this alone should be motivation enough to always stay true and honorable in your marriage. That short fling is so not worth the damage that will be done when (not if) they find out.

HONOR GUARD

~ for the firefighter ~
Commitment to Trust
In a Fire Marriage

Firefighters we definitely put a lot of the burden of responsibility on you here because we are narrowly focused in on topics related to the fire life. Please don't take that the wrong way. I hate when I hear people say "all firefighters are cheaters" because I know how untrue that is. Those few bad apples though really ruin it for many. From this wife's perspective, if you are taking heat for any kind of lack of trust issue with your spouse related to the firehouse, let me give you some direct advice.

- She just wants to feel loved and wanted by you and you only. She wants to receive the best of you and may get jealous if the best of you is being spent at the firehouse and nothing is saved to remind her of your lifelong commitment together.

- Choose to spend time with friends and when possible, crew members who share your values regarding marriage.

- When you don't have a choice and are partnered with wild single firefighter who comments on anything walking down the street on two legs, just be honest with your wife. "I have to ride with Joe again today but I'm going to try to be a positive influence on his poor choices." It's best to just be upfront about the challenge as opposed to hiding it because she may be upset.

- Don't get defensive when she shows jealousy. She's not trying to be controlling, she is feeling insecure. Insecurity is corrected by filling love tanks (and teaching her to love herself but you will go a long way in helping her to do that with the right words and actions.)

- Choose to skip the crew party if it's going to cause tension and stress in your marriage.

- You may not be a talker naturally so when you do share a little extra, she is going to really notice. Sometimes it is really that simple.

- If you've been beating your head against this trust wall for a long time, please go to counseling together. It's not scary. It's super helpful and as counselor recently shared with me, it's a way to fast forward a bit and short cycle the journey through self-growth and healing in your relationship.

~ for the spouse ~
Commitment to Trust
In a Fire Marriage

Spouses, in the fire life, this is one topic that sends frantic wives to our community over and over. It's not everyone's issue but when it is an issue, it's a big one. Here is a summary of our best advice for building and maintaining trust in your fire life marriage.

- Be confident in yourself. He picked you! Out of a bazillion women in the world. He picked you for forever. Self-doubt and insecurity are not very attractive features in any girl.

- Know his love language and keep his love tank filled up. When both spouses are satisfied in their marriage, there is way less reason for eyes to roam.

- Avoid becoming defensive, controlling and judging in conversations. Those habits will signal for him to stop communicating because it's so painful every time.

- Don't put the blame on the fire service. There's nothing "the fire service" can do about it. If you have trust issues, then the accountability is on you and your spouse to work through them together, within this fire life that you chose. Leaving the fire service is not going to correct it, nor even changing to another station. You must fix the root problem driving you apart.

- If the distrust is from your firefighter directed to you, be sure you are understanding where those hurts and doubts are stemming from in him. Are there past incidents in other relationships that could be surfacing? Vow to work through this with him with patience and respect.

– *for discussion* –

- Share some potentially tempting situations you walked through successfully with complete trust as a couple.

- In what areas of your relationship do you have complete, full transparency and trust?

- Where do you have even small doubts that you wish you could work through with your spouse?

- Who in your life is a helpful experienced married couple to give advice in this area?

- What are three things you can practice better in your marriage to keep the trust whole and complete?

RESOURCES

All resources mentioned in this chapter can be found at
HonorAndCommitment.com/Chapter11

Resources include:

- Dan Mercer—Messaging the opposite sex video
- One Extraordinary Marriage "The Trust Factor"

12 Committed Intimacy

This whole book would be incomplete if we left out an extremely important aspect of marriage—intimacy. Years ago, I may have blushed and said, "that's private," and not included this. Some of you are reading this thinking, yeah, now we're getting to the good stuff. You're right about that. I'm pretty sure when we held our first Commitment Weekend event in Atlanta in July 2013, most of the men were there due to the fact, since their wives connected with this group of women online, their sex lives had improved. So keep reading if you need to understand exactly how that works.

We've already talked about "Love Languages", one of which is physical touch. For some people, physical touch is a very legitimate love language. For some men it's their way of saying "I need more sex in my life." *The Love Languages* book goes into good detail about discerning the need there. We have long-known the emotional power of physical touch. That's why we pick up babies and touch them tenderly. Long before an infant understands the meaning of the word love, he or she feels loved by physical touch.

In marriage, the love language of physical touch includes everything from putting a hand on your mate's shoulder as you walk by, touching his or her leg as you're driving together, and holding hands while you're walking to kissing, embracing, and sexual intercourse. If physical touch is your spouse's primary love language, nothing communicates love more clearly than for you to take the initiative to reach out and touch your mate.

- Hold hands
- Greet with an embrace
- Kiss forehead
- Appropriate PDA
- Massages
- Hold hand, place hand on arm, rub back
- Fingers in hair
- Show them how much you missed them by the way you physically greet them

Literally as I write this, it's 8:30 am and my husband just returned from a 48-hour shift. I woke up around 6am to start writing in the comfort of my warm bed (my best creative hours), and now my husband and 2 children have joined us in what we like to call our family puppy pile. I was literally craving the physical touch of the warm, strong hand of my husband over my shoulder. Before he touched me, I didn't even realize how much I was missing it. Our family is very "high touch". Big, tight hugs tend to calm children down. Wrestling matches are requested often. When I can't get through my husband's tired irritability with words, I know that the promise of a neck and scalp massage will never be turned down and will soften him up to finally share what's frustrating him. But we're not here to just talk about the power of touch. This is about that special kind you share only with your spouse.

As our Fire Wife Sisterhood network began to form and girls like me were finally connecting with women who understood the nuances of the fire life, a very special bond happened I never could have predicted. When women find a safe network of other women, the conversation can get very personal. Women will say things to each other they haven't admitted out loud in decades. Whether it was a deep hurt they were experiencing in their marriage, or the topic which surprised me, talking about their sexual needs.

Teenage girls openly talk about their bodies and sex too much, in my opinion, considering they're still wrapped up in the dating scene. It's because they have a safe place to do so with their closest girl friends.

I'd venture to say that a lot of 25 - 55 year old married women don't do that as often. When this "girl talk" started to happening within the Fire Wife Sisterhood I was definitely blushing behind the keyboard and having one of those "oh crap" kind of thoughts. As the blogger behind all of this, I'm going to have to blog about our sex life. Not that it was bad, but certainly getting that transparent about our private life would be a stretch for my husband and I, who can be conservative in that space. Besides, we don't want our sex life googled by someone at our kids' school just for the embarrassment effect.

So the first thing we shared was classic Mrs. Pragmatic and Practical Lori material, "Scheduling Sex." Truthfully, when you layout the fire schedule, toss in a couple nights with sick kiddos, and a couple more for that time of the month, you have maybe 10 opportunities for intimacy a month. I wasn't into wasting any of those days. While I didn't literally schedule it or write it on my calendar, it was on my mind as I did my monthly and weekly planning. What nights are we sleeping in the same bed this week? On those nights, I made sure the evening ran to plan and bedtimes were not too late so we had some quiet time together.

■ ■ ■ ■ ■ ■ ■ ■ ■ ■ ■ ■

"Yes, the fire life has an impact on your sex life."

■ ■ ■ ■ ■ ■ ■ ■ ■ ■ ■ ■

The conversation in the Fire Wife Sisterhood however pressed onward into the uncomfortable zone. Some women are definitely more open and comfortable with this topic than others who are more of the "don't kiss and tell" mindset. The best part was that we were able to meet in the middle, and we've found ways to address this topic that challenge us to get out of our comfort zones in the bedroom without having to share details we aren't comfortable sharing. I can confidently state that even after a decade of marriage, our sex life (which we had no complaints about) kicked up another few notches thanks to the "girl talk" that was shared in the Fire Wife Sisterhood. Let's hear it for girl talk!

Yes, the fire life has an impact on your sex life. First of all, guys who are ok with running into a burning building have a lot of testosterone, probably more than the average guy. Yes that can transfer to the bedroom as well. Whoa. What are we going to do with all that sexual energy? Add it to the list of why marrying a firefighter is both exciting, a bit like winning the lottery of "sexy professions," and also once again complicated.

Intimacy is already one of the most complicated subjects individually because our views on sex are so tainted by society, media, our upbringings, and experiences. Please don't think we are trying to generalize all firefighters as one way or another here. Like any marriage topic, there are complete programs and specialized counselors for intimacy. We can't cover all of that in one chapter. If your marriage is already having some communication struggles (and most are in one category or another), then it's likely you haven't ventured too far into communication about intimacy. Let's be honest. It's easier to just turn off the lights, hop into bed naked, and let your bodies do the talking.

Let's start with this. I haven't directly stated in this book that I'm a Christian because while it's an important part of me, it's an unnecessary qualification to reading this book and getting good stuff out of it. But it helps to drive home a point in this chapter. A lot of Christians are pretty conservative about intimacy, however we believe (as do many others) that the bible shows us that sex in marriage is designed to be a hot, beautiful, amazing experience between husband and wife. Yes, Jesus wants you to have hot sex with your spouse! So we're going to be sure we are doing the obedient Christian marriage thing and ensuring our spouses are satisfied in all aspects of our marriage, including the bedroom, laundry room, shower, kitchen table, or wherever your satisfaction is met.

Back to the thoughts on scheduling sex and managing that extra testosterone. Once you understand this as a fire couple, you take a step forward in understanding and making intimacy work for you. Some wives in the Fire Wife Sisterhood used to say "once every three days is minimum wage". While there is a lot of truth to that statement, we aren't here to say how much sex is enough in your marriage. It's a personal decision. However making the realization that if you don't try to have sex at least once between shifts (one a 24-on, 48-off schedule), it could be another 6 days before you are intimate again. Long windows between physical intimacy can create wedges between spouses in a marriage. Physical intimacy, even if the act of sex does not happen each time, soften hearts, connects you as a couple, and is truly an innate need of all human beings. These are acts only shared between the two of you. It's a privilege. No one else is made to touch you like that, and no one else can fulfill that need. If you are struggling to get on the same page about parenting, house chores, finances, or pick your favorite topic to argue about, then jumping in bed together is one way to reconnect, release that stress, and remember how much you still love each other.

■ ■ ■ ■ ■ ■ ■ ■ ■ ■ ■ ■ ■

"It can be difficult to be physically intimate when the emotional love tank isn't full and there are unresolved issues to talk through."

■ ■ ■ ■ ■ ■ ■ ■ ■ ■ ■ ■ ■

Intimacy Starts With Words

Just a reminder that intimacy comes in many forms, not just sex and not just physical. Especially for women. It can be difficult to be physically intimate when the emotional love tank isn't full and there are unresolved issues to talk through. Got it? You may try everything in this section without success because you have an emotional barrier you need to break through and grow back into that place of trusted intimacy in your marriage. This is a great use of a counselor, and what a reward—to be able to be joyfully intimate with your spouse again. If there does happen to be a big fight or even a period of time when you are just in a funk with your marriage, is there any kind of sex better than make up sex?

The Who Initiates Dance

You lay down in bed and think "Does she want to? Why did she roll over that way?" Then you do a little test by running your hand down her back looking for a reaction. The crazy thing is you are married! This isn't an 8th grade date to the movie theater. If you have taken part in our Marriage On Fire training, you hear Tony and Alisa DiLorenzo share a "system" that has worked for them where they have talked about and split the responsibility for initiating. You don't want sex to feel sterile and planned. "Ok honey. It's time now for you to start our sex fun." You still want to know that your spouse desires you and wants you. So their suggestion is to set days of opportunity for each spouse to be the initiator. This avoids those moments where you are lying in bed and both of you are thinking but not saying, "I wonder if she wants to have sex? I don't want to bother her if she's too tired." What a great tip. Follow their podcasts and programs listed in our resource section for more great topics on intimacy.

Anticipation Is the Best Form of Foreplay

So you've got a 24 or a 48 hour shift until you see each other again? Game. On. Let the text message foreplay begin. Truly anticipation is the best form of foreplay. It can start with the kiss you leave him/her with before they leave for shift and continue with a surprise you sneak into the gear bag or leave behind at home. Follow it up with a trail of sexy text messages until that shift ends, and all you can think about is getting your hands on each other. (I bet you are getting hot and bothered just reading about that. Use it to your benefit. Your spouse doesn't have to know where you got the inspiration.)

I totally see this as one of the best perks of the fire life. Absence makes the heart grow fonder and fires up those hormones like almost nothing else.

Confidence Is the Sexiest Thing You Can Wear to Bed

There are a large percentage of women reading this and still feeling quite uncomfortable. I know what you are thinking. I don't like my body. I don't look good enough for him. I'm embarrassed to wear lingerie to bed. I just throw on an oversized t-shirt every night. The sexiest thing for a man to see is a confident woman who knows and loves herself right where she is. Consider if your negative self talk has contributed to a decline in your sex life. Better yet, be brave. Give it a try.

Make Your Bedroom Your Sanctuary

A common mistake that's easy to fix is putting ourselves last. Your bedroom is the one place in your house that you share personally and intimately together. If you've ever had firefighters help you to move, then you've had one of them walk into your bedroom and say, "So this is where the magic happens?" Jokesters. The whole lot of them. When we moved into our current house 11 years ago, for some reason our bedroom was the first to come together. It was a random accident but when it did I felt such relief. At night we'd walk into our bedroom and breathe a sigh of relaxation and crash into our bed together in bliss. No matter what the day held, we were in the safe sanctuary of our bedroom. We had invested in a good mattress (best ever investment!), painted it a soothing color, removed clutter, and added bedside lighting which brought a calming and romantic ambiance. Your bedroom doesn't even have to be big for this to happen. At least as a spouse, you spend a third of your life there so why not put a little more effort into it? This is one place I say go crazy on Pinterest for some inspiring ideas. Bedroom makeovers are affordable and fun. All couples need that place they can walk into that relieves the stress of the outside world.

■ ■ ■ ■ ■ ■ ■ ■ ■ ■ ■ ■ ■

"Missing that alone time for long periods is a surefire way into a difficult season."

■ ■ ■ ■ ■ ■ ■ ■ ■ ■ ■ ■

Why Is Hotel Sex Better?

Even with the best bedroom environment, you all know this is true. Hotel sex is best. Why is that? Perhaps it's the thrill of being in a new place or the fact that there is zero chance anyone, child, furry creature or otherwise, is going to bust into the bedroom. Sometimes in nice hotels it truly is the bed and linens (once you get beyond any concerns with bed bugs, right?) There is a reason hotels have catalogs in their room with a pillow menu and offering to sell you their duvet covers.

Our message here is this. Get away from the normal if you need a reconnection in your marriage. One night at a hotel with nothing to focus on but each other is the best source of love tank filling of all. Our Commitment Weekend events are in a large part designed just for that. They are meant to be a reason to connect in a fun and intimate way with a community of who gets your fire life. Honestly, I don't care where you go to get away as a couple, but I'm going to demand that you do it. That's right. I said demand. Missing that alone time for long periods is a surefire way to lead into a difficult season. Besides, marriage was meant to be fun, just like when you were dating. So don't forget that and get out there and live it up like the summer of '69 (If you aren't old enough to remember that, Google it.)

When Intimacy Goes Bad. A Warning About Pornograpy.

I'll go out on a limb here and state something for which there has been no solid research, but for which you will all likely agree. You can find some form of pornography in almost every firehouse in America. Even if it's a Maxim magazine lying around the bathroom, there is something in that chest thumping, old school, salty fireman mentality that ok'd this as an aspect of tough guy jobs like firefighting. I'm not here to demasculinize the profession or firefighters in anyway. However there are plenty of statistics and facts to show you now that pornography is an addiction that harms your sex life and does not improve it.

We aren't the only ones speaking out on this topic. Fight The New Drug is a non-profit whose mission is to provide individuals the opportunity to make an informed decision regarding pornography by raising awareness on its harmful effects using only science, facts, and personal accounts. They are driven by the facts that show how pornography truly changes our brains.

> "Neurons that fire together, wire together. Just like other addictive substances, porn floods the brain with dopamine. That rush of brain chemicals happening over and over again rewires the brain's reward pathway ultimately changing the make up of the viewer's brain. This can result in an increased appetite for porn."

■ ■ ■ ■ ■ ■ ■ ■ ■ ■ ■ ■

"Pornography does not help. It ruins your marriage's sex life."

■ ■ ■ ■ ■ ■ ■ ■ ■ ■ ■ ■

As a porn user, your appetite increases like an addict. You are no longer satisfied with the intimate personal relations with your spouse. Pornography does not help. It ruins your marriage's sex life. Yes, yes, I know someone reading this right now is saying "but we agreed together to watch pornography in our marriage." Don't throw this book down, but we challenge you to try it without. Read some of these materials, and then make an informed decision.

Pornography use is especially damaging to marriages when only one spouse participates and does so in secret. The access is so available these days with the internet, apps, and everyone having their own personal devices. Now add to that so many nights / days apart in the fire life, and firehouses being an environment where pornography use is not just accepted but expected, and you've got a recipe for big problems.

In case you're still raising your eyebrows about this topic, we encourage you to watch the videos available at 247commitment.org/pornography from organizations such as Fight The New Drug. Here are a couple more personal accounts from wives of firefighters describing what pornography did to their marriages.

> "Porn is so accepted by so many people, and many do not realize the impact it can have. I used to belong to a mom's group on Facbook, and the message regarding porn there was: ALL men watch porn. If you think your guy doesn't watch it, your head is in the sand. If he tells you he doesn't, he's lying. If you don't like it, you're a prude. Only those who watch it with their husbands and support it are "cool." My husband used to be addicted to porn, beginning as a teenager (and encouraged by his father), and it hurt me deeply. He is very respectful of my feelings about it now, and, as far as I know (and I trust him), he has stayed away from it for some time. He even averts his eyes when a Victoria's Secret commercial comes on—at least around me. ((Hugs)) to everyone who is going through this struggle right now. I know just how much it hurts."

> "I have a very personal disgust for porn because my husband became addicted as a teen. I didn't even know until after we were married, and when he confessed it to me one night. It

broke my heart. I felt betrayed and completely inadequate. And seeing how it hurt me, he was also crushed. I'm not even sure why he told me. I think he just needed some accountability and felt he had no one else to tell. It is still a daily struggle for him, even though he doesn't willingly look for it anymore, but when you work with nothing but men…it comes up. It is also a daily struggle for me to not overthink things. So no, I strongly recommend against it. For the record, I don't want my husband to go down as a bad husband or man. I seriously hit the jackpot with him! He definitely has his struggles, but he is an amazing husband and father. And he always considers my feelings, which is why I think he struggles so much in the first place! And since we have gotten to the place where we can discuss it calmly, our sex life has become so much healthier!"

We hope that left you with some thoughtful considerations.

Now let's close this topic out with our favorite tips and hints as learned in the Fire Wife Sisterhood for your intimate life.

Pineapples, Cookies, and Coconut Oil

It all began with pineapples. Yes one more "advanced' fire wife shared with us that pineapple (and other foods) can change the flavor of certain bodily fluids such as those sexual juices. You can thank us for that little giggle you will now exchange whenever you see the use of pineapple anywhere such as, on your child's homework assignment, on your church's bulletin cover, and in clever titles of recipes on Pinterest.

While some are rather open about the topic of sex, others are more reserved. You may want to have a conversation about sex while in the company of little ears and for that case, it's helpful to have a code word. In the Fire Wife Sisterhood we discovered that some couples already have code words for this. "Want to have ice cream later?" Within the Sisterhood, one wife shared that on playdates with her good friend, they chose to call it "baking cookies." That name stuck and we have gotten miles and miles of entertainment out of that code word. It's an innocent and classy way to share a bit about your intimate life.

If you take only one thing away from this chapter it's coconut oil. Thanks to the more assertive wives in our Sisterhood it has been well shared that coconut oil is the best natural additive to intimacy. Safely apply anywhere. We'll just leave it there.

What if We've Been Having Sex for 10 Years Already and There's Something I Don't Like?

It happens! You get so into a routine with your sex life and want to please your spouse, exactly how can you tell them that one position they enjoy is not your favorite or causes pain? (Women's bodies change. It happens.) Trust that your spouse wants the best for both of you and use it as an opportunity to explore something new. Ladies, be brave and find that right moment to bring this up. It's helpful to be prepared to suggest an alternative, possibly new and different. This could be where being connected with your tribe of women is helpful. It allows you to open the conversation with something like "I know we've been doing it this way forever but I learned something new from this wives community I am a part of that might make this better."

If you read all the way through this chapter with a sense of sadness and grief because you are in a marriage that is lacking sex, you are not alone. I want to share this story from one of our fire wives. There is intimacy for you too.

■ ■ ■ ■ ■ ■ ■ ■ ■ ■ ■ ■

"Do not compare your sex life to that of others."

■ ■ ■ ■ ■ ■ ■ ■ ■ ■ ■ ■

Our Marriage Is Sexless

There is no one size fits all marriage. Each and every single marriage has its differences, its successes and it's struggles. Some struggles can be too hard to share. For men and women alike, sharing that their marriage has little to no sex life can feel too heavy. Not talking to each other about it makes it that much heavier and leaves too much room for speculation.

When you aren't communicating, you're setting yourselves up to come to your own conclusions. Your mind is wandering to places of the worst kind thinking it's an affair, a matter of not being attractive enough or thinking there is something wrong with you or them. Are you chewing on these feelings and letting them affect your relationship even further? There are so many reasons why your spouse may not be interested in having sex and most of these reasons can be helped or reversed.

Do not compare your sex life to that of others.

If you and your spouse are mutually happy with not having sex as often as other couples, you have no problem! There is no room for comparison to other marriages. What is right for one is not right for them all.

If I listed everything that could affect a couple's sex life, the list would be a mile long. To touch on a few, here is a short list…

- Exhaustion
- Work schedules
- Medication Side Effects
- PTSD
- Depression
- Medical Condition
- Low Testosterone
- Low Self Esteem
- Pornography Addiction
- Bitterness
- Children

Shaking your head yes? I'm sure dozens have other things they could add to the list.

Our friends over at Engaged Marriage describe it like this:

Now I'm going to say the most obvious statement that may make you want to run…

You have to talk about this to your spouse.

How does your spouse know you want to improve your intimacy if you haven't told them? Even in a marriage where there is enough sex, there may be something you want to change up. And if you've been intimate with this person for 10 years, it may seem odd to say "Hey, I'd prefer if we…." Being open verbally about moments where you are so vulnerable and open with each other physically may not be easy. But have the courage to try and take that intimacy to the next level.

Just be sure your spouse knows that you love them no matter what but miss their touch and will do anything to help them work through what's going on. It's likely to be a challenging conversation but when you take the courage to break through that wall there is progress.

Or, perhaps you have talked about the lack of sex in your marriage but you are at a standstill.

Someone who is depressed or struggling with PTSD or a medical side effect, may just not be in a motivated enough place to know what to do. It's one of those seasons when you carry your spouse through the valley. If we don't feel whole ourselves, it's nearly impossible to give in your marriage.

Don't Be Embarrassed. This isn't something obvious everyone should know.

Some problems could be solved as easily as learning each other's Love Language and getting those love tanks filled back up. Maybe a helping hand around the house or other act of service to help carry the load. A nice massage at bedtime? Others may require a visit to your doctor for tests and options, or perhaps a marriage counselor to help wounds that are preventing you from becoming intimate with your spouse. Do not let these concerns cause you to be embarrassed or ashamed. Working on your marriage, in any aspect, is admirable.

■ ■ ■ ■ ■ ■ ■ ■ ■ ■ ■ ■ ■

"Being intimate doesn't mean strictly sex; it can mean anything that brings closeness to your relationship."

■ ■ ■ ■ ■ ■ ■ ■ ■ ■ ■ ■ ■

When there is no sex, work on your intimacy in other ways. Being intimate doesn't mean strictly sex, it can mean anything that brings closeness to your relationship. So many simple acts can build intimacy. Actions, touching, sharing, anything that helps fill the emotional and mental need to be close to your spouse. I think that intimacy is more important than sex alone in any relationship. Everything in marriage takes work and this is no exception.

■ ■ ■ ■ ■ ■ ■ ■ ■ ■ ■ ■ ■

If you read this on a shift day, don't bother with the cold shower, have fun with the warm up until you are both together again so you can "bake some cookies."

HONOR GUARD

~ for the firefighter ~
Committed Intimacy

Guys, are we wrong here? Did you like this chapter? I haven't found many who complain about our important inclusion of the sexual health of our marriages as part of the 24-7 COMMITMENT lifestyle. If your spouse is not fully on board with this, here are a few tips we can share with you.

- Pressure is the wrong tactic to take when wanting to make changes in the bedroom. An understanding viewpoint is going to be more effective than a demand.

- Patience. If their love tank has been low for some time, figure out how to fill it up. And enjoy every moment of doing that which will lead you again to physical intimacy.

- Have there been mis-steps or perception of infidelity? It takes time to recover from those moments.

- Is she a busy, busy girl? Helping her to clear her plate and get into the relaxed space is a way better mindset for intimacy than the one where she's laying in bed already going over tomorrow overwhelming to do list.

- Never compare. Never ever compare to anyone else's body or sex life.

- Tell her how sexy she is and what turns you on about her while expecting nothing in return.

- If she is not satisfied with her body, overweight, or experiencing some health problems of any sort, vow to get healthy and fit together. Sweating it up together in the gym can be a big turn on. And watching each other's bodies transform is so rewarding.

- Take care of yourself when you are off shift. Don't just shave and shower and smell good as you are heading out the door. Do so for your days at home as well.

- If she's missing that community of women, it's best to get her into something like the Fire Wife Sisterhood so she has a safe place to let her guard down and work through whatever may be holding her back.

- If pornography is an issue in your life, get help from one of the resources we share below.

~ for the spouse ~

Committed Intimacy

This is such a personal topic. You may be really open about it or it might make you blush just reading this. Let's summarize the best points for the spouse:

- Even after 10 or 20 years, don't be afraid to talk about your sex life and change things up if needed.

- Always consider satisfying your spouse's sexual needs before they head off for a long shift. Not only does it send them off on a good note, you never want to have that regret of leaving on a bad note; God forbid something were to happen on that shift.

- Dress up and feel good about yourself, even when just around home and hanging out with your spouse. A little extra attention to your hair, clothes, or accessories can be a big turn on.

- Women, get connected in a community of women you can trust for the kind of girl talk that will be beneficial for your marriage. Don't feel pressured, but be educated and inspired.

- for discussion -

- What did you learn from this chapter you want to apply in your marriage?

- Is there something you've been doing intimately for years that is no longer working and needs to be changed up?

- How do you feel about pornography use in your marriage?

- Do you have communities of same sex friends where you can have safe, healthy, educational discussions about sex?

- What is the best way for each of you to get into the mood?

- When's the last time you had a night away together? Reminisce and start planning your next adventure.

RESOURCES

All resources mentioned in this chapter can be found at
HonorAndCommitment.com/Chapter12

Resources include:

- Lori Mercer Video: Nothin' Says Sexy Like A Chart

- Our eBook "100 Love Texts" that will bring you 100 ideas to stay connected via creative text messages

- "12 Steamy Days With Your Firefighter" free eBook

  Whether you are more on the wild side or the conservative side, this eBook will light a fire in your bedroom for you sure. There is something for everyone. Looking to spice up your bedroom a little? Or maybe that thought makes you nervous and you just want to show your firefighter a little extra love. This Free eBook contains lots of ideas from just gift giving to love notes to some slightly too hot to mention ideas, all suggested by the Fire Wives of FirefighterWife.com. We're lucky if we get to sleep with him 3 or 4 nights in a row, not to mention 2 am pagers and sheer exhaustion and stress that make it difficult to find times to enjoy your firefighter intimately. If you're stuck in a rut, try some of these ideas to get your groove back on.

- 247commitment.org/pornography—Resources to inform and support you with pornography addiction.

SECTION 3

A New Level of Commitment

From the beginning to the end, I commit to be an honorable firefighter / spouse in both the darkest hours and the glorious celebrations. Let my contagious commitment expose the fire service to a new culture of honor.

13 Beyond the Firefighting Commitment
Training and Promotions

•

So you've made it this far. 13 chapters! (It's also ok to skip around in this book by the way.) When we started outlining this book and writing sections, I was shocked at how big it was getting. I asked my pre-readers what we could cut because I was worried people wouldn't pick up a big book. They said NOTHING. It's all needed. And they are so right because we've come this far and not even touched on these aspects of the fire life that most others don't understand. Just like we don't understand what it's like to be married to the on-call brain surgeon or the regional sales rep for a pharmaceutical company or a high school principal for example.

Just getting the job as a firefighter is a long dedicated journey of hard work and determination. You celebrate for a moment and get ready to pound out that rookie year. Next comes more training and additional responsibility and volunteer assignments and promotional testing and for some, medic school as well. The good news is that these are each just a season, with many "off seasons" in between. Each of these seasons is typically going to bring more benefit to your firefighting career and family. Toughing it out through these seasons can be challenging but is totally doable and the rewards are sweet. If you remember all the way back to chapter 1, a lot of the same principles apply here. There are times when you and your family can take on these extra challenges, and times when it may be better to say no, for the moment. The best approach is to do it as a team. While as a firefighter, there will be many extra demands in these seasons, your family will be picking up the extra load at home, and most of all, everyone will really be missing the family time.

Often it seems unfair. For the most part, firefighters are making these sacrifices for the love and passion for the job, as there isn't a big bonus check at the end of the season like there may be for the sales executive who pounded through 6 months of non-stop travel to be rewarded with $20 - 30K and whisks their family off to Hawaii. No one gets into firefighting for the good pay. Yes they may do it for the steady work, but not typically for big paychecks. Let's venture through these seasons and what to expect for your fire life.

First Up, Fire Academy

For some departments, when you are hired you are immediately enrolled into a fire academy. This looks like a lot of different things but to make an analogy (that our military friends will rightfully disagree with), it's a bit like a boot camp to initiate the firefighters to this department's processes and protocols, but you don't have to do it away from home. There is PT (physical training) and classroom work and lots of hands on training and yes tests. It's a test of willpower, endurance, intelligence, stamina, teamwork, emotional strength and more. To sum it up, the fire department sort of "owns you" for this season of 3–6 months on average. For a job that is so coveted with thousands applying and only a handful being accepted, no one wants to mess up the academy.

While the firefighters aren't living away at the academy, this can be a big strain on families. It's something you need to have one of those "all in" commitment huddles together as a family, come up with your game plan, and then keep up the team spirit. The days feel long but the years are short and it will be over in no time.

■ ■ ■ ■ ■ ■ ■ ■ ■ ■ ■ ■ ■

"Repeat this if needed. It's only for a season. It's only for a season. It's only for a season."

■ ■ ■ ■ ■ ■ ■ ■ ■ ■ ■ ■ ■

This season introduces different logistics challenges. If you've been doing shift work, perhaps at a couple different part time fire departments, now you must adapt to a 40+ hour Monday–Friday week. For family financial purposes you may try to fit in some part time work as well.

If you aren't yet hired on as a firefighter and are reading this to get an idea of the work, you may have considered putting yourself through a firefighting school and potentially EMS and medic school as well. This means living the college student life for a bit seeking the funding to pay for school, perhaps working a part time job and living meagerly as a family on time and money. If you are married, it's not unusual for a spouse to pick up the load while the other is finishing schooling. What an amazing sacrifice! These are the kinds of choices together as a couple that demonstrate the commitment above all others. Now, if you remember our discussion of "enthusiastic agreement", this is an important decision to be sure you are both all in for, otherwise bitterness and resentment can build up which are two very ugly feelings to have in yourself and within your marriage. The lesson of this chapter is totally teamwork and the 24-7 COMMITMENT spirit. Repeat this if needed. It's only for a season. It's only for a season. It's only for a season.

Fire Academy season leaves you with a big giant unknown as you travel this road. Where will you be assigned? What shift day? The planning personalities everywhere carry anxiety about this question as it prevents them from scheduling much of anything out into the future. Where will you be for Christmas? Will there be a summer vacation? Can your spouse switch their schedule at work? And with children involved, the planning for the right childcare. The best approach to these questions is a light hearted "we don't know!" followed by a semi-maniacal laugh. Yes people will look at you and wonder if you are ok but this carefree and whimsical viewpoint may be your only option. It's not like you can march into the big Chief's office and threaten them to tell you. (Definitely don't do that. For the love of all things firefighting I can think of very few occasions marching into the chief's office is necessary, and if you are the spouse, there are zero reasons to do that.) Anyhow at this point, you should be still in the honeymoon season of "you're going to be a firefighter" and willing to bust through anything to fulfill that gift which has just been handed to you.

The Ever Changing Fire Service

Academy ends with much celebration and then you get to experience shift life for what feels like forever and ever until 25 or more years pass and retirement arrives. Twenty-Five-Years feels like forever when you are at the beginning. Some of you reading this LOVE your job (in all caps, just like that). You don't understand this statement. I mean, you're supposed to love your job. It's the dream job for every little kid and here you are living the dream. Except that you got assigned to a crappy station with a bad attitude crew and your love for the job is overshadowed by messy people junk. It happens. It happens all over the fire service yet very few people are talking about it because this brave, heroic (most of you firefighters dislike that word and I totally get it), individual is working your dream job. There shouldn't be room to dislike it right?

I can recall so many situations where I thought to myself, "This is it. He's reached the end of his rope and is going to quit." The first few rounds of that were quite anxiety inducing for me as it touched on some history of mine with an ex-husband who didn't want to work because I had a good job. Queue the past baggage coming into play. After we survived a couple seasons of this, I learned one super important point. The structure and rigidity of the fire service in regards to promotions and crew assignments may seem like it's going to last forever, and in some stations it does. The reality is you are probably right around the corner from another change. Someone gets injured and is off for 2 months, someone retires sooner than planned or someone transfers to a different department or puts in for a crew transfer and it's accepted. Anyone of those scenarios can change up the dynamics within a crew or department significantly and bring relief to a stressful season. I must confess there have been seasons where I've prayed for some individuals to take a surprise, happy-ending transfer or retirement just to spare that crew more heartache. When it happens, relief floods my husband's face and body and we move back into that mode where we know we've got this fire life thing mastered.

Nothing ever stays the same in the fire service. When you are at your wits end and frustrated with a crew, a partner, a policy, an officer in charge, and you've taken all you can of biting your tongue and doing the right thing and your family is done hearing about it, something is bound to change.

If that change doesn't come fast enough, you can change. There are a lot of different aspects to be involved in as a firefighter to change your focus and find new purpose. Here are a few more opportunities to keep reinventing your fire life along the way.

The Union

Frustrated with decisions of the city you work for or concerned about safety or other practices at your department? If your department has a union, you can take a more active role in many ways from being an officer to assisting with the endless work that non-profit organizations always have on their to do list.

For families, here is something you may not expect to be added to your fire life. Union meetings are frequently not on a shift day. For us, they are often right after roll call requiring my husband to stay later than usual. This would sometimes wreak havoc on our childcare/work schedules, especially when they were surprise announcements at 10 PM the night before. "Oh, hey, I'm staying over tomorrow. There's a union meeting."

Deeper roles with the union include longer meetings and planning for negotiations, grievances, etc. and can also include road trips to state and national conferences.

I try to not make any judgments on union involvement in one way or another because it can be a politically charged topic and would be detrimental to our purpose in serving all fire families, unionized or not. So please don't read this in any other way except, the job never ends at just firefighting and union support is one more example.

Training, Training, Training

Training is a good thing, a very, very good thing. Training familiarizes firefighters with routines they need to know how to react to almost instinctually. The only way you learn those habits is by repetitively training on them. There are also new techniques, new risk, new equipment and tools and approaches always being developed to fight fires better and keep firefighters and the community safer. So we must be advocates for on-going training.

As a new wife, I was completely caught off guard by this aspect and it was a trigger for many arguments laced with thoughts like "He'd rather be with the fire department than us" or "Why does he get to have a job he loves so much he'll do it without pay while I'm slaving away over here working the grind?"

■ ■ ■ ■ ■ ■ ■ ■ ■ ■ ■ ■ ■

"Like any career, you must demonstrate you are willing to go above and beyond and continue to build your skills and your resume without becoming stagnant in the industry."

■ ■ ■ ■ ■ ■ ■ ■ ■ ■ ■ ■ ■

Training affects your schedule and is another time commitment outside of normal shift hours. When there is a significant training opportunity such as a live training burn or an instructor who is in the area holding a class, it's not always going to fall on a shift day, and it's not always going to be a paid activity. Oftentimes it's not mandated but still an unwritten expectation for anyone looking for future promotion. Sometimes, there is no training pay, no overtime pay and possibly no comp time offered either. Like any career, you must demonstrate you are willing to go above and beyond and continue to build your skills and your resume without becoming stagnant in the industry. Also like any career, it makes a big difference when your family is behind these commitments.

There is always a silver lining to get us through. **Those live training burns, when allowed by the trainer and safety crews, are the perfect opportunity for your family to watch firefighting in action.** Personally, the ladies really tend to enjoy this. Before I was married to a firefighter, I never really thought bunker gear was super attractive. It's big and bulky and often an ugly brown color with clashing reflective highlights. Go ahead and call me a weird girl. I may not be representing the average here. For me, it wasn't until I meet the guys wearing it and understand what they do that it becomes something symbolic of the honorable profession. Then I understood why women swoon over firefighters in gear and why they often show up to observe at a training fire. Yes it is a true statement that spouses can pick out their spouse by their swagger in turnout gear. They all may look the same when geared up aside from height and width but how they carry themselves is entirely recognizable by the ones who love them most. You don't need to be on any half-dressed firefighting calendar to fall in love with that. Equally important are the little kids in their firefighter costumes with wide eyes and a look of awe as they see how big, bad and dangerous fire really is and these firefighters grow to new heroic levels in their little minds. Lastly, there's no better place to capture amazing photography and action shots of firefighters doing what they love. Bring your camera or better yet hire a professional, because these are the memories you want to capture when you start to realize that 25 years is actually a pretty short profession.

Honor Guard and Pipes and Drums

If the Union is too politically charged but you still want to experience a fresh perspective to your firefighting career that keeps you motivated and engaged, then participating in the Honor Guard or Pipes and Drums clubs are other outlets. Both of these are honorable ways to represent your department and both also come without pay for extra time but for some of the most worthy reasons. These groups are the ones who represent to show their respects at funerals and memorials for fallen firefighters and others who are significant to that department including police or even family members.

The challenge for fire life becomes the last minute scheduling. No one ever wants to experience the loss of a loved one but of course it's a reality and when it happens, all hearts are on deck to bring support to that family. Honor Guard members are called to move on a moment's notice and be there for that purpose. Those who are able to meet this need must have that "all in" commitment agreement with their family to be able to provide this service.

Promotional Processes

Just when you get settled into a good fire life groove, it's time for another promotion cycle. Not every firefighter wants to promote, or thinks they want to promote but never say never. Also never count your chickens before they hatch because the promotional cycle is open to broad interpretation by the givers of the tests. The outcomes have been day time TV jaw droppers for decades and are a good reason more fire departments have not allowed reality TV to make it's way into firehouses.

Yes the fire service is paramilitaristic and standards and process based. However those processes can be changed on a whim by leadership and are done so for both great reasons and manipulative reasons. If you've been reading this far you know I'm not here to stroke any egos in the fire service, have my husband's blessing for these words and just want to fire families to have the truth and visibility into topics like this so they aren't blindsided. Having served fire families for the past four years, it's clear to me that the promotional processes can bring the most elated celebrations and at the same time the most unfair, trust busting, and bitterness causing decisions to firefighters and their families.

Did you know that a fire department could really have an open call for resumes to anyone and hire in whom they think is the best candidate for any position? So in theory, they could hire a Lieutenant from a neighboring department to step in as a Battalion Chief. Often there are outside candidates who are way more qualified and eager for the job than the internal prospects, especially at small departments. I hear frequently conversations such as "Well I guess I'll try for Captain when it's up because I'd hate to see _____ get it." So that department may end up with a less than enthusiastic Captain who took the job for all the wrong reasons. Why doesn't the fire department look outside it's own more often? I believe it's due to loyalty, tradition, politics, and the work it would take to officially change the written rules. It is also true that a firefighter who has been employed with you for some time is going to know and understand your department's procedures, atmosphere, crews and community better than someone new from the outside. Chief's are often hired from the outside but the recruiting stops there.

For a career that brings so much stress and pressure to an individual, the promotional process is often the light at the end of a long tunnel that will get them through one season and into the next. Competition is often high for promotion and firefighters are willing to go the extra mile to prepare. Many fire families have said "I didn't see him for 6 months because he was always studying for the promotional exam." It's that kind of sacrifice.

Even when the process is over, there is a high probability of not being promoted. In many departments, at the end of the promotional process you have a ranked candidates list that represents the order of the next to be assigned officers. Due to many of those frustrations and politics I won't go into here, it took my husband 13 years to get to the top of that list. At the time of this book writing, he's sitting at the top of that list with a strong likelihood that he will "die on the list" as no promotions were needed in this 2 year time period. This means another stressful period of retesting and aiming for that top spot.

The drama of being on the top of the list is worthy of reality TV. I could describe 4 instances where it looked like it might happen but the cards never fell as planned. One particular instance occurred during the month of December. The amount of hours my husband spent on the phone with others at the fire department during that month was absurd. I knew it was happening but I tried to be the good listening wife with the supportive but balanced input as feeding into his excitement, fears and frustrations would have only escalated the stress levels in our home, and it was Christmas time. At the end of it all, one of those "I can't believe this but I can understand why the chief took that path" decisions was made resulting in no promotions for anyone. The chief had good follow up conversations to set everyone's mind at ease and life moved on with the new assignments. But on that Christmas day, my husband said "I can't believe Christmas is already here. I feel like I didn't do anything to prepare." Honestly, he didn't. Everytime I tried to get his input on gift ideas or fun activities we wanted to do as a family, he was pulled away with phone calls and he basically missed Christmas that year. In fact, we were at a department store with all the kids doing that "divide and conquer" craziness where we each take a couple of the kids and they buy something for their sibling. (It's a complicated algorithm with 4 kids and 2 parents and knowing who can look into what shopping cart.) While we were in the middle of that trip, some emails were sent out regarding the decision for this new 40 hour position which could have created a promotion opportunity. The emails didn't tell the whole story and my husband spent half of that trip on the phone or texting trying to sort out what the decision really was, while I was half listening to his conversation just as eager to know the results. I'm just as much to blame here for missing much of that Christmas season. This promotion has been so eagerly anticipated in our home. I want nothing more than to see my husband achieve his goals. So I continued the shopping fervor allowing him to converse and dropped many holiday tasks just to sit and listen for him. It's the fire life. That's a pinnacle moment and a story we will look back on, we hope, with humor and not regret nor bitterness.

■ ■ ■ ■ ■ ■ ■ ■ ■ ■ ■ ■ ■ ■

"Leadership decisions can impact the stress levels of your firefighters and their home life as well."

■ ■ ■ ■ ■ ■ ■ ■ ■ ■ ■ ■ ■

Can We Minimize This Stress?

If you are a chief and you are reading this, I want to talk to you as a leader for a moment. Over my 22 year career as a corporate executive and business owner, I've managed multi-million dollar budgets and large teams of people and hired and fired and promoted many. You have the opportunity to set someone up for success. Leadership decisions can impact the stress levels of your firefighters and their home life as well. As a leader, you are under much stress for these decisions as well and your spouse is home getting an earful too. It's ok for promotional processes to be competitive. That's a positive. Leadership grooming is not only about the promotional process. Every member of your team should feel they are being given opportunities that match their growth needs and abilities and when the time comes for a promotion, tensions are naturally lower when everyone understands their role and their best fit and who naturally is the next best candidate for the job. That's super idealistic but to paint it the other way, when a leader plays favorites, changes the rules and practices manipulation in other areas of their leadership, no one is going to feel comfortable with the next decision coming down and the stress levels will rise. Be the kind of leader who has earned the trust of your team and built a culture of healthy fair competition.

My experience with observing the fire service says it's the rarity of the promotional cycle that elevates the stress levels around this process. In other professions, there are more opportunities to apply for new roles, change companies or laterally transfer than are offered in a fire department. So when the stakes are high, stress is high. It will never be entirely eliminated but an officer can build a culture of respect amongst all when there is trust in their actions and decisions. Frequently changing the promotional process requirements is one of the games I see played very often that doesn't demonstrate that trust. Oh, this time we're not going to use an outside assessment center. Oh, this time we are. It opens the opportunity for manipulating the results which is not a morale booster amongst men who are asked to perform to standards everyday on the job. My apologies for getting soap-boxy here. I never plan to be a fire chief but leadership is in my blood and I couldn't pass up the opportunity for explaining this from a leadership viewpoint. There are many excellent books and speakers on Honor & Commitment as a leader in the fire service and I would love the opportunity to keep pushing on excellence in that space. Leaders have the opportunity to soften the impact of many of the fire life challenges we address in this book and reverse the cultural trends we are seeing with behavioral health issues, marriage struggles and burnout amongst firefighters. The job is harder than it used to be and we must evolve together.

Passed Over, Again

So what happens when you are passed over again and again? Spouses who have experienced this can answer so well. Conversations range from complete career changes and walking away from years of pension to figuring out how to slug out another 8, 10, 15 years riding the box without your life's joy being sucked right out of you. As a wife, there is no more helpless feeling than watching your husband feel hopeless, unqualified and stuck in their job. They may go to work and say all the right things and smile and be respectful but you see their true heart and fall asleep together at night trying to comfort that broken soul.

Everything happens for a reason and hindsight is always clearer. You must believe this to lessen your disappointment. Believe there is a better alternative heading your way.

This chapter is about the seasons and this is another season. No matter how hard I try as a wife, I can't heal this. What can heal this and bring renewed hope and inspiration are the right words from an admired leader. As the one who is experiencing this let down, they may be in despair and not seeing obvious simple helps such as that. Encourage them to reach out to their leaders or others they respect and ask for feedback and steps for improvement. Ultimately it's a personal journey but no tough personal journey is easily traveled alone. We all need to be lifted up by encouraging community around us. If the culture at your fire department is more toxic than healthy, it may need to be sought elsewhere. If you need this bad, skip ahead to the next and final chapter right now. That's how important this message is. For the moment, we're going to wrap up this topic on "advanced fire life attack".

The Officer Fire Life

I'll share a secret that might be a total jinx for my husband's promotional opportunities but I have been planning in my head, since the first day he told me of his goals to be an officer, a gigantic celebration party for when it's finally achieved. I'm talking one of those parties where you rent out a hall and have food catered and invite everyone and their second cousin. Perhaps I'll feel differently when he reaches that milestone because I've not seen other fire families celebrate in this way but truly, it's been such a long awaited and desired event, it's worthy of much celebration.

> *"From the crew's perspective it looks elitist and impersonal. From the officer's perspective, it's a survival mechanism and heart breaking in some ways."*

I know why these parties don't happen though. There are expectations of officers and suddenly a divide in friendships. **People with whom you were previously friends you now must lead**, which means both praise them for what's done well and correct them for what's done wrong. That is a tough transition and 99% of fire officers who make that transition do so by distancing themselves a bit from the crew. From the crew's perspective it looks elitist and impersonal. From the officer's perspective, it's a survival mechanism and heart breaking in some ways. I'll share this story to help shed some practical light on the topic. As a friend, you want your crew to have good times together and bond over social events. As their officer, you can't sit at the crew Christmas party and watch alcohol lead to fist fights over what one firefighter said to another's girlfriend. Life happens and we're not judging that. **Officer roles require a new level of honor and commitment, and sacrifice.** New schools, more training, more phone calls off duty to be there for your crew if needed and more work taken home. It's no longer as simple as going in, riding your truck and following protocol.

Good leaders cannot turn off thoughts of the care and well being of their crew when the shift ends. Good leaders also have learned how to balance and prioritize more responsibilities but any transition to a new role is going to take a season to get used to that new normal. Don't be the officer who allows your new role to impact your family in a negative way. They still need to be your safe place to land for even more important conversations about leading people, and remember that people stuff is messy.

■ ■ ■ ■ ■ ■ ■ ■ ■ ■ ■ ■ ■

"There is nothing easy about that situation but there was no one else but you who was given that role as Officer and Officer's spouse to care for the firefighters and families on your crew."

■ ■ ■ ■ ■ ■ ■ ■ ■ ■ ■ ■

As the spouse of an officer, your role changes as well. Families you may have been close friends with could see you differently. As your husband shares concerns and thoughts about his crew with you, as happens in committed marriages, you are held to a new level to honor those conversations with respect and privacy. It's not comfortable then in some friendships. If Firefighter Jones is struggling to show up on time for shift, and you know his wife and she's complaining that he's staying out late drinking, you see what's going on. It's likely that Firefighter Jones' wife will even naturally distance herself from you knowing this information is potentially damaging to his career and suddenly it feels as though you've lost a friend. Or the opposite could happen and some desperate spouses could approach you hoping you can somehow help them, their family and influence your now Officer husband's decisions. Consider that a new honor and commitment to the fire life. There is nothing easy about that situation but there was no one else but you who was given that role as Officer and Officer's spouse to care for the firefighters and families on your crew. This topic alone is worthy of an entirely new book just for Officer's Wives. You may think you'll find friendship amongst the other officer's spouses but that's perhaps even trickier. Even amongst the other officer's wives there can be competition for the next promotion and politics.

As a leader, I can totally say that the phrase "it's lonely at the top" is absolutely truth. As my organization 24-7 COMMITMENT has grown, we went from a small, very personal group of firefighter's wives to over 100,000 followers with nearly 100 volunteers, a team of 10 people spread across the country and all the extra challenges you can imagine come with that. My heart has been broken in ways I never thought possible and then healed in ways I never thought possible as I grow into new styles of leadership. My friendly, personal style with which I am writing this book is the real me. I truly enjoy relating to and connecting to people of all kinds. As we started this journey, I was unfortunately just naive and trusting enough to realize that not everyone who wants to connect with me is doing so just to be friendly and supportive. As a leader, some people want to be your friend to influence your decisions and the moment something happens against their liking, they move on leaving a trail of ickiness. Others want a piece of the pie, either the money (FYI not so much of that in a non-profit) or some piece of the perceived glory. As a leader you know that the glory doesn't come without a lot of blood, sweat and tears and often doesn't feel so glorious. It's been a very uncomfortable season for my husband and I (and our marriage) as we learn to navigate leadership of a large organization.

I share this so those of you who are new officers, "old" officers who feel these challenges and your spouses can see that you aren't alone in those thoughts even as you feel alone in your roles. Your direct leaders should be supporting you through these phases but that doesn't always happen. Reach outside your immediate circles, especially outside the fire service or at least outside of your department, and be sure you are being filled up and strengthened both as individuals and as a couple to meet this new level of commitment being asked of you.

Your family wants to be your biggest cheerleaders in all steps of your career, yet they may not really understand what all those steps are, what they mean to your career growth and how to best support you. How do you help them to understand and still give them what they need in these seasons?

- Awareness as to what's required of these seasons is essential. Put this book in their hands with drastically obvious highlights and bookmarked pages if necessary.

- Expect the boat to rock a little and brace yourself for emotional stability as you steady it under the new norm.

- Know your limits and your family's limits. Take breaks well before you see the crash coming. How many days in a row can you go without family time?

- Keep yourself healthy. Pushing hard for a season is possible but there are limits. I know mine have been stretched when the common cold puts me on the couch for 6 days with aches and fever and loss of appetite. But that's too far. Know the signs sooner.

- Involve your family in some way in this season. Make countdown charts. Celebrate mini-milestones with special meals and activities.

- Find new ways to connect with them if they are finding you absent more. A special text message each morning is not too time consuming and can mean a lot.

- Before taking on new responsibilities, discuss it with your spouse and be sure you have enthusiastic agreement

- Planned activities always go over better than last minute "oh I forgot about this" announcements

- Understand how much your mood influences the mood of your household and find healthy ways to carry the extra stress, or in the case of disappointments, the frustration.

- Allow your spouse the occasional "break down" as you are in the midst of a season. It's tough to keep up on everything and sometimes a good cry and a sympathetic ear (and a good massage) can refuel the energy needed to carry on.

- Don't let these seasons with time away from your spouse create a desert and empty the love tank. Keep it going in "economy mode" and plan an amazing getaway at the end of this season for you to anticipate and look forward to together. 6 months of academy or medic school or studying for a promotional exam look way better when white sand beaches are a promised reward at the end of the journey.

~ for the spouse ~

Beyond the Firefighting Commitment Training and Promotions

This crazy fire life sometimes seems unfair with so much extra required. But you married someone who is committed to a career that many won't ever be able to perform and there is much honor in that. Just as they were made to be a firefighter, you were made to be their spouse and can roll with these aspects of the fire life. Don't forget these tips:

- Learn and understand these often unwritten requirements of the job. Be supportive of their need to participate in these activities

- Be honest with your feelings as you discuss moving into new opportunities. Hiding these feelings will only grow resentment. Be honest but open to compromises and solutions that will make these seasons work for your family.

- Be their best sounding board. There is no one else in the world they want to spend their time with so when you can be a good listener and confidante about their work topics, it's a very meaningful connection. (The alternative is to resent and resist what they are doing which drives wedges in marriage that are repairable but with much work.)

- There will be moments you break and need a sympathetic shoulder. Sometimes your spouse cannot immediately be that shoulder. Be ready to suck it up for just a bit until they are home and able to give you a "moment". In the meantime, ice cream and chocolate are acceptable temporary fill ins, but not permanent. They aren't friendly to the arteries and waistline in a long term relationship.

- Some spouses have helped with things like creating study cards or notecards for remembering facts for classes. Drug cards for medic school are one example. Ask how you can help. For my husband, I always help format resumes because I'm more proficient with Microsoft Office than he is and have an eye for formatting. It's the little things that save big frustrations.

- Don't let stinking-thinking convince you this season is going to last forever and you won't make it. That's just anxiety and fear talking and they need to leave on command. Go back to that countdown chart and your planned celebration for the end of this journey.

- for discussion -

- What are the career goals of the firefighter in your marriage? What may that journey look like and what sacrifices will it require? Consider time, financial, travel plans, family planning, house buying and job changing.

- What scares you about any of these steps? What thoughts bring you comfort and encouragement?

- How have you seen other fire families successfully (or unsuccessfully) navigate these seasons?

- Who is your support network to lean on as you travel these seasons?

RESOURCES

All resources mentioned in this chapter can be found at
HonorAndCommitment.com/Chapter13

14 Committed to Emotional Health
Dealing with Difficult Calls

There is perhaps not a more important chapter we can write in this book in regards to long term impact and the most serious challenges you may face as a fire family. Emotional health is essential to function in all areas of your life. No matter how much a firefighter says they're ok, they've handled it, they compartmentalize and deal with it, there is always the potential for a breaking point moment. That's what makes this topic so difficult. There are some warning signs, but often even the firefighter being affected is surprised at their own response.

The job is stressful on many levels. My husband summarized it in the intro like this:

"Doing this job can be difficult. I don't need to go on and on revisiting the topics we discuss at length that make the job unique in its stress and effort required. We can name them off the top of our head at this point. Sleep deprivation, exposure to circumstances that aren't ideal to witness, potential to miss meals, being unable to be present for a special occasion with your family, are all things we encounter that we know have an effect on us both in the moment and over time. Dealing with how you and your family make the best of each of these and the numerous other difficult scenarios that arise from our job are a personal decision."

Now let me be transparent to the most real and raw level we get with our personal story. These kind of emotional health challenges have contributed in a significant way to making our marriage a scary, unpredictable roller coaster ride that we have committed to hanging onto no matter what. Yes, even through our work here motivating and inspiring and educating marriages of firefighters, we are still right there with you in the trenches fighting every day for our own marriage. If you think that disqualifies us, well read this for what it's worth to you, but I believe writing those words are going to set someone free. This chapter represents the bravest thing anyone can do, firefighter or not. Digging into our fight, learning more about why this happens, and finding our own triggers and patterns is where we are. The battle changes often as we age, as our hormones change, as the stress thickens and lessens and with every new call he takes adding the monstrous list of bad memories piled up in his grief bucket.

■ ■ ■ ■ ■ ■ ■ ■ ■ ■ ■ ■ ■

"There are days and weeks even I need to just shut down and protect my own heart because it's too much to bear."

■ ■ ■ ■ ■ ■ ■ ■ ■ ■ ■ ■ ■

You're going to see some passionate anger flow out of me in this chapter unlike the others because I now know my grief bucket is getting filled up with the secondary effects of this. The numbers of stories of broken and failed marriages I've experienced since beginning this journey, and the impact of emotional health topics on those marriages, is simply overwhelming. There are days and weeks even I need to just shut down and protect my own heart because it's too much to bear. So when some keyboard quarterback on social media says things like "Stop over dramatizing PTSD. Not everyone has it," I get a little defensive. The last thing firefighters need is a reason to not address the issues they are facing. Defense certainly isn't the best tactic but it's a good clue to myself that I have some work to do here, both internally and externally for the cause. I can't stand by and do nothing. I'll admit, I'm a fixer by nature which is kind of weird for a woman. It pains me to see problems and know the root cause and not take any steps towards resolution. Yes, we are seeing the words PTSD and "Behavioral Health" all over the place. There are speakers and nice social media memes to share for effect. But what I am not seeing are the compelling words to drive people to actions that produce changes in their lives. Here's a fact you'll find interesting. The nationwide utilization rate of EAP services (Employee Assistance Programs that provide free counseling sessions to you and your family as offered by your employer) is 3-4%. If you have 100 employees, only 3 or 4 of them are seeking these free counseling services. Now I'm getting ahead of myself because you will see that counseling is essential to working through these personal topics.

My main point is action. How can we get you, the one reading this book, to take a step towards bettering your emotional health? Keep reading and let's see where we get by the end of this chapter.

Prevention Would Be Ideal

There are people who are good at handling this stuff, people who think they are good at handling this stuff, and people who probably break faster than others. If someone had that formula figured out, we'd put our toughest soldiers on the front lines and avoid the sad loss of life from PTSD and the subsequent suicides we are facing in the military and with first responders. Don't read this chapter and judge anyone. We've done everyone a disservice in these professions by not providing more prevention tools, screening methods, and support mechanisms. Could some people be more predisposed to PTSD and depression and anxiety than others? I believe so and research is hot on that trail. (cite research)

■ ■ ■ ■ ■ ■ ■ ■ ■ ■ ■ ■ ■

"He didn't use to be like this, isn't always like this, and what we are experiencing here is NOT my husband but an illness that has caught him in its snares."

■ ■ ■ ■ ■ ■ ■ ■ ■ ■ ■ ■ ■

How it Started for Us

Sometimes when you are in the heat of a battle for so long, you don't even realize how bad it is. Then you stick your head up, look around, get some perspective and realize life isn't meant to be this hard. Whether you believe in God or not, I bet you believe we are here live life fully and abundantly, not scared, fearful, cynical, and bitter.

I'll put it to you bluntly. There have been times in my life I was thoroughly convinced I had simply married (another) a$$. (I warned you this chapter is a little rough.) When you've been divorced once, it's easy to question yourself and think, do I attract them? But then my heart softens and my mind opens and I see things for what they are. He didn't use to be like this, isn't always like this, and what we are experiencing here is NOT my husband but an illness that has caught him in its snares. As the spouse, when you can separate the illness impact from the person's heart and soul, things begin to get clear. You are able to become an aid to the recovery and not a secondary victim to its effects.

It all starts with a few google searches these days right? You can find practically anything to support your suspicions if you google and dig a little. In this case, I didn't really have to dig as I discovered lists of symptoms of PTSD consistently everywhere. The further I read, the more clear it became.

Irritability. Bad dreams. Depression. No emotions at all. On edge. Outbursts. Trouble sleeping. Flashbacks. Anxiety. Self-destructive behavior.

■ ■ ■ ■ ■ ■ ■ ■ ■ ■ ■ ■ ■

"I don't want to retire to a hardened, embittered, cynical man whose soul was stolen by the job."

■ ■ ■ ■ ■ ■ ■ ■ ■ ■ ■ ■ ■

I read sentences like this: "Have you ever gone to a loud, energetic public place or a social engagement and you or your spouse suddenly gets tense, drinks in excess to relieve anxiety, or just wants to leave as soon as you arrive?" I thought to myself, do you mean he isn't just being anti-social but that this disorder can really have this effect? That he can hold it together for work and then come home and simply crash because we are his safe place? I may be the only one seeing this and in a position to help him. I was so relieved to have some answers! My husband wasn't just an a$$. In fact, he needs my love and support more than anything right now. His brain is literally not allowing him to function in a whole and complete way like the man I first fell in love with.

When I found that right moment, the right mood, and the right setting where I knew my husband would be receptive to my findings, I shared it with him, and for the first time we both felt some relief. We had some answers and were on a path to healing. For my husband, who is a combat veteran from Desert Storm, and a variety of other equally damaging but less well known military operations, he learned that the roots of his PTSD likely stem all the way back to his military duty. There was no single incident within the fire service as some people experience, but year after year of 20+ runs per day, in an impoverished urban district fraught with shootings, stabbings, drug overdoses, neglected elderly parents, and the saddest children's services cases ever. Add in sleep deprivation and a firehouse full of others who, whether they will admit it or not, are likely struggling with the same issues. Yet he is strong. So strong. One of the strongest men I know, so skilled in dealing with a crisis and a gigantic heart. He is a survivor and thrives there. I firmly believe like many firefighters he was made to do this but my biggest fear is that that job in this current state is slowly killing our firefighters' emotional health. I don't want to retire to a hardened, embittered, cynical man whose soul was stolen by the job. That's why this chapter we're diving into the toughest stuff head on.

None of this has been easy and there is no silver bullet. A combination of diet changes, consistent exercise, medical check-ups to be sure nothing else is going on, counseling sessions and most important for us, prayer and close connections to God and our church family, have led us through this challenging road.

Post-Traumatic Stress Disorder can present itself in many different ways depending on the person. The person affected by PTSD may not be able to or be ready to recognize the symptoms within themselves. As a spouse, some things you may notice in your loved one are:

- Irritability prior to a social event
- Restlessness in crowds or loud places

- An inability to focus
- Constantly scanning areas
- A sudden, drastic change in mood that may seem like it came out of nowhere
- Obsession over details of packing, planning, preparing for a trip, etc.
- Intentionally secluding themselves
- Drinking more than usual
- Withdrawing from usual activities
- Sleeping all the time
- Short fused
- Unwanted persistent memories
- Loss of sex drive
- Sense of claustrophobia in public places
- Loss of appetite

Not all of those symptoms mean PTSD. There could be a few different things going on, so please reach out for professional advice. However, you will not hurt yourself by practicing the basics we share here—healthy diet and exercise and constant self-awareness and learning.

The Happy Ending

The best days of my life remind me that the most important thing I may ever do on this earth is to love my husband well. I've been the one chosen to be by his side through this journey, both the good and the bad. As I reflect on my life purpose, some days this title of wife overrules all the rest and my focus lies solely there. There is no other human I have more opportunities to care for, nurture, show and be love to than any other, even my children. No matter what your spouse is going through, I hope that inspires you.

Helping Others

On our last anniversary, we snuck away for a sweet treat at our kids' insistence when they realized our anniversary had been taken over by yet another sporting event. I remember so many things about that conversation, but one was a passion of both of ours and the feeling of personal responsibility to be sure this message gets out. As we talked, we knew firsthand of too many firefighters struggling through symptoms like this. A large portion of firefighters we know use sleep aids of some sort both on and off the job. Yes, we have been very exposed to these emotional wellness topics in the fire service due to our nationwide travels with 24-7 COMMITMENT, but not everyone has seen that perspective. While it seemed so obvious, perhaps these local chiefs around us just aren't aware of what's going on. If you've had that same reaction as you read this chapter, please bring this book and this awareness to those who can help in your local fire service.

There is an article online from June 2011 by Michael Morse called "Why 20 Years of Firefighting May Be Enough For Me." It continues to be one of the best examples I've seen written of a firefighter explaining the impact of all of those years of difficult runs. Here's an excerpt to give you an idea:

> "I remember sitting in at a critical incident debriefing a few hours after I held two dead infants in my arms. My latex gloves melted into their skin their bodies were so hot as I tried unsuccessfully to revive them with my new CPR skills. I bagged the one-year-old—Savannah was her name I found out later—while doing compressions on the other, John. It was rough, but it was what I had signed on for.

> The guy who brought the babies from the fire to me was a 20-year veteran firefighter, a tough guy by all accounts. When it was his turn to speak he filled with tears, and couldn't. He hung his head and valiantly tried to express his feelings, but couldn't. He left the room. A few months later he was gone. Retired. **He told me much later that it wasn't necessarily that call that did it; it was all the calls leading up to and including that one that finished him. He simply could not do it again.**"

> - See more at: http://www.rescuingprovidence.com/editorials/ #sthash.WcTy68Zh.dpuf

It wasn't that one call but all the calls leading up to it. That's key to understand.

What if firefighters had a "run limit" expiration? This firefighter is good for up to 10,000 runs per career. Fire victims count as 10. Any loss of a child counts as 50 and any horrific incident involving someone that looks like his wife, 100. I'm only half kidding as here I am, 14 years into this life and already seeing a significant change in my 46-year-old husband's demeanor, spirit and energy. Yes, he still carries the same honor and commitment into the job he did at the beginning, but the recoveries seem longer (perhaps my patience is just thinner). The anger sometimes bubbles up a little faster. Our talks together, well, thank the good Lord he talks to me as a healing mechanism. He should be the one writing a book, not me.

■ ■ ■ ■ ■ ■ ■ ■ ■ ■ ■ ■ ■

"As a spouse, I was never there with him yet images haunt me from stories he's downloaded to me over the years."

■ ■ ■ ■ ■ ■ ■ ■ ■ ■ ■ ■ ■

In a career like firefighting, police or EMS, maybe 20 years is all the human body, heart and soul can really handle. How do you even research that? I don't know but I hope some smart people are on that research somewhere. In the meantime, we get to be the ones in the trenches slugging it out. Whether you are the first responder or their spouse or family member you are impacted. I know. As a spouse, I was never there with him yet images haunt me from stories he's downloaded to me over the years. (Possibly worse images than actually happened as I'm making them up in my own mind.)

I want to be a fixer and make the hurt go away.

There are lots of reactions to this because it's raw human emotion. It's ugly. And we just don't know what to do with that. There's the classic response "God bless all of you who do that job." Oh yes. God has blessed them all right. Because this isn't a job for everyone. I'm grateful that people recognize that, but I can't help but sometimes get irritated at that trite response. Perhaps it's because those people haven't lost days and nights and weeks to a depressed or angry spouse trying to manage day to day when his mind is stuck at that one call or simply gearing up to try to address the next. Bless those who are passing the blessing. That's all they know to do. You're reading this because you're immersed in the real life story in that article. You've got the scars to prove it and understand where I'm coming from. Or maybe you're still new at this and don't have the scars yet. Don't be scared off. Just be prepared.

As we've dissected this topic over and over in our Fire Wife Sisterhood, the comments that really stuck with me were this. "This is my biggest fear. Will there be anything of him left for me to enjoy?" That thought made me so sad. So very sad. Because what are we living for today? Right now? Oh my goodness, we must be living in these moments because tomorrow's simply aren't promised.

What if we spin it like this? Maybe I'm too logical and pragmatic and it may come across as heartless. I hope not but I sort of see it this way. This is where we are and we must make the most of it. Not just make the most of it but remember it's a privilege and honor that hasn't been given to everyone. I believe God does not give us more than we can handle. So read on, learn and have a plan.....God doesn't also put you in these battles without all the tools you need for victory, abundance, and wholeness of life. If you are reading this and not believing in God, go ahead and keep applying your "universal love" principals. It can help you, but I haven't met many first responders who haven't seen true Godly miracles at work on the scene.

So when do you know you've reached your limit? When your time in the trenches is complete? We have choices. Maybe 5 years was your limit. Maybe 25. Maybe 13. It will be different for everyone with so many factors. How many runs. How the shifts are scheduled. How tight a crew is. How well a department provides support and assistance. How strong their marriage is. Even if someone is right now stepping up with research, studies and regulations to protect people from the dangers of too much emotional stress so we need to step in and make our own decisions, it's too late for most of us reading this post. Our first responders have wounds. It's uniquely personal.

And I, for one, am not going to sit back and be a victim of that. I'm looking for those tools we were given to make it through right now. Yes, these first responders were made to be the ones to do this tough work, but I believe they were also made to live a life that honors the most people. It doesn't matter how many horrific auto crashes a first responder runs on if they are heading home and lashing out at their spouses and children as a result of the stress. Spouse and parent are the two first important titles in life, before first responder. So look for these signs and address it. Learn to deal with the emotions in a healthy manner.

I know someone is going to freak out when I say this but perhaps it's time to step back from the fire service for a bit? Or take a turn at a less busy station? Or take the pay cut to move to a lower paying department. Those who know us know that my husband had that opportunity 3 times in his career and we never came to agreement on it as a couple. Deciding to remove $20, $30 or $40K from your family's annual budget can be a tough marital conversation. Those decisions haunt us now as he's 14 years into sleepless nights of dead heroin addicts, abused children and mangled car crash victims. No time to re-hash the past and dwell there but we look at those options much differently now that we've hit our mid-forties.

Maybe I'm trying to be too much of a fixer, but when I see large communities of women with their own aching hearts over this post, I must speak up and represent and say something. There is so much "awareness" about PTSD, firefighter suicide, trainings being held, and so on. Good stuff. All of it. But when it's coming unglued right there in your living room, another training or awareness study isn't going to help. We need to take actions now. Let me try to organize this with some structure now that you've heard this emotional ramble....

Recognizing Signs of "Not Normal"

Excuse me for diving right into the emotion but it's been so real for our family and truly wasn't until I learned more about the signs that I even realized it's A. Not normal; and B. Has a name; and C. My husband isn't just an a$$.

His grief cup gets full and when it spills out it's a little ugly.

This is for you if you are new to this, or even just new to a busier station and haven't had to experience this challenging side of the fire service yet.

There is a free training available online from the National Fallen Firefighters Foundation Everyone Goes Home program. It's called Stress First

Aid and introduces you to the escalating continuum of stress levels with a focus on catching the warning signs early to practice prevention.

■ ■ ■ ■ ■ ■ ■ ■ ■ ■ ■ ■ ■

"It is important to remember that resilience means that an individual bounces eventually. It doesn't mean that s/he never feels the hit."

■ ■ ■ ■ ■ ■ ■ ■ ■ ■ ■ ■ ■

SFA incorporates the research on resilience, stress, and traumatic stress into a simple, practical framework. It is not meant to be a mental health treatment, but to restore functioning and reduce distress in service of the needs of those affected by stress, but also to make the setting in which it is employed more effective, less prone to error, and more safe.

This is a list of factors from empirical research that have commonly been related to resilience in many situations.

- Connections
- Looking beyond
- Accepting
- Focusing
- Realistic goals
- Taking decisive actions
- Looking to learn
- Developing confidence
- Taking a broader perspective
- Optimistic outlook
- Relaxing activities
- Individualized coping
- Flexibility and balance
- Looking to learn from life's experiences
- Taking a broader perspective

It is important to remember that resilience means that an individual bounces eventually. It doesn't mean that s/he never feels the hit. Learning to accommodate the things experienced in a job like this is a process that continues throughout an individual's life and career. It doesn't happen as a series of events or an episode of epiphany. The impacts never leave, but one learns to live with them, and hopefully learns to live better as a result of them.

■ ■ ■ ■ ■ ■ ■ ■ ■ ■ ■ ■

Now it's time for some actions. Remember that I'm pretty fired up on this topic and tired of the talk. Actions can make a difference in your life and others. I'm not going to sugar coat this. Some of these actions are challenging.

Pay attention to the warning signs. Be brave and bold and have those conversations. Change in mood, character, cynicism. A loss of belief in the goodness in the world. And of course other obvious issues—addictions, anger issues, etc. Have the conversation with your spouse, your co-worker, your officer. "Hey… you doing ok? Need to talk?"

The Stigma and Abuse of the Label PTSD

Many firefighters come to the career with a background in the military for good reason. The skillsets match a lot with the requirements of the job. Because of this, they have seen some military members use PTSD as an excuse for disability and give it a bad meaning. I'm not here to judge that in anyway but just to bring awareness to another reason why some won't admit they have depression or anxiety or PTSD. In fact, my husband doesn't really use that label much and I can agree. Sometimes these days we label things just because we can. No matter what you call it, if you aren't thriving, something needs to change. That symptoms list could be attributed to so many behavioral health topics and guess what else? The treatment list is pretty similar too. I'm not trying to over simplify what people spend almost a decade in school training for but, well, in some ways you can. It didn't feel complete in this chapter without mentioning this stigma. What motivates you? Your former drill sergeant yelling at you to get on your face for 50 more? Well then do it. Exercise is only going to help clear your brain.

Everyone always has a choice for how to spend their days. Always. There is always a way out. If it's too much, there are ways out. Honorable ways out. A slower station. A promotion or lateral transfer. A step out of career firefighting and maybe into a part-time position. There is that old saying "once a firefighter always a firefighter". I'm not sure the people who came up with that had maybe experienced the kind of difficult calls we talk about here. You do have a choice. A choice to get out of the profession even at a young-ish age.

This topic prompted my husband and I to solidly get on the same page about retirement. Not that we hadn't had the conversation but things became crystal clear. If nothing changes significantly at his department (promotion, schedule changes, departments merging, dream up whatever scenario you want because all kinds of crazier things have happened in the fire service) we both agree we are on the retirement countdown already.

No amount of "DROP" money (deferred retirement blah blah blah program that some states have implemented in their public employee pensions) can buy back joyful hearts and healthy spirits. He will be 58 and I'll be 54. Those are relatively young ages to still be able to really live. Give back. Start something new. Still be able to command an income. And let's be straight. There are not many industries that you can retire with a pension at that age. I've worked in the corporate world for 20+ years, and this year I have watched 3 dear co-workers retire with 38-40 years of service each, still not able to draw from their 401k without penalty. Because of the fire department pension, that won't be me.

■ ■ ■ ■ ■ ■ ■ ■ ■ ■ ■ ■ ■

"How will you balance this so these negative effects of the job are not stealing days from your family and years from your life?"

■ ■ ■ ■ ■ ■ ■ ■ ■ ■ ■ ■

How long is enough? How long until we wear out our hearts?

Think through your values and priorities. Yes firefighting is worth it but so is your family. How will you balance this so these negative effects of the job are not stealing days from your family and years from your life?

What to Do as a Family

There are so many things you can do as a family to lessen the impact of this and practice prevention. Get the help you need right now to soften the impact.

- Counseling—even if it isn't a big deal yet. Counseling for even lesser symptoms is a good practice.

- Peer support—yeah there is that industry buzzword. Not sure what they mean? Let's simplify it. Just talk to a brother or sister firefighter whom you trust. If you don't want to share it within the fire service, there are churches with open doors everywhere who will listen.

- More vacations away from the stress of the fire service

- More exercise

- More meditation, prayer, journaling

- Have your health checked—techniques, medications, surgeries for better sleep and relief from physical contributions to these stressors

- Keep learning. Look at our always updating resources listed below on our website.

Many families are impacted by these stresses on a daily basis. I want to also share a story from Jessica Jackson who has been part of the core team at 24-7 COMMITMENT since the beginning. This is a good reminder that we don't know which call or which day may affect a firefighter the wrong way.

Jessie's Story

He came in and sat the bags of things I asked him to pick up on his way home on the kitchen floor. I didn't look up or even greet him, I was "too busy" trying to fix the dishwasher tray as the kids had broken it the night before. He reached over me to grab a drinking glass and then I heard the heavy thud on the counter. I knew what it was and I hesitated to look. I stood up and finally looked at him and saw the liquor bottle on the counter and the red rings around his eyes.

In that moment my heart broke, even though I had no clue as to why, my heart was broken for him. I found my stomach in my throat and the fear I wouldn't know how to help, with whatever was wrong.

I'm normally the one who needs a rock.

I asked him what was wrong only to be greeted with a "Nothing," he knew I knew it was a lie. I'd rather be met in silence than a lie. I asked again and asked him not to lie to me. Of course he could have just avoided me but he finally said, "It's been a bad morning." and his eyes glazed over. He backed up and leaned against the counter and I hugged him for what felt like forever. All I could smell was the bourbon on his breath and the rising cinnamon dough on the stove. I choked back the lump in my throat and knew I must control my own emotions.

He had a bad morning. A bad call. Death had been working that morning. He was on duty at a one-man fire station. They aren't equipped to handle much in the way of medical calls. This morning he arrived on scene where a wife was anxious for someone to "fix" her husband. To be honest, I'll spare the details but it didn't sound like there was anything viable about the poor man anyway. BUT helping people is what they do and he was going to try.

He had done everything he knew to do and had the equipment to do. She stared at him, he said almost as if she expected a miracle and he never felt more helpless or alone in his life. I thought my heart couldn't break anymore for him but it did and continues to. He was alone. Just a wife who didn't know she was a widow, a man who had seemingly passed and himself. Alone. He has never had the burden of deciding whether there was a life to save or if there was no life left. On top of that an eager wife watching you, because you are expected to have all of the answers and all of the means to fix everything. That single decision is something that has to come with a heavy price you pay with every bit of heart and the bits of doubting yourself try to slip in too. Nothing short of a real, Lazarus moment miracle would have brought the man back, he has to know that. I hope he accepts that.

I pushed the thoughts of being a tired fire wife who was looking forward to some kind of break today to the back of my mind, and just pushed through. Being whatever he needed me to be. All I can do is listen and offer comfort that I am here and if he needs to talk about it, I can handle hearing it. The particulars never both me, it is the lives that go on even when others don't that make me sad. It's important to let them talk it out if that is what they feel they need to do. You are his other half, the one who he should be able to bare his soul to, please find a way to let him pour this out to you if that is how he copes. Sadly so many do not, I wish they all felt comfortable enough to not bottle up the things that haunt them. I wish they knew it is not a burden to their spouse.

I wish they reached out for help more often.

When a firefighter needs help, it is not a sign of weakness. It is a sign that they are real. Human. The heart that gives them the drive to enter into the fire service isn't made of stone, it's real. It beats and it hurts like every other heart in the world. Please let them know that having emotions is not being weak. Please also watch how they cope. My husband only needed a drink to calm the nerves, it isn't something he regularly turns to for comfort. All too many times, they make bad decisions in the name of coping.

If you don't like to hear some of the more detailed information, you should have a conversation about that NOW, for when the time does come that he needs to let it out, you may be somewhat prepared to listen while he may be more prepared in what to leave out. Explain that if you ever need to be an ear, that you are more than willing to listen to anything but (insert whatever it is that you don't think you can handle). Some of it, like a wife watching over him as he worked, as he had to debate over actions to take with her husband, is hard to hear but you must listen. Death is part of the fire service; it's in our lives whether we want it there or not. Don't wait until it's time to be his rock to say you don't want to hear it. You have to hear it because if he needs to say it, someone needs to listen. If not you, then who?

If your firefighter is not a talker and he seems withdrawn, it may just be his process, don't force him to share with you but take note on behavioral changes. Support him or her in other ways that you can.

If your firefighter is showing signs of depression or PTSD, please reach out and find resources to help not only him cope, but help you cope with him. Unfortunately, these situations take their toll on marriages. The stress and hazards of the Fire Service when not met head on can rip a relationship apart. Some still do not survive meeting it head on but you must try, give it all you can. My husband is an occasional drinker and while I didn't say anything about his morning nip, I also know to speak up if he consumed more than what I think is ok considering the circumstances. Don't put your head in the sand, watch for any signs of any substance abuse or other behavior.

HONOR GUARD

~ *for the firefighter* ~
Committed to Emotional Health
Dealing with Difficult Calls

Let's address the firefighters for a second specifically in regards to how this can impact your home life. We hope you are being filled to the max with information on how to get support for yourself when needed at the department, and that you are seeking out that support and watching for your fellow firefighters who also need help. The truth is the first person who may notice you are a bit "off" is your spouse. The first person who may lovingly say to you "Honey, what's bothering you?" is your spouse. The first person who's going to notice your stress overload, is the person you've vowed to spend the rest of your life with. Oftentimes, when the spouse is not knowledgeable of the impact of firefighting on emotional health, they may not be as compassionate nor understand what's going on. You hold the key in bringing awareness to them that will prevent larger problems in your marriage. It's a team effort. You can't always dig out of an emotional pit by yourself. The person who most wants you to live a healthy life in all ways, including emotional health, is your spouse.

This is your bravest moment. Admitting when you need support for your emotional health and asking for it.

■ ■ ■ ■ ■ ■ ■ ■ ■ ■ ■ ■ ■

"The most essential awareness you can grasp here that will support your marriage is to recognize the symptoms you are experiencing and be clear with your spouse."

■ ■ ■ ■ ■ ■ ■ ■ ■ ■ ■ ■ ■

We're beating a dead horse here but it starts with communication. This is another crucial conversation you need to have with your spouse about dealing with difficult runs. Your spouse doesn't need to know everything but if you don't share anything, she can't read your mind. It's helpful, healthy and fair for her to hear from you:

- Why you may be in a foul mood after a shift

- How you prefer to talk / not talk / process those difficult runs

- What you need and want for her to do in these moments

- That even if you don't want to talk about it, it's important she knows the basics. Even if you just have a code word to let her know you had a tough call and need your space.

- She'll want to hear that you do have a healthy outlet for this, even if you prefer talking to another firefighter (of the same sex, confiding in a member of the opposite sex is a slippery slope in a marriage)

The most essential awareness you can grasp here that will support your marriage is to recognize the symptoms you are experiencing and be clear with your spouse regarding what you are struggling with so they can support you, and not feel like a victim themselves. This begins the road to healing with your best partner by your side knowing you want them there. When this does not happen, a spouse can feel so trapped and hopeless in their inability to help you.

~ *for the spouse* ~
Committed to Emotional Health
Dealing with Difficult Calls

Let's keep this section super simple because the subject is already so deep and the work here already difficult. Your commitment can look this simple:

1. Take care of yourself. Have self awareness. Stay strong mentally, physically and spiritually. You will need it if your spouse is struggling with emotional health.

2. Recognize your spouse's symptoms for what they are. Have empathy but do not condone wrongful behavior.

3. Find ways and moments and the right words to have the difficult conversations that can set your spouse free towards a path of healing.

4. Practice patience in order to stay committed. It's a long challenging road but that vow you took was for better or for worse and until death do you part. There is victory ahead and you were made to be the perfect partner for your spouse to walk this beautiful road.

— for discussion —

- Are there signs and symptoms right now that you are concerned about in yourself or your spouse?

- Do the Stress First Aid training together at EveryoneGoesHome. org

- Are there others around you who may be experiencing struggles with emotional health? Do you feel moved to reach out to them or to others who can help them?

- How bad is it really? How much are these symptoms impacting your family and your home? It's easy to live in denial. It's ok to cry out a bucket of tears as you journal these thoughts out on paper.

- What lifts you up and gives you hope? How can you add more of those activities to your day?

RESOURCES

All resources mentioned in this chapter can be found at HonorAndCommitment.com/Chapter14

Resources Include:
- Jessica Jackson: When your FF needs help

- 21 days to a sober firefighter

- 247commitment.org/crisis a full list of resources for those struggling with addictions, depression, PTSD and more

- EveryoneGoesHome.org free trainings on many topics but in particular look at Initiative 13 and the Stress First Aid training.

15 *Committed to Physical Health*
Fitness, Healthy Diets and Avoiding Risks

Some job qualifications require going the extra mile not just to get the job, but to maintain the job. Firefighting qualifies as one of these. While there is no national standard for fitness levels for firefighters (although it is much debated and discussed), it's clear that no one wants an out of shape firefighter coming to rescue them from a predicament. For the sake of simplicity and this book, if the weight or strength or any fitness condition of a firefighter starts to impact their ability to do the job, it's time to make some changes.

Fire families can play a role in this. Let's start with new fire families. Here comes another surprise for you. On top of the already heavy work hours of firefighters, expect to fit in a workout on off duty days as well. While many firefighters are able to work out on the job, some at busy stations cannot do this. Being a member at a local gym or adding to your routine to go in early or stay after shift to work out at the firehouse can be a good way to fit it in.

Working out as a couple is one of our favorite dates, despite the fact that we do very different styles of workouts. Together we found a gym that offered what each of us needs. With kids, it's a great way to set that example of a healthy lifestyle.

Need another compelling reason to work out together? Staying healthy together means a higher chance of living many more years together as husband and wife. A study by the National Heart, Lung, and Blood Institute reports that adults with a body mass index (BMI) of more than 40 are nearly 60 percent more likely to die from cancer. Those with a BMI of more than 30 represent nearly 50 percent of diabetics, are twice as likely to suffer from high blood pressure, and are three times more likely to die from coronary heart disease. (See more at: http://healthy-america.org/facts-stats-and-quotes-on-obesity-in-america/#sthash.zjzyTAjO.dpuf).

First responders see all shapes, sizes and conditions of people who need help in an emergency. Many have cited their interaction with various health related conditions due in part to poor diet and sedentary lifestyle have motivated them to personally stay fit and healthy while encouraging their spouses to do the same.

One more great reason to stay fit as a couple, working out together can be an incredibly attractive and tempting activity increasing libido. So, that's settled then. Off to the gym!

Healthy Diets

You can't exercise your way out of a bad diet, and you can't simply diet without exercise. Both go hand in hand in a healthy lifestyle. Healthy diets are a personal lifestyle choice that you can make together in your home. I drive most of these decisions in our house and try to not be "that mom," but I have rightfully earned the nickname "dirty hippy" due to the slow but constant battle I've waged over the years to remove the following from our diet: high fructose corn syrup, refined sugars, gluten, and various food dyes. My husband still smiles and the kids don't starve. But what about at the firehouse? Sometimes there are crews who choose accountability to get healthy together. There are also crews who stand on nostalgia and tradition eating delicious but fat-laden, artery-busting meals. And like all of us who have experienced the yo-yo diet, there are crews who bounce violently from one extreme to the other.

■ ■ ■ ■ ■ ■ ■ ■ ■ ■ ■ ■ ■ ■

*"One more great reason to stay fit as a couple,
working out together can be an incredibly attractive
and tempting activity increasing libido."*

■ ■ ■ ■ ■ ■ ■ ■ ■ ■ ■ ■ ■

Meal Planning

As a fire family, I've seen many firefighters and spouses struggle with this dilemma. While you want to eat with the crew because it's social and relational and demonstrates you're on the same team, someone who is trying to eat healthier may opt for bringing in food from home (which adds up to a lot of food prep for 24 or 48 hour shifts).

Busy firehouses may resort to lots of fast food on the run, which adds up fast in both calories and dollars. Speaking of which, contributing to the monthly "house fund" or whatever it may be called to cover the cost of eating together as a crew can be an economical way to eat on shift, if it's the kind and quantity of food you prefer. I have seen this topic become a sore point between husbands and wives who are trying to budget. The biggest irritation from wives seems to be when a firefighter pays into this food fund, but then also partakes in eating meals out, seemingly double dipping from their family's budget. I'll just leave that point out there to digest as you need to as a couple. In summary, if you put 10 firefighters in a room you'll find 17 ways to meal plan. And then, they'll change up the crews. I secretly think there is something in the firefighting gene pool that can't sit still for very long and needs to shake things up with some excitement.

Health Risks of Firefighting and Potential Dangers for Your Family

So there are risks everywhere in life. I don't want this to read like some helicopter mama rant but I do want to be sure that where you can practice prevention, you are aware and informed.

■ ■ ■ ■ ■ ■ ■ ■ ■ ■ ■ ■

"It's a reality of the job and, while there are exposures and threats, there are many precautions taken."

■ ■ ■ ■ ■ ■ ■ ■ ■ ■ ■ ■

Infectious Diseases

Firefighters are exposed to ick. That's my non-medical professional term for it, and it sufficiently illustrates the whole gamut of viral, bacterial, airborne, bloodborne whatevers they come in contact with which you pray never enter your home. If you think too long about these invisible enemies, I'll refer you back to Chapter 3 on worry and fear. It's a reality of the job and, while there are exposures and threats, there are many precautions taken. The reality of firefighters being harmed by these seems to be rather minimal. Still it's worth knowing and understanding as a fire family the risks and preventive measures.

Real life example from our short 14-year history as a fire family. I was home with a 3-year-old and an 8-week-old who was born 7 weeks premature. My husband and his partner discover they were exposed to meningitis and put on quarantine. Quarantine was defined as going home and staying there. Hmmmmm. Exactly how does that work? Being the slightly germophobic mother of a preemie, I packed up and spent the next week at my parents, leaving without even seeing his shadow grace our doorway. My husband avoided contracting the illness but his partner (a father of 4 at the time) was not so lucky and was banished to the spare bedroom in his parent's home for a week of the worst possible headache of his entire life. Fun times and a great example of the health risks our fire families face. Also consider accidental needle sticks and the ongoing months of testing for infectious disease that follows and you have another prime example of the extra stressors of this job.

My favorite (dripping with sarcasm) moments are the awful flu and virus bugs carried home by my husband, whom we nurse back to health on his 48 hours off shift, only for him to head back to the firehouse just at the onset of the rest of us getting sick. There's another Murphy's Law example for you. To be fair, our snot-nosed youngsters probably sent their fair share of ick back to the firehouse with dad during those seasons as well. Spreading the love.

Can you prevent this back and forth germy-ness? There's one surefire health tip we recommend always. **Leave uniforms at the firehouse and only wash them at the firehouse**, including germy boots that you do not want to track the ick into and out of your vehicles. Of course, practice mega handwashing and sanitizing of anything that spends time in both locations such as cell phones, backpacks and car keys. I'm going to stop here because anyone in a healthcare profession (and lots of firefighters happen to be married to other first responders and nurses) is exposed and understands the precautions that must be taken.

Let's talk about those long term risks that aren't as physically evident as the flu and cold germs. Like that big ugly C word.

Cancer and Firefighters

I'm going to talk to you as a wife, not a researcher. The research is solid and available in our list of resources. Here is my layman's understanding that really helped me comprehend what's going on. The materials that burn today in our homes are not the basic wood and cottons of the past. There are many chemicals used to treat, press, protect and beautify our laminate floors, carpets, furniture, siding, paint, countertops and more. When these materials burn they release a lot of really nasty stuff. Firefighters are dressed in gear that is designed to protect them from the heat and fire, but these carcinogens can penetrate that gear and their skin. In fact, firefighters are sweating like mad in that gear. Their pores are wide open trying to keep their bodies cool while carcinogens can then flow freely into their bodies right through their skin. You may think that lung cancer would be a common cancer amongst firefighters, but it's no more common than for the general population thanks to the use of proper breathing equipment. Instead it's cancers like testicular, prostate, brain, and skin cancers.

From the Firefighter Cancer Support Network whitepaper "Taking Action Against Cancer in the Fire Service:"

> Some areas of skin are more permeable than others, specifically the face, the angle of the jaw, the neck and throat and the groin. Skin's permeability increases with temperature and for every 5° increase in skin temperature, absorption increases 400%. The most permeable piece of personal protective equipment is the hood. Hoods are designed to protect our head and neck from heat but are not designed to stop skin absorption through the forehead, angle of the jaw, the neck and throat.

Some studies have shown that testicular and prostate cancer are amongst the most common in firefighters. Think about that with your non-scientific logical brains. Where do we all sweat a lot? And what's the last piece of clothing to remove and clean? And where is our skin most sensitive? Just speaking as a wife, this and the findings about the hood make a whole lot of sense to me.

Personally, we have experienced cancer, specifically 2 rounds of basal cell carcinoma with my husband. Both have been on his scalp in locations where his helmet band rides on his head. Did he abuse his skin in the southern California sun in his 20s? He sure did. But to then let carcinogen laden helmets contact that skin for long, sweaty periods of time is not a good idea either.

■ ■ ■ ■ ■ ■ ■ ■ ■ ■ ■ ■ ■

The old salty firefighter wearing the worn and filthy helmet and gear has lost its sexiness."

■ ■ ■ ■ ■ ■ ■ ■ ■ ■ ■ ■ ■

Spouses, I cannot stress enough that you are the most influential person for getting your firefighter to see a doctor. In our case, there was a small scab that wouldn't seem to heal on my husband's scalp. He attributed it to being in a bad spot and always breaking open. One visit to the dermatologist later and he has a jellybean sized divot of skin removed from his head. You know that cute country song "I want to check you for ticks?" Yeah. Get your ape instincts on and give your firefighter a good looking over occasionally.

So we aren't doomed. We just haven't been so smart with some fire service traditions. The old salty firefighter wearing the worn and filthy helmet and gear has lost its sexiness like the Marlboro Man when lung cancer awareness escalated.

Fire Wife Dr. Karlie Moore (who also shares valuable tips in the next section on Cardiac Health) adds another common occurrence of cancer in firefighters due to tobacco use.

Yet another health problem in the fire service is chewing tobacco. Many years ago, firefighters smoked in the stations, and that seems preposterous in this day...yet chewing is perfectly acceptable. As a specialist in firefighter health I teach firefighters how their health behaviors affect their risk of developing disease and dying early. While all the topics are personal, since I'm also a firefighter's wife, this one is even more so because my father-in-law died of esophageal cancer and he was a firefighter who used chewing tobacco for many years. He was only 56 and died just shy of starting a second career as a pilot and meeting his first grandchild (my son). I can tell you that from my father-in-law's sickness we learned that esophageal cancer is not only very deadly, it is extremely painful. His last 9 months were excruciating for him. These days, cancer is so curable I don't think people are very scared of it...but not esophageal cancer. Another major risk factor is acid reflux, so encouraging firefighters to get their acid reflux treated (and avoid it by eating a healthier diet) could also change the course of someone's life. I hope someday soon the idea of firefighters chewing openly in the station is preposterous.

We hope this doesn't start to feel like a bunch of nagging wives telling you to change your lifestyle. If it does, we don't apologize because we love you too much. Read this as loving nudges instead.

A full list of cancer prevention tips and resources to share can be found at 247commitment.org/cancer

But the summary for fire families is simple and logical and looks like this:

- Wash everything

- Preferably wash it at the station with industrial machines designed to handle the bulk and filth

- Use wet wipes on, well everything that isn't machine washable and is hard surfaces, especially the rim of your helmet that comes in contact with your body and the insides of your truck cab.

- Keep gear as fresh and new and rotated as possible

- Do not bring contaminated gear and uniforms into your cars or homes

- Volunteers, we understand the ridiculousness of this statement but encourage you to find storage containers to help minimize the risk of exposure.

- Yes, we also love those adorable baby photos sleeping in helmets and turnout gear. Personally, I think you can do these safely with minimal exposure and using your smarts to place blankets between the baby and the gear. But we don't think it's a good idea for Daddy's old gear to be a playtoy for the kiddos.

There are many excellent additional tips on diesel fumes in the apparatus bay and wearing SCBAs for firefighters to be aware of at the station as well.

Heart Disease and Firefighters

The story I most often hear from my husband is this: a firefighter works a long solid, well-loved 25, 30, 40-year career and within one year of retiring has passed away. This is probably the saddest thought I have about my life married to a firefighter. With so much time away for the job, will there be a season when we get to have more time together? A season when there isn't so much of his time and energy given to the fire service? I wonder about these relatively young deaths of retirees. Was it a broken heart? On many levels most likely. The physical strain of the job, the constant "waiting for the tones" and burst of energy when they drop, wears on a body. You've all heard "once a firefighter, always a firefighter." The transition out of the fire service is possibly more traumatic than the transition in but let's focus on this heart issue. First of all, it's an issue in all walks of life. Heart disease is the leading cause of death in most ethnicities in the US. So on one hand, no need to call out firefighters as a special case here.

Over the last 30 years it's been shown that 45% of firefighters' on-duty deaths come from heart disease. Firefighters do not suffer a higher rate of heart attacks than the general population but there is a more interesting point. "What our study is showing is the majority of on-duty heart deaths in firefighters are work related and are precipitated by physical and toxic factors," Harvard researcher Stefanos N. Kales, MD, MPH. http://www.webmd.com/heart-disease/news/20070321/firefighter-killer-heart-disease

There are many specialty topics in this book and over the years, we've partnered with many experts in the field such as Dr. Karlie Moore of Fit For Duty Consulting. Karlie is a fire wife with a PhD in Exercise Science and Nutrition.

What's really scary about firefighters' high risk of heart attack is that you can't see or feel the majority of the risk factors: high cholesterol, high blood pressure, high blood glucose (you're probably aware if you're obese, or if you smoke, or have low aerobic fitness). As much as I write about this on my blog at www.fitfordutyconsulting.com—warning firefighters that they need to regularly monitor these risk factors – it's not as powerful as reading some of the comments I get from firefighters. After you read this, firefighters (and spouses) go schedule a physical exam if you don't have one regularly.

"Three years ago, I experienced some PVC's (irregular heart beats) on a treadmill during our annual fire brigade clearance. Even though my cholesterol and triglyceride counts had been in the normal range for a number of years and I was jogging/power walking 12 to 15 miles per week, my cardiologist ran the complete battery of test to find out the cause of the PVCs. Within hours of having a cath performed, I was being prepared for cardiac bypass surgery. I had 40, 60, 70, and a 90 percent blockages. I had absolutely no symptoms and was considered in excellent health. The fire brigade clearance absolutely saved my life. I was back on the job in 41 days and am still very active. Just thought I would share with you that there may not be any symptoms at all but, the annual physical exam can be a life saver."

Heart Attack as a Line of Duty Death

If a heart attack happens within 24 hours of being on duty, it is deemed a line of duty death. Whoever fought for this clause is a saint as it may not be evident and obvious to others what the stress of the job can do to a person.

Prevention

Diet and exercise are the best preventive measures for heart disease, and even that cannot sometimes outpace genetic disposition. This applies to you as well ladies. Heart disease is the #1 killer of women in the United States.

Google is your friend. There are many styles and formats of health and fitness resources specific to the fire service. Find one that matches your needs or go to our resource page for a list of our favorites.

A few other health risks worth mentioning follows.

Is He a Jerk or Is It Low Testosterone?

"Low T" is an old topic but with a newer resurgence of interest and treatment. I hesitate to say a lot here because of the newness but our family does have a very personal experience with testosterone treatment. You see, for a while I thought my husband was just being a lazy jerkface. (With his permission I write this.) All the while, he wondered what happened to his "get up and go" attitude. When I had enough patience, I had so much compassion and tried to help him work through whatever was going on. But when I ran out, it was so frustrating for all of us. Is he depressed? What's going on? This isn't the man I used to know. He isn't the man he used to be. This can't be what 44 feels like. At the encouragement of some other guys on his crew, he went for a screening of his testosterone (and other very important blood testing) and low and, behold, he was off the charts low. Some firefighters had some hysterically funny but crude jokes about this I wish I could mention here, but we'll keep it clean. I've finally learned that's how guys show their love.

■ ■ ■ ■ ■ ■ ■ ■ ■ ■ ■ ■ ■

"Clearly adrenaline dumps and interrupted sleep patterns are a bad combination for testosterone production in the body and soon, it forgets how to do it on its own."

■ ■ ■ ■ ■ ■ ■ ■ ■ ■ ■ ■ ■

Again, the non-medical professionals view simplified for you here. High adrenaline jobs like firefighting cause many surges and decreases in hormones rapidly throughout a day, and night. And, nighttime is when our body does a lot of hormone reproduction to keep us ticking in all the right ways. Clearly adrenaline dumps and interrupted sleep patterns are a bad combination for testosterone production in the body and soon, it forgets how to do it on its own. One method of treatment is to replace that testosterone with various methods of shots and supplements.

Before you jump down the path of medication for mental health purposes, I highly suggest you get a full physical and see what other elements in your body may be contributing to those mood swings.

Once my husband was on this treatment and had the right amounts regulated, he was like a new man. Hallelujahs all around.

This is in no way an endorsement of a specific medical treatment but an awareness of another effect the job of firefighting can have on one's body.

Sleep Issues

How many years in a row can you go with interrupted sleep, or working a night shift, before you have sleep problems? Some studies may have been done but I don't need those studies to see that this is a common problem amongst firefighters. In one particular station and crew, 75% of the crew have had sleep studies and are using some sort of supplements, CPAP machine or other medication to help them sleep better. What can you do to prepare for this?

- Consistent sleep when you are home and off shift

- Find the patterns of sleep that work best for your body. A small nap right when you get home but without sleeping all day may help you regulate better.

- Avoid dependency on unnatural sleep aids.

- Make sleeping at the station comfortable with sheets and pillows and blankets that give you a better sleep for those moments your head can hit the pillow (families, this makes for a great gift to send to the station with your firefighter!)

HONOR GUARD

~ for the firefighter ~

Committed to Physical Health
Fitness, Healthy Diets and Avoiding Risks

One of the best gifts you can give your spouse is to care for your physical health. Here are our best tips for firefighters to honor their physical health and commit to a long healthy lifestyle:

- Clean your gear. And yourself. And anything that comes in contact with carcinogens on a frequent basis.

- Be an encourager on your crew to eat healthy and workout together. Even if you are the fittest firefighter there, you may one day depend on someone on your crew to be there for you. It's in everyone's best interest to have a fit, strong firefighting crew.

- When you are getting ready to enter a new diet / exercise phase, involve your spouse in the planning. It takes their support for the time, the schedule and often the financial planning to add gym memberships, supplements or other types of food to your grocery list as well as to plan the meals together. Just like eating with your crew at the station builds bonds, eating with your family at home is how family is done best. (I speak from experience as we lived through seasons where my husband chose a different diet path and did not eat with the family and it felt a little exclusionary.)

- Listen to your spouse when they ask you to visit the doctor for a check-up. A doctor visit is less painful than those reminders and nagging about getting it done. (Yes, I do believe one of the only times nagging is acceptable when there is a health concern.)

~ *for the spouse* ~

Committed to Physical Health
Fitness, Healthy Diets and Avoiding Risks

Do you understand a bit better the importance of physical health for firefighting? We hope this has inspired you to also make the commitment to a lifetime of healthy living. Our best tips to honor your fire family's physical health needs follows.

- Planning for diet and exercise changes takes time and must be intentional. Consider this as you are thinking about your spouse's needs as a firefighter and your family's health needs.

- Be understanding if your firefighter wants to work out before or after shift at the firehouse gym.

- If you are lacking the time in your schedule to fit in a workout, have that important but sometimes difficult conversation with your spouse so you can reprioritize your family's schedule to fit it in.

- Do continue to nag (politely and kindly but with passion!) if your spouse needs to see a doctor for any concerns (and don't skip your check-ups either!)

- Take the cute pictures with turn out gear but be sure you use baby wipes and other protective means to protect those kiddos from possible carcinogens.

- You have permission to be a little nutty about hand washing and to ask your firefighter to clean their gear and uniforms at the station. If this is not possible, consider running washer cleaning cycles with bleach after washing station gear.

- Send your firefighter to the firehouse with the best linens and blankets to help in getting a good night's sleep. For years my husband took the leftovers and unwanteds from firehouse to firehouse. When we bought him nice fresh, high quality bedding and a tote to keep them neat and clean, his evenings became much more comfortable.

The most brave, courageous and powerful thing a firefighter can do is be vulnerable with their life stories. I've seen more people motivated and transformed by hearing firefighters they admire share openly about their weaknesses and how they overcome them than anything else. This story comes from Jason Brahm, founder of 1st Due Fitness in South Carolina.

◆◆◆◆ "From Fat To 1st Due Fit" By Jason Brahm ◆◆◆◆

It all started when I was hired as a full time firefighter, my dream career! I was overweight most of my life. Never really cared what types of food or how much I ate. As a kid I played sports, I was the butterball on the team. I just went through my childhood with the attitude that I was overweight and it was just how it was.

In 2006, I was hired by my local fire department after testing with them for the second time. In 2004, I did not make it through the Physical Fitness portion of the testing process. I was beyond myself to be hired and living my dream as a full time firefighter. I was still overweight and knew in the back of my mind I needed to do something to change that. It went through my mind many times while working with an extra 50 plus pounds of gear on my body, the high temperatures, the stress and workload of a "probie" in the fire service. I will never forget the day and events that took place to make the light go off for myself to step up and make a change.

It was a June day in coastal South Carolina working a 24 hours shift and it would be a test of my physical and mental abilities. We had our normal summer afternoon storm roll through. We were dispatched to a house fire from a lighting strike. Upon getting to the scene my heart was pounding through my chest as hard as you could even imagine. I was about to be living my dream, fighting fire. I was very lucky that day due to the fact that I didn't fall out or tell anyone that I didn't feel well physically and have to be transported to the hospital due to being completely exhausted. I will never forget the fact that my head was pounding so hard and I really thought my heart was going to pound out of my chest for the rest of that shift. I decided that night trying to get through the shift that something had to change if I wanted this career for the next

25 plus years. I would end up a statistic if I didn't change my life. I had to change for my family and couldn't stand the thought of leaving my wife and kids behind due to the fact that I wasn't prepared for what I had sworn in to do. Or the fact that I was putting my fellow brothers at risk every time I showed up to work.

What to do? I hired a coach. I was talking to a friend in the gym about hiring someone that works with athletes and has a background in nutrition. I did research and I found not only one of the top trainers/nutritional guys in the county I also ended up becoming true close friends with him and still am to this day. Not many coaches become true friends with clients and he will tell you I am the second client that he still talks to as a friend to this day. Hiring my coach was the best thing I ever did in my weight loss journey. He was straightforward with me and didn't sugar coat anything. He always told me, he doesn't do anything but give me the tools I need to get the results I wanted. I had to do all the work with those tools to make it happen. Not only did he help me get in the best shape of my life, he educated me and explained that I was not on a diet.

I decided to change my lifestyle. A diet is short lived. Life style change is permanent. As I went from Fat to fit under my coach's direction, I wanted to learn who and why this was so easy. Why is the rest of the county so lost when it comes to weight issues? So I decided it was time to get into school and learn the process of this. I enrolled in Precision Nutrition and Obtain a Level 1 Nutrition Coaching Certification. As a full-time firefighter and being overweight most of my life I found a way to help my brothers and sisters in the fire service.

This brings me to where I am today. I formed 1st Due Fit, which is a company that is devoted to helping the fire service reduce LODD's due to cardiovascular issues (heart attacks). 1st Due Fit is here to help fellow fire service members become healthier and better fit to do the job. 1st Due Fit is also about promoting proper nutritional intake along with physical fitness and the importance of these issues. The 50 plus brothers and sisters the fire service loses every year to these issues are preventable. 1st Due Fit is aware that everyone has to start somewhere; I fully understand the struggles of the overweight, sedentary person. Just remember you didn't become overweight and out of shape in one day or one meal. The same goes for making a lifestyle change, it will not happen overnight, or with one healthy meal. A true lifestyle change takes time.

This transformation did not happen overnight, or in some crazy 30-day crash "diet." True lifelong changes take time. For all my brothers and sisters in the fire service please look at your career with this in mind:

Your fellow brothers/sisters on the job, your crew, department, family, and the public you are devoted to serve are entitled to have a healthy, physically fit "occupational athlete" that is ready mentally and physically for the unexpected at any given time. Every firefighter no matter rank should carry themselves in this mind set.

When things get tough, your body is sore, you want to eat junk just read this quote:

"Highest Expectations Are Minimum Requirements"
-Jason Brahm, 1stDueFit.com

- for discussion -

- What do you wish you would have done to support your physical health through the years? Sunscreen, a healthier diet, better exercise patterns.

- Were you aware of the safety precautions around carcinogens on gear? What can you change right now in your home and in your firehouse to make this safer for firefighters and their family?

- Accountability time. Are you happy with your current fitness level? Together as a couple you can be such encouragers for each other. Make a plan and support each other through it.

- For what do you need to make a doctor's appointment right now? For what should your spouse make an appointment? Accountability again. You want to love each other for decades to come right?

- Who in your fire life needs a nudge in the healthy lifestyle direction? How can you be a kind truth giver and encourager to them to lead a healthier lifestyle?

RESOURCES

All resources for this chapter can be found at
HonorAndCommitment.com/Chapter15

- 247commitment.org/cancer for links to resources for Firefighter Cancer concerns with organizations such as Firefighter Cancer Support Network

- 247commitment.org/fitness for access to fire family fitness resources—meals plans, work outs and support groups such as Fit Fire Wife and our favorite firefighter fitness partners like 1st Due Fitness

- Is your fire department without the proper fitness equipment? Check out 555Fitness.org for grants to receive proper equipment at your firehouse.

16 Honor by Preparation
Line of Duty Deaths

L et's start this chapter with a very basic but important lesson that we hear often from new firefighter spouses. What is an LODD?

An LODD is a line of duty death is when a firefighter's emergency response duties, including fire calls, emergency medical calls, hazmat incidents, natural disasters, training activities, technical and search and rescues, etc., result in their death. A line of duty death can also be considered a deadly heart attack or stroke that happens up to 24 hours after the emergency incident or training activity.

Technically speaking, that's an LODD. But there is so much more to a LODD when you are living the fire life and it's not just the obvious that another brave firefighter lost their life.

I met my husband 6 months after September 11th. Before then, I really had only a general public concept of what it means to be a firefighter. Shortly after we started dating, a documentary about the firefighters who lost their life in 9/11 was released. We watched it together. He was very adamant and serious about explaining to me the risk in the job and why he feels well trained and safe to do what he does while I asked questions with a big lump in my throat. It was a crash course but I got it. And then we both moved on in agreement and understanding never make a big deal out of how brave it is that he does this, yet not needing to be reminded of the risk.

Everyone handles death and the potential for death in very different ways based on their life experiences, their personality, their faith or even how they are feeling in the moment. As I mentioned earlier, before I started blogging at FirefighterWife.com I was not aware how many women were especially fearful and anxious while their husband was on the job. We immediately went to work on resources for these ladies. What happened next really caught me, and all of us by surprise. Of course Line of Duty Deaths are a sad reality since the beginning of history, currently averaging about one every 3 days. But, unless it struck close to home, or was of a particularly dramatic event, you didn't hear about it. "The Secret List" of Firefighter Close Calls operated by Billy Goldfeder raised great awareness early on via the internet but that awareness has multiplied with the age of social media, sharing posts, videos and images instantaneously. Suddenly the awareness of Line of Duty Deaths has escalated, and somehow hurts more, if that's even possible.

More firefighter groups began to connect online in recent years across the country and grow friendships. The kinship of the fire service brings them close. So when one of them is affected, they are all affected, and the message travels so quickly when there is a brother or sister in need.

I first realized this in April 2013. I was attending FDIC, the Fire Department Instructors Conference, held annually in Indianapolis and the largest firefighting show in the country with 60,000 attendees. By then, our little Firefighter Wife site was gaining popularity. I was still in that phase of disbelief that so many other wives of firefighters were out there struggling with the same things I struggled with. Like other firefighter Facebook groups, we had somehow bonded over this fire life across the internet, and women were waking up each day and enjoying their coffee reading updates from fire wife friends across the country. Attending that first FDIC made those friendships real as we connected in person and bonded those friendships. A few days later, there was an explosion at a refinery in West, Texas, killing 15 people, 10 of them firefighters. And it was inevitable that our now large online community of fire wives was directly impacted by this event. I am grateful that none of our members lost their firefighter in that explosion as we were simply not equipped to handle it at that time. But certainly they lost friends and acquaintances, and many Texas firefighters went to serve in that city for rescue efforts for many, many days. It was one of the first moments that a line of duty death had impacted our online community with such jaw dropping force. Suddenly, nothing else seemed important to discuss. The mood was very somber.

■ ■ ■ ■ ■ ■ ■ ■ ■ ■ ■ ■

"Everyone wants to help when there's a LODD.
It's in the human nature and especially in the nature of families
of those who serve. Because it could have been you."

■ ■ ■ ■ ■ ■ ■ ■ ■ ■ ■ ■

Why does that happen? I mean, it's obvious that we all have care and concern in the face of a tragedy. Many are moved to want to help in anyway possible. Our community discussed multiple efforts to provide support from our home locations. Do the families being displaced in West, Texas need food, water, clothing, toothpaste? Do the firefighters need bottled water or energy bars? What can we DO? Everyone wants to help when there's a LODD. It's in the human nature and especially in the nature of families of those who serve. Because it could have been you.

We watch the televised memorials....or shield our eyes and intentionally don't because we can't handle the thoughts that surface. To see children and widows sobbing over caskets is a reality, not a made-for-TV moment. Of course media puts these images right in our faces because it's truly a "can't look away" moment for anyone who has even a lukewarm heart.

West, Texas was just the first of major first responder tragedies to be seen played out in our young online communities. The warehouses were soon flooded with too many supplies for that small town to manage. T-shirt vendors hawked to the crowds ready to spend money on a memorial t-shirt (something our community did as well and now refrain from due to scammers who have sadly invaded that space further deepening the wounds already felt from this event).

So where am I going with all of this? If you are new to the fire service, you may not yet be aware of the impressive display of honor and respect and fire service traditions surrounding a line of duty death. And that's just the beginning. How a line of duty death grips the crew of the fallen, the local fire department, surrounding departments and the entire fire service is sorrowfully magnificent.

More importantly, you may be caught off guard by the emotional roller coaster you experience personally even when it's not your crew, your station, your department, your city or state, or even when you're "just the spouse". There are 2 key points we want you to understand in this chapter:

1. To be prepared as a family in the case of a LODD or career ending disability

2. How to emotionally navigate a firefighter line of duty death as a family member

Preparing Your Family in the Case of a LODD

I don't want to bore you here with a long list of financial and legal jargon. Let's cut to the chase of the important stuff. We recommend working with a financial advisor and/or lawyer to be sure your insurance policies are sufficient and your last will and testament are properly prepared. Some organizations such as Wills for Heroes may offer these services to firefighters. Check with your state organization.

■ ■ ■ ■ ■ ■ ■ ■ ■ ■ ■ ■ ■

"If a firefighter dies in the line of duty, the family will be taken care of, but that doesn't mean the money shows up in the next paycheck. It could be months away."

■ ■ ■ ■ ■ ■ ■ ■ ■ ■ ■ ■ ■

If that paperwork is not in place, the family will have a lot of hassle to deal with. If a firefighter dies in the line of duty, the family will be taken care of, but that doesn't mean the money shows up in the next paycheck. It could be months away, especially if there are stepchildren, business partners, or anyone claiming rights to the inheritance. Those are more complicated scenarios which may need to be settled by a court. So what does the family live on in the meantime? Here is where the amazing brotherhood/sisterhood of the fire service often steps in. Local unions, nonprofits and other organizations will often step in with fundraising to support the family. While this is amazing, it is definitely not something that should be planned for as a preparedness step for a LODD.

And, hello obvious, but your family should also have these plans in place in the unfortunate circumstance that the non-firefighter spouse passes away. Oftentimes their income is necessary for the family to continue or even more critical, their care for the kids while the firefighter is gone for long shifts. As you are preparing these end of life documents consider all scenarios.

What Can Your Family Do to Be Prepared for the Worst?

Nothing will prepare you emotionally if that day comes when you get a phone call about a LODD that is close to home. However, you can be prepared in ways that will give you time and energy to deal with your emotions instead of details.

1. **Talk with your spouse now.** It's not a fun topic, but it shouldn't be skipped. If you can have an open and honest conversation now about what your spouse would like as far as services, burial, cremation, music, speakers, etc., it will help you be more prepared in case the day ever comes when you do need that information.

   Understand what the department will and will not do in the way of communication and support during a time like this. Departments should have a line of duty death protocol in place that includes who/how/when to contact the family. And most departments ask firefighters to complete this paperwork at the start of employment indicating who should be contacted and even preferences of who should be the one to contact them. (It's a good topic to discuss if your department does not have this in place!)

2. **Make a list of important family and friend contacts.** Write down immediate family contact information. It may be helpful to write down responsibilities you may ask of them. You might have one person make phone calls so you don't have to relive the pain every time you talk about it. Other responsibilities you can

delegate to friends and family can include: picking up/taking children to and from school and other activities, making meals, driving you to the places you will need to make funeral arrangements, or even just being close by in case you need them.

If this was a particularly public LODD with lots of media attention, you may want to consider a media spokesperson for the family.

3. **Make a list of other important contacts.** After you have had the discussion with your spouse about his wishes, you can gather contact information for funeral homes, churches, newspapers (for the obituary), and flower shops. It is also helpful to have the contact information for the officers at the station, local and IAFF unions, estate planning attorney, life insurance, National Fallen Firefighters Foundation, and any other service-related numbers. This will reduce the amount of energy you will have to spend searching for contact information.

4. **Write down important details.** Make note of any meaningful items, poems, songs, or words that you want to include at the services. For instance, do you have a special memento, ring, necklace, or photo you would like to be buried with your spouse or ensure they are with you? For firefighters, know where their Class A uniforms are (if that is their wish). Writing down the small but significant details will give you clear direction when your mind is not focused on the details.

Preparing Your Family in the Case of a Career-Ending Disability

Financially, as you are preparing documents for the loss of a spouse, consider also what would happen to your family's financials if one of you were no longer able to work. This is an often forgotten area of planning, especially in the field of firefighting which requires physical demands on the body. My husband and I frequently remind each other that every day we get to wake up and perform our jobs is a gift. Our abilities could be taken away at any moment by any kind of freak accident.

Here is a quick list of resources to consider as you prepare your family's end of life documents together:

1. Print a **Survivor's Benefit Guide** and other helpful resources from www.firehero.org to help guide you and keep you organized with helpful ideas like making sure to get at least 20 copies of your loved one's death certificate.

2. **Need help getting Class As?** Not every department issues these. Check out Lighthouse Uniforms for more information on how to get a free Class A uniform for your loved one in the case of death.

3. **Know your Fire Department Chaplain.** The chaplain can be a vital faith-based support for you and your family during this time. Reach out to them and let them walk you through the days, weeks, and months following your loss.

4. The **National Fallen Firefighters Foundation** not only has a wealth of information on where to go and what to do if you ever find yourself in the situation of losing your firefighter in a LODD, but they also have Survivor and Family Programs to help you find your way back to living without your lost love.

No, these aren't tasks that top your favorites list but they are necessary, and we want to encourage you to do this. Together. As a couple. Because it's important and it's what you make sure people you care about have completed.

~ *for the firefighter* ~
Honor by Preparation
Line of Duty Deaths

Now let's get a little more into the emotional side of the LODDs as handled and viewed differently by the firefighter and their spouse. Because we want you to live long, healthy lives together and these stressful moments can cause some serious road bumps.

Firefighter's are introduced to the LODD topic in academy and we won't dwell on those details there aside to say one more time be safe so that everyone goes home to their families every day. (Many free training resources at EveryoneGoesHome.org offered by the National Fallen Firefighter's Foundation.) There are however some unique perspectives on your family we want to share here.

When There Is LODD at Your Station/Department:

Your time and energy will be so heavily focused on your grief, your crew, your department. Your spouse will hopefully be a "soft place to land" through a time such as this, but keep in mind that the extra stress could add some tension in your marriage. And depending on how well she knew the fallen firefighter, could be a challenging time of grief for her as well.

There is also the emotional struggle of "what if it had been my husband?" She will be experiencing. Be sure during a season such as this that you are taking the necessary time for your marriage, practicing extra grace and tolerance as you grieve separately and together and find a new normal in your life.

The memorial services themselves will be exhausting, and potentially, you may not be by your spouse during the services as the crews usually are in formation together and the spouses and family sit separately. This could be so challenging depending on how well these spouses and family members know each other. Consider this as you and your spouse discuss the service plans. Even a conversation, an extra hug, a look across the room, can go a long way to let her know you are there for her too.

■ ■ ■ ■ ■ ■ ■ ■ ■ ■ ■ ■ ■

"The memorial services themselves will be exhausting, and potentially, you may not be by your spouse during the services as the crews usually are in formation together."

■ ■ ■ ■ ■ ■ ■ ■ ■ ■ ■ ■ ■

LODD inYour City/State

Many of the same worries and concerns apply when there is a LODD in your city or state, even though you maybe only knew this firefighter as an acquaintance, if that. Your spouse may need help understanding why this will take more of your time and attention even though you did not really know this person.

Covering shifts for the department that lost a firefighter may be something your spouse has not yet experienced and will need to understand.

LODD Across the Country

If you are a firefighter who is called to serve on the Honor Guard or other capacities that can support a LODD memorial service, you may be called to attend memorial services across the country. It's truly amazing the numbers of police and firefighters who show up to complete stranger's funerals to pay their respects. They're still a brother/sister.

This is so noble and respectful, but should also be carefully discussed and agreed upon with your spouse. It is a lot of time and personal expense. As a wife, no matter how much I understood the respect and honor part, I always had to bite my tongue and swallow hard when my husband mentioned taking his brief 1 or 2 days off to travel with other firefighters to a memorial service. Yes it's an awful occasion needing support but I was also a wife who had just handled the household full of little ones solo already for 24 or 48 hours. It was something else on the list of fire service related activities that weren't on the official job description. Was that a heartless thought? Maybe, but defer to Chapter 1 about priority setting and have those conversations together to be sure you are on the same page. Your wife may be thinking…. He'll travel all over the countryside to be at the service of someone he didn't know but he won't do _____ for us. It's the kind of thought that can grow a bitter heart so rapidly.

Remember Your Spouse May Be Experiencing This Too

No, she won't understand on the level you do as a firefighter, but she is human. And happens to love one particular firefighter more than any other person in her life. So in general on this topic, simply don't neglect that your spouse is also going to experience a wave of emotions as well. But she is going to experience them alone, while you are at the station with the support of your crew. Be sure you are connecting her into the fire family (if appropriate) and taking time to have these conversations together as a couple.

And, a "close to home" line of duty death or close call may be just the nudge you need to finish that paperwork.

~ *for the spouse* ~
Honor by Preparation
Line of Duty Deaths

Spouses, you have a preview here if you just read what we shared with the firefighters. But I want to expound on those emotions. They just may catch you by surprise. 14 years into this journey and running a national organization for fire families, there are still moments and stories that catch me bursting into tears unable to speak, and I wouldn't consider myself an overly emotional kind of girl.

If you've read this far, there is one thing you've already done at least once (if you haven't done it already on a regular basis) and that is to play through the scenario of your firefighter dying in the line of duty. Or even just being hurt. Or dying of a heart attack. Or cancer. Or any of those other poison pills that firefighters accept when they take the job.

I'm not writing this to plant any seeds. I'm writing this because I know you've all thought it and want you to hear.....you are normal! You've thought about how you will find out. Will it be a call or a knock? Who will it be? Who do you want it to be? You've had a late night phone call and your first thought was "is it the department"?

Maybe you've had the chief already call you late at night and your heart races like mad. It's impossible for it not to. This happened to me when our baby was 2 months old and my husband ran on a SIDS death. His assistant chief called to tell me he was sending him home and why (which was one of the nicest gestures the department ever made for our family) and still my mind went through the entire scenario of what could be wrong with my husband in the 2.5 second it took him to say "Dan is ok."

You've probably seen widows receiving flags and helmets in news coverage. Well, any funeral you've even been to is a stark reminder of the blessings in your life and brings flashbacks of what you would do if you were in her shoes.

When we can hear the awful maydays on the radio traffic play backs, we get a bit of a real sense of what may have gone wrong (never listen to those as a fire wife by the way. That's my recommendation.

No good comes out of replaying the past in your head and planting worries for the future.) It's those cases where there is first great hope. "He's trapped but we're going to get him" and then it ends with the worst possible outcome.

These emotional roller coasters are common in the lives of our firefighters and wives. I can go to work for 2 months in my office and hardly elevate my blood pressure over any topic. But my husband will text me about a pediatric call or house fire and my heart races away. And in the case of a death, my heart sinks. Even when it's a stranger. But the hum drum day-to-day life goes on around me as if nothing changed. There is zero awareness unless I share, and when I do, it brings an uncomfortable silence around the room. My co-workers just aren't used to facing life and death on a daily basis.

■ ■ ■ ■ ■ ■ ■ ■ ■ ■ ■ ■ ■

"I confess that I go through a little brain game where I think about what that widow must be feeling right now in this moment."

■ ■ ■ ■ ■ ■ ■ ■ ■ ■ ■ ■ ■

You can't deny that every time there is a LODD, you run through the game plan in your head. What if it was me?

What if it was someone at his station?

I confess that I go through a little brain game where I think about what that widow must be feeling right now in this moment. And the next day. And the next day. And the planning the funeral day. And the funeral itself. And a few weeks later when she might be finally alone in her thoughts.

I have found much personal growth in myself by learning to recognize this pattern. Learn from it. Grow from it. It is a necessary part of the grieving process (yes there is a grieving process of sorts even if you didn't know them), but I think we sometimes forget how much energy and strain it puts on our bodies. You must plan some time for your personal recovery a few days after the event has passed. After you've gone through your cycle of emotions. After you've dissected it in conversation with your friends. After you've cried. After you've stayed strong for your husband and for your kids. After you're done praying for strength to get your through. Your body is simply exhausted and needs to be renewed.

#1 most important thing for you to do is to NOT get down on yourself for feeling exhausted and not staying strong. You are human. Sister, you WERE strong. And you still are. Every warrior has rest and recovery. No one goes non-stop all of the time.

■ ■ ■ ■ ■ ■ ■ ■ ■ ■ ■ ■ ■

"We sometimes forget how much energy and strain it puts on our bodies. You must plan some time for your personal recovery a few days after the event has passed."

■ ■ ■ ■ ■ ■ ■ ■ ■ ■ ■ ■ ■

One of the biggest productivity tips I learned recently is that there is that it doesn't matter what method I use to track and micro-manage my to-do list, track my hours, and watch the clock. What matters the most in my productivity is watching my energy levels. If I have an especially busy and emotional morning, I don't try to pack 6 more hours of writing into the afternoon.

If I'm throwing a birthday party on Sunday afternoon, my Monday better include some of my normal Sunday rest and relax time. So if there is a LODD that hits particularly close to home, immediately re-construct your to do list and add:

- Talk to my husband.
- Extra playtime with my kids.
- Read a book and relax.
- Go to bed earlier.
- Cancel that extra event and stay home for more family time.

It sounds trite, but we do want to hug them a little tighter and a little longer.

And the next time he does leave for his shift, you know it crosses your mind again. Be ready for it and punch fear in the face. Don't let it zap your energy with worry.

You will keep your firefighter safer when you stand strong and face a LODD with grace and dignity and don't collapse in a pile of tears in his lap.

Why does this keep him safer? Because he needs to go to work and focus on his safety and doing his job well. If he left you at home in a pile of tears, his mind is not going to be fully on the job. Don't deny or hide your emotions but learn to deal with them. It's ok to show you are human. We have the ability to grieve and cry without letting fear and worry carry us away to that place that makes our husbands not want to tell us things for fear of sending us there again. Find support groups of women like the Fire Wife Sisterhood to help get you through these times.

Recognize your needs. Find another fire wife who gets this because your neighborhood friends, sister-in-law, or fellow soccer mom will possibly not connect on the same level, nor understand why the death of this "stranger" is so impactful.

You ARE strong. And don't let emotional exhaustion tell you otherwise. And when you aren't feeling strong, confess safely to your Fire Wife sisters and we'll take the load for awhile.

– *for discussion* –

---

1. Are your end of life plans in place? Are you ready to discuss them? Schedule time to talk just for this topic.

2. If you have experienced a LODD that was close to home, open up to each other about how the experience went. What felt right? Where did you struggle with the logistics or emotions or stress as a couple? If you haven't experienced this, use these stories to help you talk through it together.

3. For the firefighter, share your views on the honor and respect paid during a memorial service and your feelings on wanting to participate in those events. Clearly communicating your "why" will help your spouse be your biggest supporter in those needs and make space for it to happen. Spouses, share your concerns and your support.

4. Forget the paperwork aspects. What do you want for each other? If one spouse dies tragically young, what are your wishes for your spouse and family after you are gone? Discuss this for both the husband's and the wife's perspective.

RESOURCES

- National Fallen Firefighters Foundation FireHero.org
- 24-7 COMMITMENT LODD Support Resources 247commitment.org/lodd

17 $\;$ *A Community Commitment*
Your Support Network

This is it. The big finale. If you are a book skimmer and skip to the end to get the message, be sure to read this whole chapter. It's important for how you move forward through the fire life as a game changer. We need some game changers on this mission.

Firefighters are notorious for being independent problem solvers and over givers and not reaching out to ask for help. This may be fine for a single guy who can tough it out but when a family is impacted, it's much more difficult.

How is it that firefighters can pick each other out amongst a crowd at Sea World while you are on vacation (the fire department t-shirt and cargo shorts are a dead giveaway) and chat like they've known each other for years but then retreat when the tough topics come up in life?

Before I created FirefighterWife.com, I really felt alone in the fire life. So alone I didn't even realize what I was missing except that I was really praying for some girlfriends who understood our schedule a little better and could empathize with how many nights I spent away from my husband. The reality is that I started that website only as a test bed for my web development business and had not idea this is what it would become. I needed a blog and website where I could play around and try things for my clients. I knew I'd need to pick a topic I could be passionate about and staying married is definitely that topic. The firefighting aspect was almost just a whim as I didn't have strong connections in the fire service then but I noticed a lot of people liked things that were firefighter related, and it made for some really cute graphics, so I thought I'd give it a go.

God had other plans (call it destiny if that makes you feel better). The firefighters and wives who began to contact us felt the same way as I did. They were broken and alone and missing interaction with girlfriends and advice from other firefighters and wives on how to get help for their marriage. The need was overwhelming and without a second thought, we launched straight into our free Facebook community.

Suddenly my work on web development and marketing for other non-profits was overridden by the needs of the fire service community to connect, bond and heal together and I wouldn't change that in any way. Often there are convoluted paths to purpose and I just wrote 200+ pages encouraging a profession that used to be placing great strain my marriage and family apart. **Be committed.**

For my husband, his eyes are now more opened to the fact that he isn't the only firefighter frustrated with many aspects of the fire service, while still being an honorable and committed firefighter and husband. He still loves the job and works hard to keep his love for it larger than his frustration with aspects that need improvement. There's a tension there but it can be a healthy one. Our pastor gave him the book "Holy Discontent". It's good for people like us who are both driven and who want to see and do and be good and drive for better but can get stuck in the frustration of our discontent. There needs to be someone who isn't too content to see the opportunities for improvement, have those difficult conversations and take the steps towards improvement. Here we are in the name of stronger marriages and families. Having both been divorced, we know the pain and see it in those around us who are in the midst of it. A little discontent keeps us on the growth trajectory while a lot of discontent creates a cold, bitter heart that loses hope. Surrounding yourself with the right people helps you to walk that fine line.

If you have not been a part of those online communities we built, it may be tough to appreciate that I can't even write the words here to describe it. I'm talking about the online communities we have built at 247commitment.org via our Facebook groups. There were many copycats, which is flattering and indicative of the high need for these communities. We have put much effort and structure into making our communities healthy and effective and without as much internet drama as possible. **Be honorable.**

Honor and Commitment are self values we believe we all should strive for both in the fire service, in our personal actions and in our marriages. Now we add a third goal that is required to do this well because it's really hard work. **Be in community.**

This Book Is Not Yet Complete with Every Aspect of the Fire Life

Before I explain community, I need to share a bit of the dark side we've tried to optimistically encourage you through in this book. Bear with me while I unveil this dark side so you can either relate or be prepared and then we're going to quickly move on to being game changers.

If you are a new fire family, there are many more stages of fire life you get to venture together and we cannot promise they will be easy. Most every firefighter or spouse I've spoken with has said the following:

- This job isn't what it used to be.
- Sometimes the brotherhood is a lie.
- If I could quit I would.
- I hate how this job has made me so bitter.

Let me clarify and state that none of those statements have been truly about fighting fire. I don't know a single firefighter who complains about that. These statements are typically due to toxic environments within their station or crew, poor leadership, a heavy stressful call volume (that isn't recognized by leadership to make changes for better health), and a lack of the brotherhood they expected when taking this job. Of special note, a firefighter who is leaving a tight-knit brotherhood within the military to join the fire life seems to face these views more commonly. **If you enter a profession with the bar set so high, your disappointment is deeper.**

At first, I used to think only my husband felt that way and I encouraged him to change his view and look at the positives. As I got to know fire families better over these past 4 years, I learned once again that this is a common issue. For a variety of reasons, many firefighters have said they wanted to quit at one time or another. Those words bring immediate lumps to my throat and panic to my heartbeat. Those are dark days for sure but you see here we are still fighting the good fight.

We're probably not going to fix this problem with the fire service here but I'd love to make a big dent in those kind of morale and culture issues. We can learn how to respond, with honor and commitment, to the fire life we willingly took the oath and vow to join. This is only going to be accomplished in community. There may be hand-to-hand combat we each individually participate in but our refueling and refocus happens in community. One of the most favorite quotes my husband shares that lifts me up is this: **"The efforts of good men will prevail."** This is a variation of a popular quote attributed to Edmund Burke and shared by John. F. Kennedy "The only thing necessary for the triumph of evil is that good men do nothing." Powerful. Let's close this book out strong with encouragement and a challenge to take this on.

Let me introduce you to another brave firefighter named Ben Martin. Ben has been a contributing writer for 24-7 COMMITMENT and sharing bravely the thoughts inside his, and many firefighter's, head about how to be a husband AND a firefighter. A Dad AND a firefighter. A leader AND a firefighter. Ben boldly bares his soul as you hear his internal battle with being honorable and committed to all that is asked of him. Let's let Ben's story remind us, that even if we aren't feeling this struggle, many firefighters are and if we are truly "family" and a "brotherhood" then we need to go take care of this.

◆◆◆◆◆ "Quieting A Heart At War" By Ben Martin ◆◆◆◆◆

"Sometimes I Hate this Job"

Family is a word I hear used a lot in the fire service. We recognize that in our profession, family transcends bloodlines, last names, and race. When we graduate recruit academy and swear the oath, we are congratulated on joining something "much larger than ourselves". We are promised that in our dark times, both professionally and personally, we can come to rely on this new family. Over our careers, our family at home will often come in contact with our family at work. Our children will visit us to see the fire trucks. Our loved ones will come celebrate a cold meal over a Christmas holiday, while we try to eat between calls for service. I have so many memories of days like this, that it starts to feel normal—but it's not.

I start to become numb to the fact, that my job gets in the way of "our lives"—a lot. It's a sacrifice that "we" must make, in order for me to do what "I" love.

I fool myself into thinking that my wife knew what she was getting into ,since I was a fireman when she married me. With a promise of only having to work 10, twentyfour hour shifts per month, just how hard could this be on our marriage, especially when we made the decision to have children? But, every firefighter seems to have a part-time or side job. Mine was running a construction company part-time, that ended up being more hours than my full-time fire department job. The consequence of all this work is having no recollection of my first child for the first two years of her life, because I was never home to hold her.

As my children grow older, and their activities and interests compete for my time at work, I begin to realize that some days I don't feel as though I love this job anymore. It's hard for me to kiss them goodnight, and not be there when they wake up. I tell myself it's only ten nights a month away, but that ends up becoming twenty mornings, as I rarely make it home in time to help my wife get the children ready for school.

I want to be great at my job. I take training classes because I want to be knowledgeable and have as many answers as possible. It's the cost of wanting to be the "go-to" guy. So I keep taking classes and signing up for overtime teaching assignments. I keep volunteering for projects, and if anyone needs anything I'm there to help.

As I write this I'm sitting over 100 miles away from my family attending a conference (the irony abounds). All of this should help me to have a great career, and make my family proud. But, the idea is starting to creep into my head, that if I keep this up I may not have a family to come home to. All too often I hear the people we help and come in contact with while in uniform say to me, "you sure are brave to go into burning buildings". I don't feel brave because I'm paid and trained to do that. **Running into burning buildings isn't scary. Scary is hearing my wife suggest, "this isn't working, perhaps we need space"**

Postpartum is something that my wife and I experienced in our marriage after having our second child. When I say experienced, I mean my wife went through it alone, and I blew it. I failed her as a husband, and as a leader of our family, because I allowed work to compete with the needs of my family at home. I have a strong work ethic, high standard, and at times exhaust myself trying to meet my own professional benchmarks. When I started this job, I was taught to not take sick leave, unless you couldn't drag yourself into work. And even then, when you reported the day after, it felt as if you were under scrutiny for taking a personal day. So when my wife asked me to "just stay home today", I said no. I wasn't sick, so why would I? Family sick days were for when her or the kids are sick, and my wife didn't "seem" sick. But I wish I could have extricated my head out of my ass sooner, and saw how alone she felt. If I could redo just one thing in my life, this is the moment I would choose. I would go back in time, and tell the younger version of myself, "You're wife is in pain and needs you, pay attention." But I can't, and no amount of apologizing or marital counseling, will ever repair the holes in her heart. Every time she asked me to stay, I chose to leave.

I struggle more than I'd like to admit I struggle as a dad at times, because of the fears that come with being a parent. It started with a single question: can we become pregnant (so many couples face this challenge), and once we were, we started praying we would avoid a miscarriage. I hoped each ultrasound showed ten fingers and ten toes. Two pregnancies and two very tiny, premature, but healthy, babies later, I wondered how could I protect something so small and precious. I have a fear of strangers around my kids, mostly the future 16 year old boys who I know will break my daughters' hearts. I'm scared of not knowing what to say when they start to ask tough questions, and what happens when my kisses no longer heal their boo boos. And those are just my fears.

If I wasn't so selfish, I would have realized sooner that I have been hurting my wife for a really long time, by the things I didn't do and say, as much as by the actions and words I did. So I better get this out in the open now. I'm sorry. I'm really, really sorry. I struggle as a husband at times, because I can act self-centered. I hide, from helping at home as much as I should, behind the agenda that I need to work more to pay for the stuff we own. When I come home, I've fooled myself into thinking that I've "earned the right to relax", even as the kids run around dancing on my wife's last nerve. **I love my job at the firehouse, and it has stood as rival to loving being at home with my family.** I've failed to remind my wife how beautiful a mother she is, because I'm preoccupied with satisfying my own goals. The public tells me all the time that I am brave to be a fireman, but does letting me wife go to bed mad because I refuse to say I'm sorry make me a coward?

Why do I let ego occupy so much space in my life….The reality is I'm not as brave as my wife. So many leaders lose sight of what's really important. Unfortunately it's really easy to do, especially when you experience a lot of success at work. But the reality is, we should take the extra time to see our family's perspective more often, and to ask about their fears and hopes.

I'm a stubborn man and I don't ask for her help when I should. I've realized anger masks people's hurt and fears, and it's obvious even to my four year old, that my wife and I are scared and angered for our marriage. My opportunity to lead, and to have impact is with my family. My absence is felt every second I am away from them. **As a result, I show up to work everyday conflicted that I am unable to fill my obligation to my real family. I am a professional fireman, and my heart is at war.**

If this is hitting too close to home for you, please don't beat yourself up: struggling to balance family and work is more common than you think. But you should realize that the struggle is not just about you—it's about your significant other and children. I've admitted to my wife recently that I have anxiety some days when I'm not at work. I don't want to miss company training. I don't like missing a work day and feeling out of the loop. But the reality is the fire service never needed me anyway. It allows me to show up and feel valued for a few hours out of the workday. But, if the fire service never knew Ben Martin, fire engines would still answer the 911 calls just the same.

I realize that as I grow in my career, and seek additional leadership responsibilities and promotion, I risk continuing to grow further away from my family. There are always "more" classes that I should take. More so, as I continue to see "bad people do bad things", and "bad things happen to good people", I compartmentalize my feelings and experiences more and more each day.

As I seek additional leadership responsibilities, and engage employees at work in the name of the fire service mission, I continue to encounter resistance from people who don't care. I hear rumors about me that barely resemble the truth. Firefighter suicides are higher than the general population. I don't find it coincidental, that people who give so much to their communities, are quietly hurting inside, until there is no hope left. It certainly reinforces my belief that many of us who serve in a public safety profession are also suffering from hearts at war.

■ ■ ■ ■ ■ ■ ■ ■ ■ ■ ■ ■ ■

That's a bit heartbreaking isn't it? You see the good in his intentions and the failures in his flesh, and it stings because it's a bit like all of us. How do we approach this community thing and elevate everyone to a level of more self-awareness, more confidence and less tension between all the "good things" you want to be in your life?

You're First Going to Try to Fight this on Your Own

Our first instinct when facing frustrations like this is to do the honorable thing and not complain nor grumble outwardly but to keep it to ourselves. We're strong. We can get through this. This is exactly how we get stress headaches, knots in our shoulders, stiff necks and TMJ just to name a few physical expressions of stress in our body. It's also a good way to bring work induced irritability home and share that mood in our household. We do our job, try to smile through it, grit our teeth and move on, especially if you're the junior guy or it's your rookie year.

■ ■ ■ ■ ■ ■ ■ ■ ■ ■ ■ ■ ■

"If you are lucky, there's a salty older firefighter who's really a big softy underneath who gives you a safe ear right away."

■ ■ ■ ■ ■ ■ ■ ■ ■ ■ ■ ■ ■

Those who are self-aware enough as to what is happening pour themselves into exercise, motivational books, church and our spouse's unconditional love to seek relief and they do bring some. You're strong and so is your family so you should be able to master this right? **All those other firefighters and wives have got it together and so should**

we. Your wife likely lifts you up and tries to maintain a voice of reason and encouragement (or she completely doesn't understand in which case having her read this book could be a help.)

If you are lucky, there's a salty older firefighter who's really a big softy underneath who gives you a safe ear right away, or at least when he recognizes these issues are starting to wear you down. If you're super lucky, he's got a wife who's been there ready to chat with your spouse as well.

We all know that firefighters don't reach out to talk right? Thank you to John Dixon who bravely pulled the veil back on that perception. **Everyone likes to hide behind the statement that firefighters don't talk but they do talk when they find the right, safe person to be vulnerable with.** When the right person recognizes what's going on, firefighters have a way of reaching out and doing a check in for accountability. No firefighter wants a stressed out, high strung, irritable firefighter on the front line next to them when duty calls. The bravest firefighters are the ones who share openly these struggles with a safe confidante and tackle them head on with communication and by building an accountability network. How often do you see these thoughts shared on your favorite firefighter Instagram account? Almost never.

These days it's not as natural to lean on others for support. Our family units are living farther apart and communities are not as tightly integrated. It's easy to hole up and do it on our own. There's no need for communal farming and sharing of resources to stay alive. We got this on our own right?

■ ■ ■ ■ ■ ■ ■ ■ ■ ■ ■ ■ ■

A rope with more strands is more resistant to damage than a single filament rope. Any individual filament in the rope can break but it won't affect the overall working load of the rope.

■ ■ ■ ■ ■ ■ ■ ■ ■ ■ ■ ■ ■

I wish it were that easy. We preach a lot about being strong individuals and want that for everyone, yet that's not enough. You know about rope theory as firefighters right? **A rope with more strands is more resistant to damage than a single filament rope. Any individual filament in the rope can break but it won't affect the overall working**

load of the rope. You'll see this in wedding ceremonies from Ecclesiastes 4:12 "Though one can be overpowered, two can defend themselves, a cord of three strands cannot be quickly broken." You are individually strong. Together as a couple you are stronger. When you add in the third, even more so. In this verse used in wedding ceremonies that third cord refers to God in your marriage. Let's take it further. When you have an even bigger team of cheerleaders and support around you, you have a much better chance of success. This must, however, be the right team, not a team that is a bad influence, in it for their own interest, or that tears you down.

This community you chose to be around you can fulfill social, inspirational, spiritual, fitness, leadership, personal growth and motivational purposes. It will take a wide variety of people and we have found that in those moments where you start to despair, when you have a wide variable community, somehow that next phone call is just the one you need to give you perspective and renewed purpose. The efforts of good men DO prevail.

∎ ∎ ∎ ∎ ∎ ∎ ∎ ∎ ∎ ∎ ∎ ∎ ∎

Who is your core group of people who know you well and can speak into your life in encouraging and truthful ways.

∎ ∎ ∎ ∎ ∎ ∎ ∎ ∎ ∎ ∎ ∎ ∎ ∎

If you want to thrive in anything you choose, this team is essential. Some people call it a network but that feels way less personal to me. You can have a professional network of people all in it for themselves or who are trying to "fake it until they make it". In this case, I'm talking about that core group of people who know you well and can speak into your life in encouraging and truthful ways. Their own issues don't cloud their judgment of of what they share to you. They have baggage, because we all do, but they are self-aware and emotionally mature. How do you ever find these people?

First You Need to Ask and Seek Them Out

In rare cases, you will find those mentors who just appear to guide you along the way. Like Rafiki the wise monkey in "The Lion King" who suddenly appears with wise words, humor, guidance and just the right amount of pushiness. You know the saying, "When the student is ready, the teacher will appear." Oh if life played out like the movies!

It's more likely you will need to reach out and ask someone. Scary, yes. Brave, very. Wise, without a doubt. I've recently sought this in my life (after a giant personal red flag caught me by surprise) by getting specific about what I was looking for, asking a couple of trusted friends if they know anyone who may be interested and then meeting with those who were willing. Both women I met with were flattered, honored and eager to impart their wisdom on me. Both were a decade or so ahead of me, had taken their own bumps and bruises and were not wanting to see another woman experience the same. Men can do the same, probably with fewer tears and fewer words. Good people are out there. You must seek them out. (Everyone has good in them. Not everyone has cleared out their own emotional baggage to be wise counsel. Trust your instinct.)

Where to Find Your Community of People

It's quite easy to write about. The hard work comes as you seek, meet and get to know people a little better than just their facebook status. You have to be a bit vulnerable yourself and open up to others. It's likely these people are already within your circles. Seek others who:

- Have marriages you admire

- Share your values. If you are into health and fitness (if you aren't, please re-read those chapters!) then seek others who can respect healthy diets and an active lifestyle.

- Share common interests

- Have a work schedule similar to yours or at least margin in their calendars. That eliminates barriers to meeting up.

- Are not necessarily in the same life stage that you are. It's ok for families with young kids to want to connect with empty nesters, especially if your own family has not been the supportive wisdom givers you had dreamed about.

- Aren't just rainbow and sunshine throwers but can discuss the tough topics with an encouraging edge.

Trust your gut and observe the actions of those you begin to interact with. Many talk a big game but fail to execute. This community of people can come from churches, your neighborhood, local clubs and organizations or be friends of friends. Yes, you can even meet them online and test the waters before meeting in person. Online connections are not just for dating but also for friendship (with members of the same sex so you are honoring your marriage!)

■ ■ ■ ■ ■ ■ ■ ■ ■ ■ ■ ■ ■

The fire service leaders are very accessible to firefighters, especially those who are seeking self-improvement."

■ ■ ■ ■ ■ ■ ■ ■ ■ ■ ■ ■ ■

Do you know how we connected with all the wonderful contributors within this book? We simply reached out. Whether it was an email, message or phone call or we were at a conference where they were speaking and took the time to meet them in person, the fire service leaders are very accessible to firefighters, especially those who are seeking self-improvement. Like minded people tend to seek each other out naturally.

Get Outside Your Department

One of the biggest concerns we receive in the Fire Wife Sisterhood is not wanting to post anything because "someone from my department is also in the group and it will get back." To help this concern, we opened small groups. This created smaller communities for discussions which feel safer and do not include other locals. It's not that these women are gossiping or complaining, but if your husband is up for promotion, and together you are struggling with weight loss, pornography addiction or a parenting challenge, you don't want to put anything out there which could potentially hurt the chances for promotion. It's a wise step. Most women in the Fire Wife Sisterhood sought it out because they were not receiving this support locally and found it here in our nationwide communities and small groups.

For firefighters, we recommend the same. Talk to other firefighters a couple cities over. Let me shortcut the cycle for you and summarize quickly what you're going to find:

- Many departments struggle with similar issues.

- Your department is (usually) no worse off than the others.

- The grass is often not greener. If it is, there are different dry patches they struggle with.

- You will learn something new from each other.

- Both of you will walk away with a renewed sense of "It's going to be ok. We're all in this together" mentality.

If you are stuck in this rut, it's easy to assume that all firefighters are like the ones you are working with. I prefer to believe that all firefighters can become honorable and committed but until they are there, it's tough to survive a 24 or 48 hour or longer shift in that atmosphere. We all have rough seasons where we aren't the nicest to be around. It's easy to believe everyone is like that.

In our national events held by 24-7 COMMITMENT, **the most powerful experience has been the connection made between firefighters across the country who would have never met each other had their wives not convinced them to attend** a "Flame Fest" (that was our old name, when we thought it was only going to be a girls event. Bravo to all those men who attended with much ridicule!) We now call these Commitment Weekends, much to everyone's preference, and my husband has stated he could easily build his "dream crew" of firefighters from the quality of men attending these events. We've created and found that support network which extends well beyond our own local departments. Here's a quote from one of our male firefighter attendees:

> "I humored my wife like many do and agreed halfheartedly to go to a conference with her. I mean, she had gone to FDIC with me, and it was an opportunity for us to spend a few days away out of town. In a town we both enjoy, Chicago. What happened was the opposite of what I expected. I not only enjoyed myself, I was looking forward to the next year. So, now I am sitting on a chairlift in Tahoe. Very anti-climatic, right? Except, I am sitting with two firefighters I met at her conference. AND...there is NO, I repeat, NO conference going on! We are here because we want to be here with each other."

I'm not saying you have to attend a Commitment Weekend to achieve this (although we'd love that!) but you do need to stretch outside of your own department and there are many opportunities to do so with local trainings, regional fire conference events or the many national fire service trainings and conferences which are held. For the wives, you are always welcome in our nationwide Fire Wife Sisterhood where we promise the same special connection to other fire wives. My vision is truly for everyone to have a fire wife "BFF" in their backyard. In the meantime, we'll lean on each other for encouragement in our online communities. If you are blessed with a tight knit crew of fire families at your department, by all means, keep on keepin' on! Realize the rarity of that blessing and enjoy.

■ ■ ■ ■ ■ ■ ■ ■ ■ ■ ■ ■

"The most powerful experience has been the connection made between firefighters across the country who would have never met each other had their wives not convinced them to attend."

■ ■ ■ ■ ■ ■ ■ ■ ■ ■ ■ ■

John Dixon on Firefighters Connecting with Other Firefighters

John Dixon shared that when communicating with firefighters who aren't at your department, you have to start with a debriefing of a recent event for which you want feedback. The act of simply debriefing together allows you to replay the event, communicate new thoughts in a new way and will shed new light on the topic. When you are forced to describe a situation, saying it out loud can paint a different picture than the thoughts running around in your head and your heart.

■ ■ ■ ■ ■ ■ ■ ■ ■ ■ ■ ■

"The act of simply debriefing together allows you to replay the event, communicate new thoughts in a new way and will shed new light on the topic."

■ ■ ■ ■ ■ ■ ■ ■ ■ ■ ■ ■

John went on to share with us that he doesn't believe we should be shielding rookies from these issues. (Um, John, I hope you love the ugly and beautiful truths we splash throughout this book in the name of preparing everyone and raising the bar for the future generations of firefighters!) He states "We tell rookies to keep their mouths shut. How do they learn that way? They need to be able to ask questions, seek advice and have a supportive ear for the challenges they are facing." As a leader of people, I agree. Training a new employee to not speak up their first year on the job, sets a pattern and precedence for moving into the future. Improvements are not made if no one has the "holy discontent" to state hard truths and seek improvements in cancer rates, divorce rates, suicide rates, and even bitter heart rates. I made that last one up. No one but me has ever tried to quote that statistic right here and now but we all know it's painfully true. You've seen firefighters who later in their career who have simply checked out and are hanging on for the ride to retirement. How do we capture the spirit of pride and passion and eagerness that every new firefighter begins with in the profession and make it last for 25 or 35 years? I've seen it and you've seen it so we know it's possible but indeed a rarity. Let's be the game changers.

■ ■ ■ ■ ■ ■ ■ ■ ■ ■ ■ ■ ■

"How do we capture the spirit of pride and passion and eagerness that every new firefighter begins with in the profession and make it last for 25 or 35 years?"

■ ■ ■ ■ ■ ■ ■ ■ ■ ■ ■ ■

One individual who has been part of our team of game changers that keep each other lifted up and encouraged is Ryan Pennington. Ryan is a husband, father, firefighter, training officer and the founder of ViewsFromTheJumpSeat.com where he writes, speaks and podcasts across the country. Here's his view on how building that support team is critical to your personal motivation and growth.

••• "Get Out Of Your Firehouse" By Ryan Pennington •••

Today's fire service has evolved into a network of associates that can interact over various means of communications. Gone are the days of fire departments and firefighters whose group of contacts only involve their local area. Technology has opened doors and made communication instantaneous. Having an issue at the firehouse, send a text. Need a outside perspective, post a Facebook Question. If all else fails there are devices where you can actually dial a number and speak to a person, I think its called a telephone, but who uses those anymore.

Having these connections prove to be a sounding post, information source, and an outlet to let us know that we are deal with similar issues. Whether it's a direct fire department question or a family issue reaching out for outside views and opinions can help save the day when you feel the end of the rope is quickly coming. Holding the frustrations and concerns in is NOT the way to deal with any issue, period. Most of the time when you share these concerns the person on the other end has either gone through or is going through the same issues.

Do the outside folks replace our station members or our family, absolutely not. But, they have one advantage in many cases. We don't live with them! Whether that is living with them at the firehouse or in our house folks from outside can give us humbling true perspective. Getting away from the folks involved in an issue can give you a new perspective on it and hopefully an honest evaluation. **Honesty can often be a painful word, especially when dealing with issues that many have deep seated views and opinions on.** Isn't that why you reached out to them in the first place? I would rather a friend be BRUTALLY honest when discussing an issue. Don't sugar coat it! The answer may hurt, stir up emotions that are not pleasant, but it should help us grow as firefighters.

Not long ago I had an issue that my outside network helped me work through. After being assigned to a new, slower, company I found myself surrounded by negativity. Not the normal run of the mill "Chief is not doing the right thing" kind, it was more like "the sky is falling" response to everything mentioned. "We are losing staffing, closing companies, running more calls, truck wont be fixed, and we are losing vacation days." All unfounded and untrue.

Being in that environment was making it tough to show up with an attitude of service, preparedness, and eagerness to serve. Moral was beyond low and it was similar to being in the movie groundhog day, over and over and over..........

Nearly at the end of my rope, ready to explode any day I reached out to my network for suggestions. Can I whip someones butt and not get fired? How can I influence the Eeyores assigned with me? Looking for anything that would save my sanity and keep this funk from intruding into the family life the texts, calls, posts, and face times went flying faster that a jet plane.

Their responses HURT! Yelp, they didn't sugar coat anything. My great friend Andy Starnes from the Charlotte North Carolina area sent me on a mission of self exploration. Finding out where happiness comes from for Ryan. During this exploration he asked questions, made suggestions, and continually checked in. Was is a fun process, NO. Did it work, sort of. You see sometimes it takes more than one outside source. Enter three more fire service connections. John Dixon, Dan Kerrigan, and John Hayowyck each brought new perspectives to my issue.

Amazingly each person's suggestion had one constant, Ryan! Sparing the details their suggestions cut to the core and stirred communication that brought change to that constant variable. Being removed from the situation gave them a neutral perspective that lead to true insight. They were brutal, honest, and it worked! It didn't take long to make a neutral decision that corrected the issues. Having these wise men proved more valuable than any anything.

How does one find folks like this, that is THE BEST PART. Technology has made it possible to reach out to anyone at anytime. Want to talk to a fire service legend like Bobby Halton, Editor in Chief of Fire Engineering Magazine, follow his twitter feed. He often post comments and even his cell phone number. Funny thing about that is he will answer it. Can we all have folks like Chief Halton to guide the way, no, but you can start to build a group of friends this way.

An example of this came while I was writing my book on Hoarding Fires. Through twitter I met Chief Gary Wiess from Wisconsin. The chief and I have never met in person, but through the twitter universe we developed a friendship. Interacting on the social media platform lead to his assisting in editing and helping directing the writing process. Three years later and we hope to meet face to face this year at FDIC.

His contributions to my work are worth more than gold to this firefighter and for someone to help that much without ever meeting face to face speaks to the values of the chief. He is always one text away and we have developed a strong friendship thousands of miles removed.

We can start by using social media, conferences, and friends of friends to start building our networks. You will need to follow a few simple guidelines.

- **Always be honest**
- **Be there**
- **Care**
- **Offer advice and support**

These are rules we should follow in our station and family lives. Using these values in building a long distance network will be amplified because they don't have any personal attachments to you. A network of advice is a treasured achievement, period. To keep it constant requires integration and input from both ends. Use technology to keep the interactions consistent. Through texting, slack app, Facebook, or the good ole telephone make sure to reach out, even if to provide a status check.

Some of the best reach outs come in the form of a "Status Check". "Hey Ryan, its John, just called for a status check and updates." I can't tell you how much these will perk up a day! Why? Because I know the guy on the other end cares enough to reach out!

You see we are NOT alone in this business, period. **The days of huge egos, brash personas, and macho men need to go. We need to develop of system of family and friends that are there on a moment's notice to help us when we are nearing the end of our patience.** Start building your network now! Reach out to other firefighters and families and you will be amazed at how far you can reach. From sunny California to the frozen tundra of Newfoundland I cherish each and everyone of the folks in my network that I casually call the #JumpseatNation. Each and everyone of these folks are priceless in their direction, wisdom, and friendship. Heck, when you're finished reading this chapter shoot me an email jumpseatviews@icloud.com and start a friendship/network! I always welcome more!

Stay safe and Always #JumpseatReady
Ryan Pennington
Training Officer
Charleston WV Fire Department

■ ■ ■ ■ ■ ■ ■ ■ ■ ■ ■ ■

Patience. Everything Changes Eventually

If you find yourself in an especially challenging season where you "can't believe the chief is actually going to go through with that," call your positive reinforcement community and remind yourself these 2 things:

1. I don't have his full view on the matter and need to trust leadership.

2. Even if I don't agree with that change, chances are it won't stay that way forever.

Crews change. Rules change. Promotional processes change. I wasted too much time early on in our marriage fretting over how we would manage the _____ change coming.

Just to state the obvious, **no spouse should ever intervene by calling the chief or an officer**, unless you feel your firefighter is potentially going to self-harm and that chief or officer is able to speak light into their darkness. No other exceptions. If you are a spouse and think you have a case, come talk to the Fire Wife Sisterhood and someone will talk you off that dangerous ledge.

Your Personal Accountability Report

One tool that the fire service uses to manage the unknowns involved when fighting a fire or in any IDLH (Immediately Dangerous to Life of Health) scenario is the PAR (Personal Accountability Report—All the best professions have a lot of important sounding acronyms.). We've expanded this tool to take a personal accountability report for your fire family life.

I can stretch my brain and think of a few IDLH moments in our fire life, at least relationally thinking.

- Emotional meltdown of a toddler or teen

- The moment you realize there was a big financially impacting event

- The walking on eggshell days with irritable spouses

- Anytime one goes without food or sleep for too long

- When you make that smart aleck comment to your spouse and immediately regret that it came out of your mouth

- When you make that smart aleck comment to your spouse without immediate regret but a sense of vindication

- When one is caught in a lie

- A season of medical disability

- Caring for a sick family member

- Dealing with a special needs child

- Almost any blended family topic

- Addictions, yes, even to SmartPhones

- When multiple forms of chaos break loose on a shift night

- When your spouse seems to be an alien life form and you have no clue what would make them say/do/think what they just did

The list could go on but this analogy is going to help us shore up our case for community here in this chapter. Firefighters work in teams on the job, and we encourage you to do so for personal support as well. Spouses who try to go this alone and independent know what a tough road this is and can apply the practice as well.

Here is an official fire department description of Personal Accountability:

Accountability involves a personal commitment of all personnel to work within the accountability system at all times. Accountability is more than an accurate passport. Accountability is an accurate roster, companies keeping together, staying on the hoseline, working in teams, leaving when low on air, having your portable radio, and knowing what to do if in trouble or separated from your crew.

Basic concepts of accountability

- All department members are responsible to utilize the accountability system

- The minimum size team when operating in an IDLH shall be two (2) persons

- All teams will go in together, stay together and come out together

- Team members operating in an IDLH shall always be in contact through either voice, vision, or touch. Radio communications is not an acceptable method of maintaining contact with the exception of apparatus operators, command or sector officers or other situations where the location of such personnel is constant and known by the rest of the team.

Even when firemen are responding to a scene of a fire, there is a lot of excitement and emotion. "SOGs" are Standard Operating Guidelines like these we've written here provide structure and routine in an attempt to maintain accountability and control in the heat of the moment.

Let me suggest some things for you to think about as you create a mental PAR for the fire family life:

- Who is your team? Who are your go to people for when you are facing a fire in your life?

- Do you let this team carry you into and out of the fire? Or do you just skirt around issues and take bits and pieces? Who are you letting dive into the details of your life?

- How are you in contact with your team? Online connections like we have in the fire wife sisterhood are good but what about face to face or by phone?

- What tools are you using? Texting, chatting, emailing, phone calling?

- What mental tools are you using? Meditation, prayer, Pushing your pause button, taking a timeout for mama.

- How are you communicating your situation? Are you staying in constant communication? Are you being vague? (Are you vague-booking? "Today was a really challenging day. Thank goodness it's over!")

- If you are communicating with your team throughout the fire, how do they know you are in trouble? What's your mayday signal?

Even if this feels a little cheesy, the concept is spot on (and for the wives reading this, may be a really effective way to connect to your right hand team member, your firefighter, with a concept they are fully on board with.)

But Sometimes You Need to Get Outside the Fire Service

Even though, I'm not a firefighter, "just" married to one, I have experienced this frustration with negativity in the fire service as well. Our community of firefighters across the country and men like Ryan and John and many others have been of great support to us personally. I know full and well that many of these firefighters I am dealing with are stressed out, hurt from years of emotional wear and tear, and have been hurt by the system too. Our organization is here to bring care to them. However those who are in this condition may not have the best overall perspective on your life as they are bringing advice through their own bitterness and frustration with the fire service. It can be a real downer. I've had my own moments where I've felt how heavy this negative culture can be and questioned whether we should continue the fight. (Yes, yes we continue the fight. Don't let those moments break you. It's the moment you must call that person who can talk you back into the light.)

When you try to care for those who are struggling, you can find yourself with something called "Care Fatigue." There's only so many times you can hear burdensome struggles before your grief cup gets a little too full. Practicing good self-care is necessary for anyone in these mentoring roles. One way to do that is to take a complete break from the fire service. **As a non-fire service person who's been rapidly indoctrinated over the past 4 years into the industry, can I boldly say that too many fire departments try to recreate the wheel by themselves?** Those who do look outside their own department, are only looking at other departments. In the meantime, a lot of fabulous ideas and techniques are available in thriving industries that could really benefit the fire service. I imagine someone could write a few books like "What Teaching High Schoolers Has Taught Me About the Fire Service" or "How Surviving Entrepreneurialism Has Taught Me New Insights For Firefighting."

In my corporate job, whenever I got out of the office and traveled to a customer site or a conference, I came back with renewed energy and a fresh perspective. As a couple, when we break away from our day to day routine and spend a night away together, we have new insights. This may go against all cultural tendencies in the fire service, but exposing yourself to others outside the fire service can have that same effect. Wise counsel can remind you of your purpose and the bigger picture. They can broaden your perspective and give you a fresh set of eyes with which to look at challenges. Sometimes you just need to leave a situation that is challenging to refresh yourself so you can go back in even stronger for the fight.

Be a lifelong learner no matter what the topic.

If You're Still Reading, Consider Yourself Part of the Community

I imagine some of the most traditional firefighters who have read this far may be crying hogwash on my words now. Who am I? Just a girl who fell in love with a firefighter and somehow compelled a community of over 100,000 followers to say "Yes. I have been waiting for someone to understand our fire life forever now." Will you all give this a chance?

For those are already in the huddle and grateful for this long missing resource, welcome. We naturally share a common connection.

Why We Feel What We Do

My heart is so proud to be married to a man willing to do the work firefighters do. Every spouse and family member of a firefighter feels this and knows this so much that I'm in tears writing these lines. **At the end of the day, the fire life takes a firefighter who's already done the most courageous thing by saying yes to the responsibility, a supportive spouse and family and the commitment to it all through thick and thin.** That's the common bond which immediately pulls us into the fire life community. Even those who resist being identified as a fire wife or fire family cannot deny that when the tough times come for a fire family, you would be there to support them. The support in fundraising dollars and care for fire families who have lost a loved one or are dealing with a sick child or spouse or who lost their own home in a fire is a model example of a caring community.

hon · or

noun

1. high respect; esteem.

   "his portrait hangs in the place of honor"

   synonyms: distinction, recognition, privilege, glory, kudos, cachet, prestige, merit, credit

2. a privilege.

   "the great poet of whom it is my honor to speak tonight"

   synonyms: privilege, pleasure, pride, joy

verb

1. regard with great respect.

   "Joyce has now learned to honor her father's memory"

   synonyms: esteem, respect, admire, defer to, look up to

2. fulfill (an obligation) or keep (an agreement).

   "make sure the franchisees honor the terms of the contract"

   synonyms: fulfill, observe, keep, obey, heed, follow, carry out, discharge, implement, execute, effect

Now we are pushing you one step further. **Let's care for each other in the dark seasons, through the chaotic moments, through the little** annoyances and laugh together in between it all as we strengthen our community and knock down divorce and stress and PTSD and anger and all those other topics stealing our joy.

It's really still a small town fire service connected now by the big wide world of the internet. Who are you going to reach out to today and offer your encouraging words for their honorable fire life commitment?

com · mit · ment

noun

1. the state or quality of being dedicated to a cause, activity, etc.

   "the company's commitment to quality"

   synonyms: dedication, devotion, allegiance, loyalty, faithfulness, fidelity

   "her commitment to her students"

HONOR GUARD
~ *for the firefighter* ~
A Community Commitment
Your Support Network

Connecting in community is likely not your favorite thing to do. Often you want to leave the firehouse at the firehouse. At the same time, those guys really get you and you share many commonalities. Having seen many firefighters try it alone, we insist you give this community thing a try, especially for your family.

- When your spouse doesn't understand some of the stressors of your job, connect them with resources (this book, our website) or other understanding wives within your fire community.

- Do not be afraid to reach out before you're feeling too frustrated or alone or like you want to say those words "this isn't what I thought it would be." Every firefighter has thought that at one time or another.

- Get your head outside of your firehouse and the fire service in general every once in awhile for a break and a fresh perspective.

- Vow to be there for each other more times than just the worst moments such as a LODD or loss of a loved one.

- Seek out the positive influences in your profession and life and stay accountable together. It's as simple as a text message.

Advice from Ben Martin on "Quieting a Heart At War"

1. When we talk about leaders, we are talking about those who can instill hope in our situations and problems. Whether things are great at home, or on their last leg, you always possess the ability to do just that—make things better. It's time to recover our work and life balance, and put our families first.

2. This job is about helping others. Our mission is to save "them". Make sure you understand "them" includes our families too. Too often they are the exposure on our fireground, that simply needs a little cooling off, but too often ignites due to a neglectful focus of the main body of fire (our careers).

3. Your children are your legacy. Make sure you do everything in your power to be the one who gets to put them to bed, and be in their lives. Remembering this may help you find humility and the words "I'm sorry", sooner than later. Don't let your spouse or yourself go to bed angry.

This chapter is not about trying to build a great fire family group at your department (unless you want to). Experience and feedback show us those have been quite challenging to pull off. (If you have one, that's awesome! Keep it up!) This chapter is about the right community for you and your family and a commitment to not try to do this alone, especially when those challenging seasons arise.

- If you've heard your spouse share any of the scary statements above, stop right now and just give a shout out that you aren't the only one.

- Be sure you are aware of the warning signs when you have tried to walk it alone for too long and reach out, even if just for a short phone call. It's amazing how that can really lift your mood and change your perspective.

- Create your own PAR team. Don't go into those fires alone.

- Learn how to connect to the communities out there for support of a fire family such as the ones at 247commitment.org and within your own department.

- Be a game changer. If everyone reading this book just did one little act of kindness for another fire family, what joy that would bring.

— for discussion —

- What has been your "safe place" to vent and connect with others who understand the ups and downs of the fire life?

- If you had to name your top 3 go-to friends who know you well and would be there for you, who would they be?

- How have you dealt with the waves of bitterness and negativity? If you haven't experienced them, how do you think you've avoided that?

- Where are you looking for continual learning both within the fire service and outside the fire service?

RESOURCES

All resources for this chapter can be found at
HonorAndCommitment.com/Chapter17

- John Dixon—InstructorJohnDixon.com
- Ryan Pennington—ViewsFromTheJumpseat.com

{I feel a little sad right here. It's the end. I want to meet you and look you in the eye and tell you that you can do this too. I've had that opportunity with so many in our communities and meeting in person solidifies that soul connection and boosts our energy. Be sure to reach out to us at 247commitment.org. Join one of our free communities. Organize a workshop with us for your department. We'd love to share this message in person with a big smile on our face. This is tough work but we know we aren't alone and neither are you.}

Fire Family Love,
Lori

COMMUNICATION
COMMITMENT
COM(PASSION)

247COMMITMENT.ORG
COMMUNITY ACCOUNTABILITY

on FIRE

Marriage

Did you enjoy this book? Consider our online, self-paced video series, Marriage On Fire, created by Dan and Lori Mercer specifically for firefighters wanting to intentionally strengthen their marriage.

CONNECTION.
Remember why you fell in love. Have fun together. Keep each other's love tank filled up. Marriage is meant to be fun and fulfilling (even with the work it takes).

CONFIDENCE.
In yourself. When you love yourself, you can better love your spouse and your spouse better love you.

COMMUNICATION.
You don't stuff emotions. Expect mind reading. Talk out in anger. Hide or withhold from your spouse. Give up when you feel like you are talking two languages. And the fire life presents it's own challenges with long time away and interrupted phone calls. Communication must be intentional.

CONFLICT RESOLUTION.
No hurtful words. Break bad patterns. Learn to forgive, in whatever language that needs to happen. Seek out resources to help you through the valleys.

COM(PASSION).
Have great make up sex even when there's nothing to make up about. Make the fire schedule work for your love life. Understand that intimacy isn't just physical.

COMMUNITY.
Surround yourself by people who honor marriage, encourage and lift you up. Spend time in the company of others that make you smile and love each other even more.

To register go to 247commitment.org/marriageonfire
To access this program for your department, go to
247commitment.org/departments

247Commitment.ORG

Our Mission is clear and simple:

Less divorce. To create a safe, encouraging community of people to connect with and walk through the highs and lows of life - and a place to reach out and get help when your marriage or fire life is spinning out of control.

We are a federally approved 501(c)3 non-profit providing resources to firefighters and their families. We are funded in a large part by individual donors. To support this cause visit 247commitment.org/donate

Resources for Fire Departments

We know the pressures firefighters are under on the job. PTSD and suicide are very real issues. Do you know what trigger often pushes them "over the edge"? It's not the one bad call. It's home life.

If the home life is stable, they have a safe place to rest and recover from the stress of the fire service. When it's in turmoil, suddenly everything is too much.

While there are no official statistics regarding divorce in the fire service, the evidence is around you. Count the members of your crew who are separated, divorced or on a second or third marriage. Even the marriages that survive have many scars along the way.

Home life can in fact be the healer and difference maker in a successful fire service career simply because of the support and stability they receive allowing them to endure the difficult runs, long hours and often politically charged environment.

24-7 COMMITMENT offers:

- Workshops and Training for Firefighters and / or spouses
- Self-Study training on marriage and fire life topics
- Bulk orders of this book and other resources

Visit 247Commitment.org/departments or
Email contact@firefighterwife.com
for more information

CPSIA information can be obtained
at www.ICGtesting.com
Printed in the USA
FFOW02n0135141217
44080806-43351FF